Africa Now

Africa Now is an exciting new series, published by Zed Books in association with the internationally respected Nordic Africa Institute. Featuring high-quality, cutting-edge research from leading academics, the series addresses the big issues confronting Africa today. Accessible but in-depth, and wide-ranging in its scope, Africa Now engages with the critical political, economic, sociological and development debates affecting the continent, shedding new light on pressing concerns.

Nordic Africa Institute

The Nordic Africa Institute (Nordiska Afrikainstitutet) is a centre for research, documentation and information on modern Africa. Based in Uppsala, Sweden, the Institute is dedicated to providing timely, critical and alternative research and analysis of Africa and to cooperating with African researchers. As a hub and a meeting place for a growing field of research and analysis, the Institute strives to put knowledge of African issues within reach for scholars, policy-makers, politicians, the media, students and the general public. The Institute is financed jointly by the Nordic countries (Denmark, Finland, Iceland, Norway and Sweden).

www.nai.uu.se

Forthcoming titles

Mats Utas (ed.), *African Conflicts and Informal Power: Big Men and Networks*

Maria Eriksson Baaz and Maria Stern, *Sexual Violence in African Conflicts: Perceptions, Prescriptions, Problems*

Titles already published

Fantu Cheru and Cyril Obi (eds), *The Rise of China and India in Africa: Challenges, Opportunities and Critical Interventions*

Ilda Lindell (ed.), *Africa's Informal Workers: Collective Agency, Alliances and Transnational Organizing in Urban Africa*

Iman Hashim and Dorte Thorsen, *Child Migration in Africa*

Cyril Obi and Siri Aas Rustad (eds), *Oil and Insurgency in the Niger Delta: Managing the Complex Politics of Petro-violence*

Prosper B. Matondi, Kjell Havnevik and Atakilte Beyene (eds), *Biofuels, Land Grabbing and Food Security in Africa*

About the editors

Prosper B. Matondi is the executive director of the Ruzivo Trust, a not-for-profit organization based in Harare, Zimbabwe. He holds a PhD in rural development from the Swedish University of Agricultural Sciences. He has more than 15 years' experience of researching on land, natural resources management, environmental policy and planning in Zimbabwe, in southern Africa and internationally. He has published widely and contributed to many national, regional and international networks on land and agrarian reform issues. He sits on various research boards and is currently supervising PhD students working on land issues in Zimbabwe and beyond.

Kjell Havnevik is senior researcher and head of the research cluster on rural and agrarian change at the Nordic Africa Institute. He is also professor of development studies at the University of Agder in Norway. He holds a PhD from the University of Bradford (1988) and has been working with universities and research institutes in Norway, Sweden and Tanzania. From 1996–2005, he was professor of rural development at the Swedish University of Agricultural Sciences. He has published a number of books and articles on African development issues, with a special focus on rural development, natural resource management, and international financial institutions' strategies in, and development assistance to, Africa. He has wide experience as a teacher and lecturer on African rural and development issues.

Atakilte Beyene is a researcher in rural development. He is based at the Stockholm Environment Institute. His research focuses on institutions and the relationships between smallholder agricultural systems, property rights and national agricultural policies. He has facilitated and conducted extensive empirical field studies on livelihood systems, food insecurity and risk management strategies, natural resources management, and recent developments in commercial farming, including biofuels. He has also been a lecturer at the Swedish University of Agricultural Sciences, where he doubled up as coordinator of an international MSc programme in Integrated Water Resources Management.

Biofuels, land grabbing and food security in Africa

edited by Prosper B. Matondi, Kjell Havnevik
and Atakilte Beyene

Nordiska Afrikainstitutet
The Nordic Africa Institute

Zed Books
LONDON | NEW YORK

Biofuels, land grabbing and food security in Africa was first published in association with the Nordic Africa Institute, PO Box 1703, SE-751 47 Uppsala, Sweden in 2011 by Zed Books Ltd, 7 Cynthia Street, London N1 9JF, UK and Room 400, 175 Fifth Avenue, New York, NY 10010, USA

www.zedbooks.co.uk
www.nai.uu.se

Set in OurType Arnhem, Monotype Gill Sans Heavy by Ewan Smith, London
Index: ed.emery@thefreeuniversity.net
Cover designed by Rogue Four Design
Printed and bound in Great Britain by the MPG Books Group, King's Lynn and Bodmin

Mixed Sources
Product group from well-managed
forests and other controlled sources
www.fsc.org Cert no. SA-COC-1565
© 1996 Forest Stewardship Council
FSC

Distributed in the USA exclusively by Palgrave Macmillan, a division of St Martin's Press, LLC, 175 Fifth Avenue, New York, NY 10010, USA

A catalogue record for this book is available from the British Library
Library of Congress Cataloging in Publication Data available

ISBN 978 1 84813 879 7 hb
ISBN 978 1 84813 878 0 pb

Contents

Tables, figure, boxes and maps

Acronyms

AAG	ActionAid-Ghana
ARDA	Agriculture and Rural Development Authority (Zimbabwe)
ARU	Ardhi University (Dar es Salaam)
BIPPA	bilateral promotion and protection agreement
BRICS	Brazil, Russia, India, China, South Africa
CAADP	Comprehensive Africa Agriculture Development Programme
CSR	corporate social responsibility
DRC	Democratic Republic of Congo
DTZ	Development Trust of Zimbabwe
EIA	Energy Information Administration/environmental impact assessment
ESIA	environmental and social impact assessment
EU	European Union
FAO	Food and Agriculture Organization
FARA	Forum for Agricultural Research in Africa
FDI	foreign direct investment
GHS	Ghana new cedi
ICRISAT	International Crops Research Institute for the Semi-Arid Tropics
IEA	International Energy Agency
IFAD	International Fund for Agricultural Development
IFPRI	International Food Policy Research Institute
IIED	International Institute for Environmental Development
IMF	International Monetary Fund
IPCC	Intergovernmental Panel on Climate Change
MME	Ministry of Mines and Energy (Ethiopia)
MNC	multinational corporation
NEMC	National Environmental Management Council (Tanzania)
NGO	non-governmental organization
NOCZIM	National Oil Company of Zimbabwe
OECD	Organisation for Economic Co-operation and Development
OPEC	Organization of the Petroleum Exporting Countries
PGU	Politik för Global Utveckling (Policy for Global Development)
RAINS	Regional Advisory and Information Network Systems (Ghana)
RBZ	Reserve Bank of Zimbabwe

RED	Renewable Energy Directive (EU)
SEA	strategic environmental analysis
SEI	Stockholm Environment Institute
SEK	Swedish krona
Sida	Swedish International Development Cooperation Agency
SOE	state-owned enterprise
SWF	sovereign wealth fund
TAC	Technical Advisory Committee
TIC	Tanzania Investment Centre
TNC	transnational corporation
ToR	terms of reference
UNCTAD	United Nations Conference on Trade and Development
UNEP	UN Environment Programme
UN/SRRF	UN Special Rapporteur on the right to food
VLUP	village land use plan
WB	World Bank
WCED	World Commission on Environment and Development
ZAPU-PF	Zimbabwe African People's Union–Patriotic Front
ZBE	Zimbabwe Bio-Energy Ltd

Acknowledgements

This book is a result of the efforts of many people who have been engaged in African rural and agrarian issues over the last decade or more. During this time, a number of scholars in Africa and Europe have networked and met to share ideas and experiences of a range of issues – agriculture, land, environment, sustainability, institutions, poverty, biofuel development, etc. A major international workshop in Harare (November 2006) and several follow-up workshops in Sweden and Norway in recent years have contributed to this book. Biofuels, food security and land grabbing have slowly emerged as the major global topical issues, and have become the focus of this book.

Engaged as we were with these issues through North–South research networks, we benefited greatly from the support of the Nordic Africa Institute (NAI) in Sweden, the Swedish Interdisciplinary Research Network on Livelihoods and Natural Resource Governance (SERN), funded by Sida/Sarec, and the Ruzivo Trust in Harare. The NAI and SERN were instrumental in generating the knowledge from the various research forums, including the Harare workshop and seminars at the Royal Swedish Academy of Forestry and Agriculture (KSLA), Stockholm (April 2008), at Stockholm University (20 May 2009) and at the Nordic Africa Institute, Uppsala (17 September and 4 December 2009).

The authors of the chapters have, through multi- and interdisciplinary research approaches, addressed various contested issues related to biofuel development, food security and land grabbing.

The editors are grateful for the support provided in connection with the research and publication of this book. We would particularly like to single out our former colleague, the late Nontokozo Nemarundwe, and to thank Opira Otto, Torbjörn Rydberg, Otavio Cavalett, Simone Noemdoe, Peter Roberntz, Linda Engström, Melinda Fones-Sundell, Deborah Bryceson, Bertil Odén, Amanda Hammar, Mats Hårsmar, Göran Holmqvist, Terje Östigård, Eva Tobisson, Carin Norberg and other colleagues at NAI. At the Ruzivo Trust, we acknowledge the support provided by Esther Paradza, Mukundi Mutasa, Sheila Chikulo, Tandiwe Musiyiwa, Sheila Jack and Alfred Mafika. Colleagues at the University of Agder, Norway, also provided immeasurable support. We are grateful for the support in publishing the book from Birgitta Hellmark-Lindgren at NAI and Ken Barlow at Zed Books, and for the very competent language editing of Clive Liddiard.

The financial support provided by SERN and NAI made it possible to arrange the workshops and seminars and to publish this book.

Preface

Africa has seen a whirlwind of development models constructed, implemented and evaluated from one decade to the next. These have had mixed outcomes. But what is not contested is the fact that Africa badly needs to see the standard of living of the majority of its people raised. The issues of what and who will contribute to the Africans' quest to drag themselves out of poverty and misery, and of how this will be achieved, are highly contested. The introduction of biofuels in Africa has raised debates about their meaning, and about whether their presumed benefits will help Africans. At the same time, the last two to three years have witnessed unprecedented land grabbing, not just for biofuels but also for food production.

In 2008, intense debates on biofuels emerged on the back of the energy crisis, which seems also to have triggered the world food crisis. As these issues dominated the global debates, climate change issues also emerged at a time when the world financial system (and hence also the economic system) was likewise in dire straits. Our major preoccupation as researchers was to try to make sense of these multiple and complex crises in relation to Africa and its people. Our view was that the rights of smallholder African farmers were under siege, because the direction of change did not inspire confidence that Africans would ultimately benefit. Today, there is a lack of confidence in world food trade. At the same time, oil markets are unstable, because the dynamics keep changing from day to day. In Africa, there is a new propensity to venture into large-scale farming as a response to the global crisis; yet the basis for Africa's livelihoods is smallholder farming.

However, the problems that Africa faces are uneven, given the rising and unstable commodity pricing. The 'tacit' pressure placed on Africans to open their countries up to agro-investors in biofuels, food and other agricultural commodities is creating new relationships. In this book, we demonstrate how the issues are being framed in terms of areas of origin (Middle East, Europe, the Americas, Africa, Asia); the scramble for a variety of resources (food, energy, labour, water, mining, tourism, etc.); the range of investors (state, sovereign funds, private sector); and strategic interests (developing export model away from the home country, search for markets, pure profit motives). Clearly, as the cases in this book show, land grabbing has become a key security issue.

On the other hand, there are different conditions and patterns emerging in Africa: unclear deal-making; various kinds of contracts (land lease and outright land acquisition); strategic interests of domestic elites; issues to do with compensation (or lack thereof, in some instances). We have, therefore, performed a first systematic analysis of the various interests and issues that are emerging in Africa. We present the stories behind the headlines, in an attempt to provide information that might contribute to action on alternatives that can leverage benefits for Africa.

In this book, we have opened the debate beyond the underlying issues, to call for a deeper understanding of the African environment and people. At the same time, our work is not anti-development, as is assumed by proponents of land grabbing. Rather, we question the 'win-win' paradigm that is externally driven, which resembles development for and not with Africans. We are also clear that Africa requires development that not only protects the poor but also attracts technological advances and investments that can benefit all African people. We hope this book will stimulate further research and debates on these issues, and that policy-making processes aimed at balancing external investments and the internal development of Africa will begin to feature prominently.

Prosper B. Matondi, Ruzivo Trust, Harare, Zimbabwe

Kjell Havnevik, Nordic Africa Institute, Uppsala, Sweden, and University of Agder, Kristiansand, Norway

Atakilte Beyene, Stockholm Environment Institute, Sweden

We dedicate this book to our colleague, the late
Dr Nontokozo Nemarundwe, born Nabane, who
passed away in 2010. We worked with our friend,
whom we fondly called Nonto, for the past ten
years on various issues that are pertinent to
Africa. May her soul rest in eternal peace.

Introduction: biofuels, food security and land grabbing in Africa

Prosper B. Matondi, Kjell Havnevik
and Atakilte Beyene

Introduction

Land grabbing for growing biofuels and to ensure food security is capturing the imagination of multilateral institutions, donors, non-governmental organizations (NGOs), land activists, academics and the media worldwide. The subject has also become popular on e-discussion fora, in the electronic and print media, at regional and international conferences and at workshops. In the last few years, climate change, peak oil and rising food prices have made energy and food security the primary global political issues. This has spurred the search for alternative renewable energy sources and has resulted in a global push for biofuels from various agricultural feedstocks, as well as for land in order to enhance food production and food security. This development has generated new frictions and tensions both globally and within African societies (Borras et al. 2010). Active resistance to land grabbing for biofuels and food for export is growing among those local communities in the South that are affected, among NGOs and among concerned researchers in the North and South (see the Declaration of the Harare Conference of 24–25 November 2010). The resistance to land grabbing is affecting moral, economic and political relations between and within nations, classes and communities both inside and outside Africa.

Land grabbing has acquired various definitions, reflecting the positions of players globally. The term 'land grabbing' has gained popularity, alongside a plethora of terms such as 'green colonization', 'new land colonization', 'climate colonization' and 'water plunder' (see chapters 1 and 7). In the African context, we find land grabbing to be a more useful and generic concept, which we define to include exploration, negotiations, acquisitions or leasing, settlement and exploitation of the land resource, specifically to attain energy and food security through export to investors' countries and other markets. This does not preclude land grabbing by domestic or regional commercial, state and other interests; however, the major tendency is for these domestic interests to be in collusion or alliance with external interests, often through minor share holdings in local companies so that legal and other regulatory aspects can be

I

circumvented. In this context, the implication is that local people and producers have to contend not just with external, but also with domestic interests.

The significance of the concept thus also needs to be seen in relation to the 'unsettled' character of the governance structures of African land ownership, and to control of and access to natural resources. As a result, the roles, legitimacy and stakes of different actors, including the state, are contested. Land grabbing in its wider sense thus relates to changing access to, and control, use and ownership of, African land and the products generated from it, including what happens to them on the domestic and export markets. The actual process by which land is 'grabbed' by foreigners ranges from outright 'illegal' acquisitions, based on secretive negotiations, to rapidly concluded binding contracts that, though legal, are characterized by a strong asymmetry in power relations, by risk taking and by limited access to information, particularly among the weaker stakeholders, who are potentially most affected by the deals.

As a preamble, this chapter examines the complex aspects of biofuels, food security and land grabbing in Africa, as the continent competes for investments at a time of global economic recession. Peak oil and climate change have led to a resurgence of the search for alternative fuel, as well as to varying and competing discourses on climate change and on ways of mitigating it. This has generated fresh debates (and revived old ones) about the place and the role of Africa in international and global developments. The debates are expanding, as critics level the charge that 'rich countries are buying poor countries' soil fertility, water and sun to ship food and fuel back home, in a kind of neo-colonial dynamic' (Leahy 2009).

Multiple pressures towards commercialization of land in Africa converge – both historical and current – and these need to be differentiated and contextualized in relation to the recent wave of land grabbing. The concession of large areas – often as part of wider agreements for investment in infrastructure, the provision of services and job creation, as part of economic growth and the 'development' of Africa – motivated the authors of this book to present an in-depth analysis based on current research and informed observations of what is happening in Africa. As we observe and seek to understand the features and mechanisms of land grabbing and the initiatives at the international level to develop voluntary guidelines to 'do it right', we gain fascinating insights as to how Africa and the African rural population and smallholders are perceived by investing countries, international institutions and even external research communities. Our opinion is that Africa requires investment in many areas (economic, infrastructure, institutional and social) for the benefit of its people. The key question is whether land grabbing and the associated agro-investments can contribute to the development of Africa in such a way that benefits its people, or whether it will lead to their further impoverishment.

Unmasking land grabbing in Africa

A general theme running through most of the recent publications on land grabbing in Africa is that it is an integral part of the rise of commercialization within the context of globalization. The widespread view is that it is the West, with its strong, market-based econ̲___ ___ ___ ___ ___ ___ ___ ___ while the East is also angling to d̲___ ___ ___ ___ ___ ___ ___ intensity and secrecy have caused ___ ___ ___ ___ ___ ___ have also been local protests on di̲___ ___ ___ wave of press reports illustrates the magnitude of these trends, and a recent World Bank report (2010: vi) showed an annual average of less than 4 million hectares of land being sourced before 2008, as opposed to 45 million hectares in 2009. At least 70 per cent of this land was sourced in Africa. Nevertheless, in only 21 per cent of the deals announced was there any activity or implementation. The large gap between reported deals and activity on the ground in 2009 (World Bank 2010) indicates both that land grabbing-related projects have a long gestation period and also that projects (at least in the early phases) may end in failure (see Chapter 6). This does not, however, undermine the conclusion that land grabbing today is a significant and accelerating process that needs to be understood deeply from various angles and perspectives. The World Bank's conservative estimate is that 6 million hectares of additional land will be brought into production each year until 2030, and that: 'Two-thirds of this expansion will be in Sub-Saharan Africa and Latin America, where potential farmland is most plentiful' (World Bank 2010: xi, xvi, table 2). In this book, we aim to provide an African perspective on land grabbing, with reference to the globalized system of exchange and production in food and energy that is being shaped by the failed neoliberal history and agenda for Africa of the 1980s and 1990s.

In our search to understand the original motives for seeking out African lands, we are reminded of the unpleasant history of land takeovers and the colonization of Africa by Western nations aspiring to create empires. The contemporary land-grabbing process in Africa matches this history, insofar as it constitutes an increasing control over the benefits of Africa's land resources, ecology and water by non-Africans. The similarities between the colonial historical legacy and the key issues that arise from the current land-grab discourse are remarkable. The implications of land takeover involve political absorption, economic change, redirection of societal change and social dominance. Land grabbing is a response to the insecurity and vulnerability generated by the liberalized – and increasingly global – agro-food, fuel and financial systems. On the other hand, foreign investments in African land force certain social categories to the periphery of the economic system. In Africa, land is a resource that engenders phenomenal power, and the current land grabbing can contribute to processes of discrimination and marginalization that are similar to the dislocations during the colonial period.

Borras et al. (2010: 575) state that the starting point for understanding land grabs is 'who owns what? Who does what? Who gets what? And what do they do with the surplus wealth?' Anuradha Mittal (2010: 3) adds: 'What is grown? For whom? And how?' In our view, wealth and power are shaping global systems of production and exchange, as is demonstrated by the current biofuel investments in Africa. Over the last decades, there has been growing technological confidence in the West related to the exploitation of agricultural feedstocks for energy, but also for supplying food to Western and Asian markets and nations. Modern technology is contrasted with the simple techniques of a barren and poverty-stricken African agriculture. On this basis, it is easy to argue that Africa requires foreign investment as a shock therapy to modernize its agriculture and speed its 'development'.

In the rush for African land and biofuel production, non-African nations have given themselves the role of bearers of the right scientific and engineering approach. This perspective is obsessed with large-scale monoculture production systems that use advanced machinery to harness Africa's 'nature'. The perception of a barren Africa reconceptualizes the image of colonial Africa held by Sir Charles Eliot, Commissioner of the East Africa Protectorate:

> Nations and races derive their characteristics largely from their surroundings, but on the other hand, man reclaims disciplines and trains nature. The surface of Europe, Asia and North America has been submitted to this influence and discipline, but it has still to be applied to large parts of South America and Africa. (quoted in Mackenzie 1997: 216–17)

Contemporary land grabbing is shrouded in similar attitudes about unexplored, underutilized and uninhabited African land. This echoes in a subtle way the past colonization of Africa. Worse in the current context, however, is the existence of willing participants on the African side who negotiate concessions with foreign interests under a veil of secrecy, and often in alliance with domestic actors. It has been noted that there are no proper guidelines or policies on land transfer processes in most African countries, and that investors take advantage of this lacuna, and of weak land governance, in what the World Bank terms 'a race to the bottom' to attract investors (World Bank 2010: xv). The purveyors of the land sales are the people, whose stand Frantz Fanon (1965: 38–9) described thus:

> at the beginning of his association with the people, the native intellectual overstresses details and thereby comes to forget that the defeat of colonialism is the real object of the struggle ... The people on the other hand, take their stand from the start on the broad and inclusive positions of the Bread and the Land: how can we obtain land and bread to eat? And this obstinate point of view of the masses, which may seem shrunken and limited, is in the end the most worthwhile and most efficient mode of procedure.

The voice of the African policy-makers caught unaware has provided mixed signals as to their understanding of the land-grabbing phenomenon. Some actually believe that in their own countries there is 'too much land' for the size of the human population. They do not find it problematic to cede some of it to foreign investors, arguing that their countries need agricultural investment (capital) more than this land, which is assumed to be underutilized. This time, in biofuel-associated land deals, unlike during colonial times, the voice of African policy-makers can be heard from time to time. However, the weapons employed in land conquests have changed: the struggles take place in corporate boardrooms and on stock markets, rather than through physical war, as in the pre-colonial and colonial periods. In what seems to be justification for land acquisition, Palmer (2010: 5) has catalogued a series of self-serving statements from Africa in support of biofuels and land acquisition:

> Mozambique's Minister of Energy, Salvador Namburete, for example, stated that '36 million hectares of arable land could be used for biofuels without threatening food production, while another 41 million hectares of marginal land would be suitable for raising jatropha'; Zambia's Minister of Agriculture, Brian Chituwo, boasted 'we have well over 30 million hectares of land that is begging to be utilised'; while his counterpart in Ethiopia, Abeda Deressa, suggested that pastoralists displaced by land grabbing 'can just go somewhere else'.

Yet in Africa there are also voices that have taken a cautious approach, given that many governments see foreign private investment as a panacea for economic development (Chapter 4). At this stage, one gets a sense of leadership inaction, as responses have come from lower-ranking government officials. In addition, there are no specific policy positions emanating from regional and continental bodies on land-grabbing policy. It is clear that if land grabbing is to be stopped, or even if it is to be channelled to the benefit of rural people and African smallholders, there is a need for towering leadership in Africa that can see beyond the 'guided' optimism.

The narratives of Western colonialism convey a message that foreigners take out more than they give Africa, especially in relation to resources. Whereas in colonial times it was about people being settled, today it is about machines on large-scale monoculture farms displacing African smallholders. A new form of 'settler' society is being created, which is not numerically dominant but which uses wealth and money to transform Africa's agrarian spaces. The issue of local benefits persists in the arguments of advocates for biofuels. However, the cases offered in this book, apart from in the chapter on Ghana (Chapter 8), demonstrate promises yet to be fulfilled in terms of employment creation, infrastructure, higher standards of living, etc. In the colonial period, these promises of 'civilization' for Africa resulted in an exclusive benefit for the colonizers that created structural tremors of conflict in Africa which are persisting to this day.

The drivers and face of land grabs in Africa

The companies investing in large-scale land acquisitions are the products of complex social forces in their own countries (or sometimes transnationally); but Africa has only partial and fleeting glimpses of these social forces, made up of complex interests of transnational companies, governments under pressure to supply cheap food and politicians willing to satisfy affluence by approving policies that can damage other nations and people. Such companies as D1 Oils, Daewoo and SEKAB, identified by the media for land grabbing in Africa, are part of a complex social and political web, in which capital and the forces behind it shape global policy paradigms exemplified by biofuels and the search for food security. At this juncture it is easy to get a generalized description of what they do in Africa, but some of the descriptions are aimed rather at hiding than at revealing the true nature of the companies (Chapter 6). In addition, many companies adhere to proper and accepted ethical and moral values in their operations in the North, and in so doing retain their prestige and standing; in the South, though, including in Africa, this is generally not considered necessary.

It is difficult for Africans to understand the private-sector biofuel companies – not just because of their secrecy or 'hidden agendas', but also because their ideological and philosophical orientations are the products of complex historical forces within their own countries. The four hundred years of Africa's association with the West has been shaped by a history of resource plunder. And in colonial times that plunder was at the behest of private companies. Palmer (2010: 1) illustrates this history:

> the motives of those who joined the Company's invading Pioneer Column in 1890 were unambiguous: 'the main reason we are all here is to make money and lose no time about it'.

Whereas in the colonial period private companies were blunt about their intentions, this is not so in the current discourse. A view that Africa badly needs investment and that foreign aid has largely failed seems to imply that foreign companies should have unfettered access to Africa (Chapter 4). In the colonial period, European governments were 'reluctant to spend large sums of tax revenue on the conquest and administration of tropical lands' (Palmer 2010: 2). Yet nowadays governments that worry about the sustainability of development aid tacitly encourage private companies to invest in Africa's lands. Under this arrangement, multiple benefits are envisaged: reduced foreign aid and thus reduced taxation of their own people, plus food and energy for the European and Asian markets.

However, when we look at the private companies that are taking over land in Africa, who are they and what are they doing in Africa? Public understanding of these issues seems to be both superficial and uncritical. Are they the forerunners of the real 'scramble' for Africa in a global contest where new forces (China, India, Brazil) are emerging to seek a stake in the African land? The companies at the forefront of investment in Africa are secretive. In Africa, very little is known about them, their linkages with their governments and their direct and indirect 'control' of markets. Much of the criticism in this book stems from this very opaqueness, which fosters suspicion. The generally hospitable and welcoming culture of Africa has been exploited by these companies. Yet, they are unaccountable and are under no public scrutiny in terms of their history, their operations, or their linkages and alliances.

The private sector in Western countries has largely been in favour of biofuels, stressing the energy and climate benefits that accrue from reducing a country's reliance on oil. At the same time, some governments support biofuels because they are regarded as 'strategic' in terms of energy security and of reducing the cost of oil imports. A huge campaign to promote clean and renewable energy is also seen as a direct contribution to reducing the emissions of greenhouse gases. In developing countries, it is argued that biofuel production is likely to lead to income generation, to the creation of jobs, the promotion of trade and industry and to alternative domestic uses for crops that may not be absorbed by global market competition.[1] In September 2007, the managing director of the Ouagadougou-based International Institute for Water and Environment Engineering, Paul Ginies, concluded that: 'No matter what we say, today biofuels represent a pragmatic solution in light of the energy problems in relation to soaring oil prices' (Hien 2008).

Myths about land availability in Africa

Large-scale land grabbing has led to a renewed academic interest in struggles and conflicts around land in Africa (Cotula et al.; 2008a Cotula et al. 2009; World Bank 2010). Whereas current studies have looked at continent- and country-wide tendencies, the global-level analysis strips them of much of their content and nuance and mutes realities at the micro level. This book responds directly to this gap by providing national and micro-level cases on the complex impact of land grabbing for biofuels in Africa.

Africa's land question cannot be understood on the basis of the mistaken perception that the continent has abundant land resources that are either not utilized or else are underutilized (Cotula et al. 2009; also see Chapter 1). In terms of the agrarian basis of the land question, it is notable that the extent of developed arable and irrigable land available for agriculture is limited, despite the continent's large size. In general, there is apparent consensus on the centrality of land to African livelihoods, and the dismantling of colonial rule in Africa was about redressing the skewed land ownership patterns inherited from colonialism. In some countries, the efforts to address imbalances in African land ownership through land tenure reforms, land redistribution and land restitution have failed to improve the land situation, which remains distorted in favour of big commercial interests. This implies that agricultural support (subsidies using finance or inputs) is also skewed towards the large-scale commercial sector, rather than smallholder farmers (Lund 2001).

One key argument for biofuels is that such production will occur on 'marginal' rather than prime agricultural land (Cotula et al. 2008a; 2008b). It has been indicated that in Africa, unforested marginal land amounts to 154 million hectares (ibid.). Meanwhile, the growing evidence on the subject raises doubts about the concept of 'idle' land. According to Dufey et al. (2007), in many cases lands perceived to be 'idle', 'underutilized', 'marginal' or 'abandoned' by government and large private operators provide a vital basis for the livelihoods of poorer and vulnerable groups, through arable crop land, grazing areas, and ecosystems with a variety of biodiversity resources (ibid.; see also Chapter 1). In Africa, livestock production forms the backbone of the rural economy in the agriculturally marginal areas (Engström 2009).

Even though the policy preference (where policies exist) is to plant crops aimed at producing biofuels on marginal lands, many land deals in Africa relate to fertile lands. The 'modern-day' land question is characterized by extensive degradation of fragile land resources and by increasing elite control of the prime lands through exclusion from the land of the majority of its former users and rights holders. In practice, no profit-driven investors would target marginal and degraded land. Instead, they would aim for fertile land, since there is a higher probability of making a profit that way than if they were merely 'environmentally sensitive'. For instance, in Ethiopia the spatial distribution of land deals shows a concentration in regions with more fertile lands and/or closer links to markets (Cotula et al. 2009).

In Tanzania, sugarcane plantations for biofuel in the Bagamoyo and Rufiji districts (Chapter 6) aim to draw water from the adjacent Rufiji River. In the Bagamoyo case, smallholders were using some of the project land for rice production and other parts were used for grazing by pastoralists, although formal ownership of the land is with the government of Zanzibar. In Rufiji district, some of the planned biofuel plantations were located in wooded areas, in forest reserves or on village land designated for food production (Chapter 6). Other ongoing or planned large land allocations in Tanzania have been reported as involving the displacement of local farmers (ABN 2007).

Africa's challenge today lies in the fact that the conditions of poverty and the increasing conflict levels are largely a result of limited access to natural resources, including agricultural land, pasture and water. In the post-independence era, many African states have generally failed to redistribute land or to protect the rights of the indigenous communities in the face of competing interests for land from foreign investors (as well as from domestic interests). These weaknesses have contributed towards the general failure of African states to effect sustainable natural resource exploitation policies that benefit the majority of their populations.

The African crisis has historically been one of the 'reproduction of labour', i.e. social relations and the forms of organization of agriculture, and its contribution to livelihoods. There seems to be a continuation of the same livelihood risks in the context of land grabbing in Africa. Increasing competition among outsiders for land in all parts of Africa has already been noted. This is linked to an intensification of generalized commodity production (under neoliberal structural adjustment programmes), a generalized crisis of social reproduction and global security concerns. These reforms are changing the structure of agricultural production, land holding and natural resource use patterns, and in many instances exacerbate the conflict situation.

The four triggers for land grabbing

Unprecedented economic growth in transition countries The unprecedented economic growth in the transition countries (India, China and Brazil) has led to a rapid increase in the demand for energy (Coyle 2007). Consumers in these countries are demanding a higher standard of living and are hastening to catch up with Western welfare standards. Is this model of development sustainable, and what are its implications for the world energy stock? In addition, what does it imply for Africa, which is generally the slowest-growing continent but which is currently being heavily targeted for biofuels and food production for external interests?

The combination of higher (and more volatile) global commodity prices, the demand for biofuels, population growth and urbanization, globalization and overall economic development implies that such investments will increase in importance in the future (von Braun and Pachauri 2006; ABN 2007). In many contexts, the large-scale acquisition of land highlights renewed interest in plantation-based agriculture, which is also fuelled by scepticism regarding the effectiveness of market and trade mechanisms in guaranteeing access to basic food supplies. In addition, there is the belief that large-scale production can help modernize the agricultural sector. As Hollander (2010) observes, agrofuels are products of a globally organized system of production, exchange and consumption that provides distinct patterns and alliances within and outside spaces in intricate and complex ways. In this way, transition countries are also developing complex economic and production linkages with Africa. However, many of the deals are shrouded in secrecy, and also involve land takeover and the import of humans to Africa (as technical experts), in order to oversee production on behalf of the agro-investments and investors.

Food security Biofuel production is being introduced in situations of food uncertainty for rural and urban areas. The absolute number of undernourished Africans increased by about 20 per cent between 1992 and 2002 (FAO 2006; Kidane et al. 2006), and has further increased with the financial crisis and the increase in global food prices since 2008. Globally, more than a billion people, mostly in rural areas of the South, live in food insecure situations (IFPRI 2008). What is needed is increased food production and employment, as well as lower consumer food prices. This requires continued support for agriculture in order to improve soil fertility, water availability and crop yields. However, in Africa the agricultural systems remain rudimentary. Rukuni (2006: 2) points out that:

> The circumstances of the African farmer remain perilous today. The typical farmer in Africa is a woman with a family who has one hectare or less of low fertility land with erratic rainfall and little or no irrigation. If the farmer wanted to buy fertilizer it would be more expensive than in Europe or America. Her farm faces numerous pests, crop diseases, and environmental stresses that would severely annoy a typical farmer in the United States of America (USA) or Europe. Modern equipment, backed by dynamic information technology and more resources for a European as compared to an African are the norm rather than the exception. Average crop yields in Africa are the same level as pre-industrial Europe. Even if there is increased productivity or yield improvement, farmers in Africa face dysfunctional markets, and find it difficult to compete with farmers in Europe and America.

Biofuels have been affecting the production of traditional food crops, and thus further raising world food prices. The FAO (2008: 72) argues that 'the rapid growth in biofuel production will affect food security at the national and household levels mainly through its impact on food prices and incomes'. This affects the poor, who are mainly found in the developing nations (chapter 1). Biofuel production is also changing the traditional agricultural landscape, leading to monoculture. There is a need for concerted global action on how best to tackle the issue of biofuel production without compromising the livelihoods of rural and urban dwellers. However, so far most recommendations and guidelines are of a voluntary nature and seem to have little effect on actual practices (Chapter 1).

Small farmers are traditionally dependent on their land for their own food production (Chapter 5). One can easily picture the current situation, with poor farmers, most of whom lack access to the necessary resources (land, credit, infrastructure and inputs) and already struggle to feed themselves, being lured into engaging with biofuel crops. For a variety of reasons, most poor rural households are actually net consumers of food, rather than net producers. When the price of food rises, they become worse off because they have limited supply, given the weak competition in food retail in rural areas. At the same time, governments have weak rural development programmes and hence cannot generate significant income on a continuous basis. The assumption is that when smallholders turn to biofuels they will be able to acquire food.

Global peak oil and alternative fuel energy sources Since the 1970s, African economies have experienced a decline in trade as their agricultural exports have become uncompetitive. Africa now faces a renewed oil crisis as global prices move upwards. Analysis of the trends on global peak oil (Chapter 3) demonstrates the fallacy of biofuel production by industrialized nations. Biofuel production can certainly contribute to damping down the rise in oil prices and can marginally improve national energy security. On the other hand, though, it is highly questionable (to say the least) whether biofuels can contribute to abating the climate crisis.

Biofuels are renewable, are clean burning and can be mixed with petrol to reduce oil dependency or used to generate electricity. Chapter 3 demonstrates that peak oil has generated a global surge in interest in alternative forms of energy, of which biofuel is central. This fuel is seen as a clean source of renewable energy that can make up for some of the declining access to fossil energy. However, the analyses and perspectives on biofuel as a provider of net energy are questioned.

Although biofuels constitute a small share of global energy consumption, a slight increase in biofuel production necessitates a significant change in land use – such as the conversion of different land uses to biofuel feedstock production. So rising food insecurity is to be anticipated, as large tracts of land are used for biofuel rather than food crops. This has a disproportionately negative impact on the rural poor (Msangi 2007; Runge and Senauer 2007; and see Chapter 1).[2]

Climate and environmental concerns Biofuels are being sought as an alternative source of energy, at a time when climate change issues are prominent in world politics. Yet biofuels also pose risks, particularly with respect to impending global warming. Scientific enquiry has revealed that each biofuel plant type varies considerably in terms of its energy efficiency and environmental impact. More generally, the net climate benefit outcomes of ethanol production from biofuel crops are questionable. As more forest and bush land is opened up for cultivation, a major source of carbon sink will be destroyed, and this will contribute to climate change. Forested areas of Africa are likely to be a prime area for biofuel investors, which would further deeply compromise Africa's available carbon sinks for greenhouse gases.

Climate change will bring rising temperatures worldwide and increasing desertification in many places. On balance, African agriculture is likely to suffer most from global warming, with growing numbers of people likely to be at risk of hunger. African smallholders' finely tuned food systems are already experiencing difficulties, with the disruption of seasonal climate patterns, freak storms and increased weather variability. Simultaneously, climate change will bring irregular weather events, rising temperatures and increasing water shortages. African agricultural systems – both small- and large-scale – are very vulnerable. In welfare terms, poor rural communities are likely to suffer greatly from the negative impacts of climate change, since their lives and livelihoods depend directly upon the fragile natural resources around them (Cline 2007; Prowse and Braunholtz-Speight 2007; Giles 2007). Furthermore, the irregularity of output could also jeopardize rural non-agricultural livelihoods, given the inevitable decline in rural purchasing power that follows climatic setbacks.[3]

Other environmental issues that arise in connection with biofuel expansion include the risk of introducing invasive species, changing water usage patterns, potential sources of pollution from biofuel processing and the decline in local biodiversity as a result of mono-cropping. When biofuel production relies on the use of crop residues that are normally left on the ground to replenish the soil, soil fertility is adversely affected. Biofuel production may also overtax local water supplies, or be wasteful if rising fertilizer prices preclude the use of sufficient fertilizer, thus causing low yields and sub-optimal use of land otherwise available for food production.

This book promotes the issue of biopolitics, implying that biophysical resources have now become central to the global policy discourse. The 2009 Copenhagen Conference on Climate Change did indeed amplify geopolitics and the role and position of the South, as the North seemed unwilling to give up its superfluous energy needs, which were placed upfront as some sort of privilege. Africa in general finds itself 'between a rock and a hard place', because many countries lack policy mechanisms on climate change. Therefore, when the North argues for collective responsibility and discipline in the modern governance discourse (Foucault et al. 2003), it is on the basis of unequal advances in knowledge and technology. This means that the South is expected to share responsibility for problems caused by the North's higher energy consumption (Chapter 3). The North is thereby seriously undermining the path towards climate justice. The North is seen to use the morality of collective responsibility for the environment as a tacit strategy for market deregulation (Chapter 2), which in this case is coming via biofuels.

Hegemonic dissonance in governance over biofuels

For a variety of reasons, Africa has for many decades struggled to meet a wide range of basic needs, including food, income, infrastructure, techno-logy and investment. The challenges that Africa faces take different forms for different countries and people, and there is no single answer to the myriad problems and challenges. To try to mitigate some of these challenges, African governments usually seek to attract foreign direct investment (FDI), which is assumed to contribute to the modernization of agriculture (and certainly does so in certain contexts). However, in the current discourse, the benefits of land grabs seem to be outweighed by the damage to the livelihoods of smallholder farmers, leaving the latter worse off.

In most African countries, the regulatory and institutional frameworks for private agribusiness investments are not adapted to current trends. The role of smallholder producers in biofuel expansion has been severely neglected (Mwamila et al. 2008), because most African states have not yet established the institutional and policy mechanisms to support the biofuel expansion (Chapter 5). Yet, in Africa, ambiguous land policies and inadequate tenure rights for African smallholders exist amid the efforts by African governments to attract biofuel investments. The key issues are that there is considerable contestation over land rights, the distribution of land, and the role of foreigners in land ownership and use. In Chapter 2, Widengård argues for a broader understanding of the strategic interests of the North in Africa's land that is emerging through the biofuel expansion. Boamah also addresses this issue, in a case study of jatropha in Ghana (Chapter 8).

The key discourse in these two chapters is how to balance private and public interests, as well as the role of globalism or the use of 'eco-governmentality' in the governance of biofuels. There is a growing body of organizations that are resisting some of the counter-hegemonic discourse that emerges with biofuels and agro-investments. While, in some instances, African governments are not so certain about what they have been told, they have largely accepted biofuels and agro-investments based on precautionary principles. In Africa, over time, resistance to biofuels and land grabbing has been noted (e.g. chapters 6 and 7). At the local level, smallholder farmers realize that they are not part of the projects or that they are promised benefits that do not materialize. Havnevik and Haaland (Chapter 6) document the resistance that made SEKAB retreat in Tanzania. At a session of the All Party Parliamentary Group on Agriculture and Food for Development in the UK House of Commons on 27 January 2010, Robin Palmer asked Tanzanian High Commissioner Mwanaidi Sinare Maajar:

> what if, at a time of great food insecurity, a foreign company working in your country exported food back home?

She replied:

> we would not allow it; in fact we are in the process of drawing up a code of conduct which would prevent such a thing happening, and if any company refuses to sign it, then they won't be allowed to operate.

In the case of some countries, the domestic economic pressures would seem to imply that they have limited options to negotiate on agro-investments. The case of Zimbabwe described by Matondi (7) clearly illustrates this trajectory. Pressures emanating from both the domestic and the global economies have created a cruel dilemma for African governments. In future, this will lead to serious questions of how to manage the political costs and pain.

This book is also framed towards understanding the global governance and techniques that are being employed to sell biofuels as a cleaner energy. This brings to the fore, in poignant ways, the North–South relationship, where inventions (machines and management systems) from the North are used by the South (for African lands and water resources), but strangely the North reaps the benefits (through export products). The diversity and complexity of land-grabbing forms and mechanisms for food and biofuels, identified in chapters 1, 4 and 8, suggest that these links are very varied. Chapter 4, on biofuels and FDI, demonstrates the construction of the relationship between the North and the South, in which the smallholders are either victims or potential beneficiaries of economic globalization. When foreign investors acquire land for biofuels, they tend to pocket most of the gains, as they repatriate foreign currency to the investing countries. The case studies in this book suggest that global governance and eco-governmentality, in particular, circumvent the notion of nation states having control over their territories and/or political agendas.

Narratives and sticking points in smallholder farming

African smallholder agriculture has experienced over 25 years of mixed fortunes: there has been underinvestment and productivity decline, but there have also been achievements in some countries (Havnevik et al. 2007). The *World Development Report* (World Bank 2007) stressed the difficulties that African farmers face in trying to compete in the global market. The scale of poverty in rural Africa remains higher than in any other region of the world, in spite of decades of programmes and strategies to address poverty, both domestic and based on external development assistance. The greatest fear related to the push towards biofuels is that smallholders in Africa, who are the core of the producers (at least 60–70 per cent of the people live and work on small family farms), would be alienated from their land. However, the enigma is that African states, which are supposed to be the protectors of the poor, could be acquiescing with foreign investors and governments in such land displacements. Promises of economic development from foreign investors and technological innovations in agriculture give some African governments grounds for optimism.

Agriculture in Europe and Asia is synonymous with technology and infra-structure, and many African countries would also like to see this. However, at this stage in Africa's development, technological advances in countries with a poor skills base and low literacy levels are likely to lead to the majority of the African rural poor ending up as spectators, watching the export of agricultural production from their own countries. The failure of the Green Revolution in Africa in the 1970s provides examples of the fallacy of the biofuel and land-grabbing agenda. Smallholders are at the tail end of production, and rarely have any power to influence the control and management of world consumer markets, where the energy prices are decided. Would it then be morally right to make African biomass crop-production enclaves to meet the affluence needs of the North?

Africa, however, badly needs to raise food production, create employment and reduce consumer prices (while low in absolute terms, food prices are often high relative to income). This requires continued investment in, and support for, agriculture. Low soil fertility and lack of water are the most fundamental biophysical constraints to raising agricultural productivity. The smallholder farmers in Africa face numerous other challenges, such as inadequate land and financial resources. Governments, on the other hand, have struggled to prioritize agriculture, even though it provides the greatest scope for an escape from poverty. Recent agreements to allocate at least 10 per cent of African national budgets to agriculture have not generally been implemented, in spite of numerous conferences.[4] The prospects for increasing resources to African smallholder agriculture are slim, given that this sector remains on the margins of the state and markets. Yet smallholder agriculture, led mostly by women, does provide the bulk of the food needs in African families. In many countries, smallholder farms are further characterized by a low level of technological innovation, and by poor market orientation and infrastructure. How, then, can smallholders faced with these challenges produce biofuels?

African farming has developed along two different trajectories: smallholders (who use mainly rain-fed cultivation, adapted to the local natural resource bases) and large-scale mono-cropping in capitalized plantation farming (Djurfeldt et al. 2005; Gibbon and Ponte 2005). Previous research has argued that small family farms are often more efficient than large-scale agriculture (Berry and Cline 1979; Binswanger and McIntire 1987; Bruce and Migot-Adholla 1994; Djurfeldt et al. 2005). However, the current trend, not least in biofuel production, is for the promotion of large-scale units. Large-scale monoculture farms are the most blatant manifestations of these deals where machines displace the poor and the powerless. Anuradha Mittal (2010) argues the case strongly: 'We have an agricultural system, which is upside down and backwards, which has replaced diversity with monocultures and self sufficiency with increased dependency on markets.' Arguments in support of large-scale agriculture in Africa are once more gaining currency (Collier 2008). Africa is most likely to witness a gradual shift in land use from the cultivation of crops for biofuels. The change in land use on a larger scale will happen at different levels and gradually, through the conversion from one crop to another, and from pastoral land to cropland.

The current trends in agribusiness and global value chains promote 'efficient' large-scale, capitalized biofuel production units over scattered, small-scale peasant farmers' efforts. On the other hand, the equity and livelihood of large segments of the rural African population could suffer if narrow measures of economic efficiency were prioritized to the exclusion of welfare considerations. Therefore, places that were characterized by low-intensity land use will be converted to high-intensity and expansive use of land. As the economic opportunities linked to biofuel production improve, so agricultural producers may shift from food or cash crops to feedstocks.

Since the biofuel industry needs economies of scale, it will tend to bypass smallholder farmers and lead to rising food insecurity (Msangi 2007; Runge and Senauer 2007). For instance, the jatropha crop is generally grown in large, monocultured block plantations. The economic value of biofuel crops may also increase the value of land, which in turn may derail government public resettlement programmes. However, on the other hand, this may provide an opportunity for indigenous people to renew their interest and investment in the land. Boamah (Chapter 8) shows how chiefs in Northern Ghana leased the land areas to BioFuel Africa Ltd and voiced optimism in jatropha because the livelihoods of the affected communities are vulnerable. Particularly as the communities have large areas of 'unused' land, the chiefs expressed the hope that the project would improve livelihoods without creating competition with such land-based livelihoods as farming or other local business. However, generally speaking, when small-scale farmers suspect that they may lose their rights, they try to negotiate political channels in order to seek more secure individual or communal tenure over their land resources. The case of Zimbabwe shows that smallholders do not accept agro-investments without first negotiating their rights and potential benefits (Chapter 7).

Spatial distribution of biofuels across Africa

The case studies in this book are drawn from south, east and west Africa. Chapter 4 on biofuels and FDI argues from the perspective of the effects of economic globalization on smallholder agriculture. When foreign investors acquire land for biofuel production, they tend to capture most of the gains through repatriation of profits to their host countries. Local governments and partners are left with meagre benefits, yet they are the ones who provide land and labour for the production activities. Farmers' land rights are also compromised, as most of the companies get long-term leases that may end in outright purchase. Chapter 4 shows that FDI may also lead to the development of infrastructure on the land – for example, through investment in irrigation, which can provide employment for the surrounding rural communities.

The Ethiopian case (Chapter 5) introduces us to the way in which biofuel production has been undertaken by multinational companies and smallholder farmers. Biofuel production is a new phenomenon in Ethiopia; there are considerable pros and cons for the farmers, since it is premised on contract farming. A major shortcoming of the current policies and strategies that promote biofuels is that they are not framed in relation to rural development and the livelihood needs of the rural areas. The potential of the rural energy supply to reduce poverty, the need to secure household energy across rural–urban contexts, and the creation of conditions (institutional, financial and technological) to facilitate such processes within the country are major areas that need to be considered in biofuel and energy policies.

On the other hand, the Tanzanian case (Chapter 6) focuses on the inconsistencies inherent in the environmental and social impact assessment (ESIA) related to an investment plan for biofuel in Bagamoyo district. SEKAB, a Swedish municipally owned company, was challenged by local NGOs and stakeholders, despite the fact that the company had claimed to have adopted a sustainable development approach. However, contradictions arose between SEKAB and various stakeholders. This was partly related to the lack of clear Tanzanian policies or a legal framework related to the biofuel sector (a feature typical of many African countries). However, governance problems also emerged in the ESIA process due to lack of regulation and clarity in the process. SEKAB had launched other large-scale biofuel investment plans, such as in Rufiji district, but faced problems in accessing land, and came in for criticism from researchers, NGOs and other stakeholders in Tanzania and Sweden for overlooking environmental issues. SEKAB ended up by pulling out of the projects, after having invested US$25 million in the project planning, but without much having happened on the ground. However, the company did receive an investment licence for the Bagamoyo project that was taken over by the buyer of SEKAB's activities in Tanzania and Mozambique. The experience of SEKAB and its biofuel investment plans in Tanzania reveals the complexities that surround biofuel expansion in countries where the government supports such production, but where land is owned by the state but managed by local communities and villages.

The Zimbabwean case shows that biofuel expansion has led to the establishment of the third-biggest bioenergy processing plant in the world. This investment is only good when it is fully utilized; since it was set up, however, it has not been fully utilized because of jatropha production problems. The government has also been very reluctant to use food as a feedstock for the plant, thus rendering the investment dysfunctional. At the same time, agro-investments need to be looked at within the context of the peculiarities of Zimbabwe's land politics. The politics and history of land in Zimbabwe recast memories of conflicts precipitated by the land redistribution exercise, especially after 2000. Chapter 7 demonstrates how issues of smallholder farmers, livelihoods and the right to land are critical issues related to the land question and the formalization processes in Zimbabwe. This has an effect on the policy- and law-making process in the country, which has been blurred over the past decade.

Chapter 8, on Northern Ghana, suggests that the implications of biofuels on food security should be seen in a context that takes account of local conditions, such as land use patterns, population density and local livelihoods, as well as the biological characteristics of the biofuel feedstock. In the case of Ghana, the local conditions – in terms of low population densities (availability of 'unused' land), economic vulnerability of livelihoods, the existence of sharing in the households and the suitability of the jatropha plant to infertile land areas – created an enabling environment, which had positive spin-off effects of the project on food security. The case study concludes that investing companies should have a social responsibility strategy and a participatory investment approach that involves the local populations. The case of Ghana differs from most of the countries, where the companies are in conflict with local leaders.

Conclusion

This book examines the various impacts of biofuel production on African economies, the environment, agriculture and rural livelihoods. Biofuel pro- duction and manufacturing have a symbiotic interdependence with land use, land grabbing and land management. As developing nations embark on the growing of sugarcane and jatropha for fuel, smallholder farmers are coming under threat, and there is a real possibility that they might lose their land to large-scale plantation activities. Biofuel politics emerge as smallholder farmers in most African countries do not have written legal title to their land, because the African customary and the European legal systems imported by African states do not dovetail. The politics around biofuels can be regarded as a power game, where the elites decide on behalf of rural smallholders, who cannot easily voice their concerns in relation to bilateral agreements, investment or trade policies made within the regional and international systems. Women smallholders are presented as the most affected, since, more often than not, they lose their user rights or access to land on account of policies that further discriminate against them.

Land grabbing directly affects smallholder farmers, as multinational cor- porations come in and acquire huge tracts of land. The negotiating field is uneven, as the bigger companies tend to gain more from the investment, while the local populations experience little or no tangible output from the deals. Many governments in Africa have neither policies nor guidelines on how rights to land, livelihood and food should be balanced in agro-investments, to which biofuels are central. By moving towards the production of biofuels, African states are entering the new terrain of bio-economies, which are driven by the neoliberal agenda and the North's conceptualization of the world. Yet even the world policy arena is fragmented, and there are no proper agenda-setting targets that take account of climate change and environmental issues. Biofuel production, in its present context, is likely to prove a fallacy, because developed countries are the users of the energy produced, and this has a negative impact on the environment, biodiversity and smallholders. In addition, the food produced for external interests through agro-investments will further undermine land control and land access by African smallholders. The beneficiaries will be the investing countries and companies in the North, as well as emerging nations, especially in the Middle East and Asia, which will enhance their energy and food security at the expense of African smallholders and nations.

1 | Grabbing of African lands for energy and food: implications for land rights, food security and smallholders[1]

Kjell Havnevik

Introduction

The process whereby external investors acquire land for the production of food and agricultural feedstocks for biofuel (such as sugarcane and jatropha) has accelerated globally in recent years, particularly in sub-Saharan Africa. The African continent remains in deep poverty and has witnessed a deterioration in the conditions of smallholder agriculture over the past three decades, due to neglect by African governments, international financial institutions and donors. The international media have, over the last few years, reported a picture of ongoing massive land grabbing in Africa, which is connected with the need for non-African governments and people to enhance their food and energy security. Some of the land deals reported – concluded, in process or aborted – are spectacular. However, information on the broader process, as well as details of actors, the terms of contracts and the implications of the land deals for host and investing countries, governments and people, remain unclear and are in need of systematic data collection and assessment.

Nevertheless, some information has emerged about the dynamic process of land acquisitions and leases in Africa by foreign states and investors. Recent research related to the character and volumes of the large-scale land deals or leases (over 1,000 hectares per unit of land) provides a first approximation of the dynamic changes taking place regarding control, ownership and use of African lands. There have been responses to the large-scale African land deals from non-governmental organizations (NGOs) in the affected African countries and globally, and from research and specialized United Nations (UN) agencies such as the Food and Agriculture Organization (FAO), the International Fund for Agricultural Development (IFAD) and the UN Special Rapporteur on the right to food (UN/SRRF) (De Schutter 2009).

Most of the advocacy, research and human rights-related initiatives and activities have attempted to get a better understanding of the background, driving forces and outcomes of this process by conducting fieldwork, and by sourcing, systematizing and analysing data. Although many of these initiatives have been short term and have used methodologies that leave many uncertainties, they do illustrate the fact that the process of land acquisition and leases has accelerated over the last years, alongside a growing concern about the implications of this process. This concern is clear from the formulation of a number of proposals, recommendations and principles that are expected to guide the land acquisitions and leases, in order to safeguard the interests of rural people and communities in Africa and their rights to land, food and decent livelihoods, as well as to protect aspects of environmental sustainability.

In fact, research institutes such as the International Food Policy Research Institute (IFPRI)[2] and the International Institute for Environmental Development (IIED), in cooperation with the FAO and IFAD and the UN Special Rapporteur on the right to food, have all provided recommendations to guide the land acquisition and land lease process (von Braun and Meinzen-Dick 2009; Cotula et al. 2009; De Schutter 2009). Although both the number and the nature of the recommendations vary, they show consensus on the following aspects that relate to the large-scale land acquisition and lease process:

1 There should be transparency in the negotiations.
2 The rights of local communities, including customary land rights, should be protected.
3 The benefits should be shared between local communities and investors.
4 Environmental sustainability should be ensured.
5 Food security in the African countries and communities should not be compromised.

Beyond these locally oriented recommendations,[3] the increasing concentration of land and the scale of operations have critical implications for (i) the balance between smallholder and large-scale farming and the future livelihoods of African rural people; (ii) the relative importance of African subsistence and domestic food supply versus export-led agriculture; and (iii) the role of global agribusiness in African countries, connected with vertical integration in agricultural production, processing and distribution (Gibbon and Ponte 2005).

Driving forces

Food prices increased rapidly worldwide during 2007 and 2008. Global maize and wheat prices doubled between 2003 and 2008 (von Braun 2008). It is estimated that the increased demand for biofuels between 2000 and 2007 contributed 30 per cent to the weighted average increase in cereal prices (ibid.). A recent empirical study indicates that a rapid increase in index fund investments in agricultural and energy commodity future markets was not a major cause of food price volatility during the period 2006–09 (Irwin and Sanders 2010). In 2007, 18 million tonnes of grain were used for industrial purposes, compared to 100 million tonnes for biofuels and other industrial purposes in 2008 (Chakrabortty 2008). A relevant factor for the current and longer-term food demand is changing food consumption patterns in emerging economies, and in particular an increase of meat in the diet. The food conversion required means a considerable loss of calories: currently more than 40 per cent of world grain is being fed to livestock, rather than going to feed people directly (Aal et al. 2009). Although food prices have dropped since mid-2008, they were still 30–50 per cent higher in mid-2009 than the average of a decade ago. A new wave of food price rises started in 2010. The food import bill for the world's poorest countries, including many in Africa, was expected to rise by 11 per cent during 2010. It was also reported by the FAO that rising sugar prices, which reached their highest level for 30 years in November 2010, had played an important role in the increase in food prices (FAO 2010b).

Concern over food security in those countries that are highly dependent upon imports, or that have limited or declining natural conditions for production of their own food (such as many of the Arab states), is also an important driving force for the acquisition and lease of African land. This fear is also connected with deteriorating global conditions for agriculture and food production due to soil erosion and soil mining, depletion of water resources, etc.

Food is unlike any other commodity: without it people cannot survive. Lack of access to food (or a limited or declining supply of it) can translate into immediate popular demonstrations that may lead to serious political instability. The political implications are also important in producer countries because of the sensitivity over food exports in the context of growing food insecurity. Through recent food price increases and the ongoing conversion of land to non-food production, food security has emerged as a critical global issue that governments need to prioritize.

Uncertainties related to volatility in the provision of food globally have also led to a protectionist stance among important food-producing countries that have large populations to feed. Many governments are no longer willing to trust the role assigned to international trade as a levelling mechanism for food prices and global food distribution. Hence, increasingly states are trying to secure food through inter-state agreements and various forms of investments and leases conducted by state-owned enterprises (SOE) or sovereign wealth funds (SWF), or in cooperation with private enterprises. The growing fear of states about increased food insecurity, and its association with hunger and political instability, has led to a rapid increase in the engagement of state-controlled entities and agencies in food-related investments and agreements. This has also led to major changes in the governance situation related to the food and energy sectors.

Over recent years, increasing oil prices and growing concern about climate change have led to a burgeoning interest in switching to non-fossil fuels, such as ethanol (from sugarcane and other feedstocks) and biodiesel (from jatropha). Government consumption targets for non-fossil fuels, which are linked to increasing oil prices and the peak oil scenario, have led to rapidly growing interest in biofuels and their production, and this is likely to continue in the longer term, as the scarcity of fossil energy makes itself felt. However, uncertainties linger as to the role of agriculturally based biofuels (based on sugarcane, jatropha, etc.) when new and second-generation technologies become commercially viable. At that point in the future, many African countries will have converted considerable areas of their land to large-scale mono-cropping of agricultural feedstocks, with the associated consequences for water use, ground water tables, biodiversity, etc. This is a process that is not easily reversible to achieve sustainable agricultural food production.

The global community is facing a dilemma: it needs to cut greenhouse gas emissions at the same time as the demand for energy is increasing in the world. This global dilemma, coupled with national and regional political priorities about national energy security, has led to a shift in interest towards alternative energy sources, including biofuel. The European Union (EU) has already committed itself to reducing greenhouse gas emissions by 20 per cent, compared to 1990 levels, by 2020. The Swedish government, which held the presidency of the EU between July and December 2009, was, however, working to push this EU objective up to 30 per cent, given that similar commitments are likely to emerge from such major global economies as the USA and China. This process is establishing firm global markets that are driving development of the alternative energy sector, including large-scale biofuel developments in Africa.

Concerns about the sustainability of alternative energy production, including biofuels, have, however, increasingly been raised by researchers and advocacy groups that have taken a closer look at the 'net energy' contribution and the environmental and social impact of various large-scale biofuel production projects. In 2008, this contributed to the endorsement by the EU of a directive on the promotion of the use of energy from renewable sources.[4] In Article 15, the sustainability criteria for biofuels and other bioliquids state that they shall not be made from raw material obtained from land with high biodiversity value, including primary forests and other wooded land – Art. 15, 3(a) – and areas designated by law or by the relevant authority for nature protection purposes – Art. 15, 3(b).

African governments also see an increasing potential for rural development and agriculture thanks to higher land and commodity prices, as well as a major export potential where land endowments are substantial. In recent years, there has been renewed interest globally in the role and potential of agriculture, and this has translated into an increase in donor commitments to the sector. African government budgets have also increased their allocations to agriculture in recent years, although many countries have not reached the target set by the Comprehensive Africa Agriculture Development Programme (CAADP), launched in July 2003 under the auspices of the African Union and the New Partnership for Africa's Development, of having 10 per cent of government budgets allocated to agriculture.

The Forum for Agricultural Research in Africa (FARA) forms the secretariat for CAADP's fourth pillar. In early 2008, in its bi-monthly bulletin, Monty Jones, the executive director of FARA, emphasized both the opportunities and the problems related to large-scale biofuel production in Africa, arguing the need for comprehensive research programmes to address these issues in depth (FARA 2007/08: 2). A FARA discussion paper of April 2008 states that the opportunities related to African biofuel production present risks 'that must be managed'. Further, it argues that: 'Provided sustainability criteria are met, the biofuel market represents an opportunity for marginal and unused or abandoned land for development' (FARA 2008).

Rising land values and the rise in prices of agriculture-based commodities (food and biofuels) are key drivers for the engagement of the private sector in African agriculture. Though they are rising, the still relatively low land prices mean that among many companies – domestic and foreign – there are high expectations of competitive returns from agriculture and land. This process is further compounded by the increasing tendency of large-scale international food and supermarket chains to extend their processing and sales to the production of commodities and raw materials themselves, often pushing smallholders off their land without proper compensation. This vertical integration of food and supermarket chains is also an important driver in the acquisition and lease of African land. Some agribusinesses that were traditionally involved in processing and distribution are also pursuing integration strategies into direct agricultural production, in order to reduce the risks – e.g. Lonrho's recent land acquisitions in Angola, Mali and Malawi; see Cotula et al. (2009: 57). The processes mentioned complement – or at times are integrated with – government-backed objectives and initiatives related to food and energy security.

Key assumption: availability of African land

A key assumption behind the rising interest and investment in the acquisition and leasing of African land is that there are large reservoirs of unused or underutilized land. The *Global Agro-Ecological Assessment* provides the most comprehensive survey of global and African agricultural potential (Fischer et al. 2002).[5] It is suggested that 80 per cent of the global reserve of agricultural land exists in Africa and South America. Satellite imagery from the mid-1990s indicates a total cultivable land area in Africa of about 800 million hectares, of which 25 per cent are under cultivation. The study itself indicates that the underreporting on use ranges from 10 to 20 per cent.

According to Cotula et al. (2009: 60), it is not 'clear how land under shifting cultivation and fallow systems is included' in the *Agro-Ecological Assessment*. In order to make the assessment more realistic for African conditions, Cotula et al. assume that agricultural systems on average have five fallow plots for every plot in use. Due to various and increasing pressures on smallholder land in recent decades, by my assessment it is unlikely that the current ratio of cultivated land (i.e. 200 million hectares) to fallow land in African farming systems is 1:5, as Cotula et al. have indicated. Assuming that cultivated and fallow land plots are of the same size, this would imply that the land use of African farming systems is nearly 1,000 million hectares, which exceeds the estimated potential cultivable land area of 800 million hectares by 200 million hectares. Most likely, land under cultivation is higher than the estimate of the *Agro-Ecological Assessment* (including the underreporting mentioned), and the amount of fallow land lower than Cotula's assumption. This implies that the estimate of potential available uncultivated sub-Saharan African land of 202 million hectares offered by the World Bank recently (World Bank 2010) may be reasonable. But it would be wrong to assume, for the reason given below, that this land is unused or unoccupied.

Since the mid-1990s, there has been a rapid expansion of land cultivation both by smallholders and by investors in large-scale food and biofuel production. In the case of smallholders, this is partly due to the average annual rise in the population of Africa of about 2.5 per cent between 2000 and 2005. Other factors are relevant when declaring land to be available, idle, not in use, etc.: pastoral systems rely on large areas of land for grazing, and villagers make use of land for the collection of firewood and medicines. Although some fallow land does exist, particularly in low-intensity agricultural systems, the increased pressure on land since the mid-1990s is likely to have reduced both fallow and grazing areas considerably. Given the importance of agriculture to African economies, 'unused' land belonging to clans, communities or villages is often looked upon as land to be provided for future generations.

Within African governments and agencies there is often an eagerness to declare land to be unused or unoccupied in order to attract foreign investments, although there may be multiple claims on the same land. In countries with state-owned land systems, such as Tanzania and Ethiopia, where the management of land is delegated to villages, major conflicts may emerge due to a wrong classification of land. In Tanzania, 70 per cent of all land is under the jurisdiction of 11,000 villages. In such a context, large-scale production of biofuel and food will necessarily impinge on village land. Detailed legal procedures exist as to how external investors can access such land through land leases of between 33 and 99 years. The remaining land is reserved land of various categories (28 per cent) and general land (2 per cent), which is under the direct jurisdiction of the government. Governments eager to provide land for lease or acquisition by foreign investors tend to take shortcuts that overlook national legislation and the land rights of the rural people (Cotula et al. 2009: 62; this volume, case study on Tanzania, chapter 6).

For the above reasons, there is a need for governments to be cautious about providing land for large-scale investment, given the complexity and multiplicity of claims on rural land. Most likely there is a certain amount of unused and unoccupied African land that could be used for large-scale land investments. However, to avoid conflict and the alienation of smallholder farmers, the identification of land for large-scale investors must take account of the factors mentioned above.

For some, including governments, investors and certain academics, the alienation of smallholder land is defended by claims that smallholder farming systems are ineffective, and that large-scale farms will provide better utilization of the land and higher productivity (Collier 2008). Numerous studies, however, have found that smallholder farming systems are in fact efficient, or could enhance their productivity considerably through various types of support to improve production conditions and market access (Byerlee and de Janvry 2009; Djurfeldt et al. 2005). Others have reported on the potential smallholder 'Green Revolution', fostered by the policies of several African states during the 1970s, that was nipped in the bud.

Trends in large-scale land acquisition and leases

Several recent studies have provided quantitative estimates and trends for land acquisition and leases globally and in Africa. An IFPRI estimate, depicting the trend since 2006, claims that 15 to 20 million hectares of farmland in developing countries have been subject to transactions and/or negotiations involving foreign investors (von Braun and Meinzen-Dick 2009; De Schutter 2009: 3). This is exclusive of a recent land offer of 10 million hectares (reported by Reuters, 15 April 2009), allegedly made to South African farmers in the Democratic Republic of Congo (DRC). According to the UN/SRRF, the major target countries in sub-Saharan Africa include DRC, Cameroon, Ethiopia, Madagascar, Mali, Somalia, Sudan, Tanzania and Zambia (see the case studies on Ethiopia, chapter 5 and Tanzania, chapter 6).

China is reported to have acquired 2.8 million hectares in the DRC for an oil palm plantation,[6] and Libya has leased 100,000 hectares in Mali for rice production. Meanwhile, in the Sudan, South Korea has acquired 690,000 hectares for wheat growing, the United Arab Emirates have invested in more than 400,000 hectares to grow corn and other crops, while Egypt has secured a similar area to grow wheat.[7] In Madagascar, negotiations over a 99-year lease of 1.3 million hectares with Daewoo Logistics Corporation of South Korea for maize and palm oil was aborted due to the role the unpopular deal played in the overthrow of the government in 2009 (von Braun and Meinzen-Dick 2009). A major lease of 465,000 hectares of land in Madagascar has been given to Varun International, an Indian company, for the growing of rice for export to India (ibid.; Cotula et al. 2009). Saudi Arabia is seeking to lease 500,000 hectares, and a subsidiary of SEKAB, a Swedish ethanol company, had planned 400,000 hectares of biofuel production in Tanzania (see case study, chapter 6).[8]

It is difficult to come by precise information about the content of the African land deals, due to secrecy and a lack of transparency. Therefore the information must be treated with caution. Cotula et al. (2009) attempted to undertake a systematic study of acquisitions and land leases of more than 1,000 hectares in the period 2004 to March 2009 in five case-study countries – Ethiopia, Ghana, Madagascar, Mali and Sudan. In addition, qualitative field studies were conducted in Tanzania and Mozambique. The study was carried out by IIED, London, with partners in the seven countries.[9]

The national inventories in the five case-study countries document about 2.5 million hectares of approved land allocations for investment in agriculture, including foreign direct investment (FDI) and domestic investment, whether private or state-led (Cotula et al. 2009: 49). Madagascar reports a total of about 800,000 hectares, Ethiopia about 600,000 hectares and the Sudan about 470,000 hectares. The sizes of the approved land allocations range from 100,000 hectares to about 450,000 hectares, in Madagascar and Ghana, respectively. Total investment commitments linked to the land areas and investment projects amount to about US$920 million. The numbers of approved projects from 2004 to March 2009 were: in Ethiopia – 157 (with investment commitments of US$78.5 million); in Sudan – 11 (US$440 million); in Mali – 7 (US$292 million); in Madagascar – 6 (US$80 million); and in Ghana – 3 (US$30 million). Nearly all the data, however, are said by Cotula et al. to be incomplete.

In terms of the investment commitments recorded in four of the countries (Sudan excluded), about US$250 million were directed towards food production for the domestic market, compared to US$44 million for export. Yet all the biofuel-related investments (US$117 million) were geared to export. Hence, we see that large-scale investments in food production for the domestic market far outweigh those for export. This implies that food needs in the countries in question are translated into actual demand for food, which can be a dynamic impetus for growth of the basic food production sector.

In terms of land area, food for the domestic market was recorded at 230,000 hectares, while food for export was more than double that – about 520,000 hectares – and fuel-related investments were allocated about 1.1 million hectares. Hence, in those four countries (Ghana, Madagascar, Ethiopia and Mali), the land allocated to biofuel (solely for exports) exceeded the land allocations for food production (domestic supply and exports) by nearly 50 per cent (calculated on the basis of Cotula et al. 2009: 51, table 2.3). This may reflect the fact that energy-related land acquisitions and leases are more extensive in terms of area than are large-scale allocations to food production, which are likely to target better-quality land.[10]

Governance issues

All investments and deals documented in Ethiopia and Madagascar are privately owned, while in Mali major government-backed investments exist, including land allocations to an SWF (government-owned funds with financial objectives, but separately managed from other government funds) with a base in Libya (Cotula et al. 2009: 49). When comparing the shares of FDI and domestic investments in Ethiopia, Ghana, Madagascar and Mali, Cotula et al. found that the major part of the investments involve FDI. However, it was also found that national individuals and companies were acquiring land in a number of countries. Ethiopia showed domestic investors accounting for land allocations of 362,000 hectares and US$54 million in investment, compared with 240,000 hectares and US$24 million in FDI (Cotula et al. 2009).

The findings from Ethiopia and other countries imply that the context of large-scale land acquisitions and leases cannot be understood properly unless the domestic investor aspects are included. It would be particularly interesting to learn what proportion of the domestic acquisitions and leases relates to aspirations to go into partnership with foreign investors. The involvement of domestic elites or investors may imply that, in their struggle to retain their rights, rural smallholders are faced not only with external investors, but with domestic ones as well, or indeed with a combination. The 'combination' possibility is particularly relevant where external investors are not allowed to own land in the host countries, as is the case in Ethiopia and Tanzania (see chapters 5 and 6).

An alliance of external and domestic investors linked to host-state agencies may prove similar in outlook to the alliance of African states, international institutions and donor agencies in the 1970s (and into the 1980s) that also overlooked the interests of African smallholders (Ellis 1982; Havnevik 1987; Gibbon 1992). The hypothesis that smallholders are increasingly facing an alliance of external and domestic investors in land acquisitions and leases would possibly imply weak consultation with local communities and interests, and lack of transparency around contracts. This was the case in Mozambique, in spite of a rather strong policy that emphasized consultations with smallholders. Nhantumbo and Salomao (2009) found that national economic priorities give district authorities stronger incentives to promote the interests of investors over local communities. They further state that: 'Local interests are also undermined by the fact that policy does not include terms for benefit-sharing. In addition, the actual legal weight of community consultation processes is unclear.' As a result, 'community consultations during land acquisitions by investors are in practice fairly limited' (Nhantumbo and Salomao 2009: 72). (See also chapter 9.)

Cotula et al. (2009: 74) conclude that:

there is little sign that efforts are made specifically to include significant social groups such as women, or user groups such as pastoralists. Indirectly affected communities, for example those affected by migration out of project areas, have not been included to date. Consultation tends to be a one-off rather than an ongoing interaction through the project cycle.

In addition, 'Lack of transparency is a major challenge in the negotiations of land deals as well as the broader government-to-government arrangement in which individual deals may fit' (ibid.: 68). Given the empirical evidence presented by Cotula et al. of weak or nonexistent consultation between investors/government agencies and local communities, it is surprising that they ascribe the underlying problem not so much to reluctance on the part of local government and companies to 'do the right thing' as to a lack of experience and guidance to shape better practice. The World Bank's (2010) thinking as to the future development of biofuels runs along the same lines. The findings presented in this book, however, show that it is not just a question of governments and companies gaining experience and receiving guidance, but that there is a lack of respect for rural livelihoods and smallholders' land rights. In such a context, voluntary guidelines for biofuel expansion, as presented above, may rather serve the function of legitimizing new forms of colonialism (Havnevik 2010).

The emergence of food and energy issues as top political security priorities for an increasing number of states implies that current economic analysis, including trade analysis, may weaken the potential to explain economic growth and global trade, since political aspects tend to overshadow issues of economic efficiency. Understanding of the process of land acquisitions and leases related to food and energy may, therefore, require deeper insights about the governance system around food and energy and, in the wider context, scarce natural resources.

This perspective is further supported by the increasing number of bilateral investment treaties (BITs) as a framework for FDI in African food and energy production. According to Cotula et al. (2009) and the United Nations Conference on Trade and Development (UNCTAD), there has been a veritable boom in BITs with African countries (UNCTAD 2008). These had increased from 193 in 1995 to 687 by December 2006. The seven countries covered by Cotula et al. (2009) signed 71 treaties in the period 2000–09, compared with five in the 1960s and 42 in the 1990s.

Although BITs vary, they usually provide legal protection to investments by nationals of one state party in the other state. The BITs define investments broadly, 'which would cover investments in agriculture and land acquisitions' (Cotula et al. 2009: 32). The overall outcome of the new governance system may imply that states pursuing food and energy security through large-scale land investments in Africa have been able to attain quite good political and economic guarantees for their investments.

The above framework for security for state and state/private investments in individual African countries may also help explain the rapid increase in FDI in Africa over the past few years – from US$17 billion in 2005 to US$22 billion in 2006 and US$30 billion in 2007 (UNCTAD 2008). There has been a parallel acceleration in the investments abroad by SWFs. According to UNCTAD (2008), investments abroad by such funds over the last 20 years reached nearly US$40 billion, of which as much as 75 per cent was committed during 2005–07. The increasing dominance of SWFs has led to concern about their activities and impact. Recently, both the OECD and the International Monetary Fund (IMF) have provided guidance to host countries on SWF investments, so that they can strike a better balance between their own national security concerns and the continued flow of SWF investments.

Alongside SWFs, SOEs are also important players in large-scale land acquisitions and leases. SOEs can be seen as profit-making companies, registered under company law, that are wholly or majority owned by the state. Such firms often operate in tandem with non-state or private companies. The importance of SOEs is growing – for example, all major Chinese transnational companies are state owned. In addition, many strategic private companies are influenced by states or are able to expand because of their links with SOEs or other state agencies. SOEs usually disclose limited information about their operations, thus blurring their actual role, as well as understanding of the governance system associated with large-scale land acquisitions and leases related to food and energy. Both formal and informal links exist between private companies and SOEs, and such relationships are of particular importance when states pursue energy and food security or wish to access other strategic natural resources.

The nature of land transfer contracts and benefit sharing

Important insights towards understanding the character and distribution of the benefits of land transfers may emerge through a scrutiny of the contracts that guide such transfers. In the African context, however, it is not so straightforward to identify the nature of the land rights concerned and who the contracting partners are. This is because of the complex nature of African land ownership, where state ownership, customary ownership systems and private land ownership may exist side by side or be intertwined with each other (Toulmin and Quan 2000; Havnevik et al. 2007). Even in Kenya, where private ownership and individual titling emerged in the early 1960s, the system is currently in disarray due to lack of proper records, various forms of land grabbing, and conflicting and overlapping claims to land.

It has been estimated that formal land ownership or tenure in Africa exists for at most 10 per cent of the land (and probably less), and the major part of such land lies in urban areas. International donors and financial institutions, including the World Bank, and others seeing Africa from outside, have for decades argued and supported the process of formalization and privatization of African land, seeing this as a precondition for increasing agricultural productivity and economic development. More insightful analyses have documented and argued that individualization of African land ownership can best come from an evolutionary process of commercialization of African agriculture (Platteau 1996). Even more recently, the World Bank analysis of African land issues has come to an understanding of the virtues of customary land ownership systems, which see land not simply as an economic, but also as a social and cultural category (World Bank 2007).

It is particularly problematic to determine whose land rights are being transferred in land deals in those countries with state ownership of land or where the management of land has been delegated to rural communities and villages through complex laws and regulations. Tanzania, Ethiopia and Mozambique are among the countries where reported land transfers – sometimes of significant hectarage – are increasing. In these countries, foreign ownership of land may be prohibited or complicated, leading to long-term leases, often of 33–99 years. The implementation of such deals may be helped by the establishment of joint companies, where the domestic partner has a stake. Most African countries with communal-type land ownership systems aspire to develop a 'one-stop' agency to serve foreign investors and their partners who are in search of land. Investors seeking large areas of land clearly also need to access village land – a cumbersome process that easily gets tangled up (Cotula et al. 2009: 73–4; this volume, chapter 6).

Both customary land ownership and community- (or village)-managed land systems easily translate into insecure land ownership systems when the state decides to 'free up' land on behalf of, or in cooperation with, external and domestic investors. This can happen in spite of the fact that customary and village land is protected by law (as in Mali, Tanzania, Mozambique and Uganda). A key mechanism used by the state and state agencies to 'free up' land for itself and investors is to claim that the land is 'waste land' (as in Ethiopia) or is unused or underutilized, so that productivity and incomes can be increased through investment. The offer of such land for investor-based land acquisitions and leases signed by the state and the investors frequently results in land conflicts on the ground, since the investor is not considered to be the legitimate manager or owner of the land. It should thus be a central issue for all partners involved to address land tenure uncertainty in a proper manner.

Compensation for the acquisition and lease of land associated with local land rights reportedly varies both from country to country and within the same country. In cases where the state holds the ultimate title to land, legal contracts are most often limited to compensation for loss of harvest and land improvements. Such cash compensation is normally insufficient for households to acquire replacement land. Problems surrounding the implementation of contracts can also obstruct compensation to restore affected rural livelihoods. Compensation is supposed to be paid by governments; however, because of budget and administrative problems, investors often pay affected local land rights holders and users direct.

Compensation in kind may thus be preferable to rural people, since that may at least guarantee some livelihood security. One example reported by *L'Essor* (2008) is the compensation offered of five hectares (two hectares offered free and three to be paid off over two decades) of irrigated land to each of the 800 households affected by a large-scale irrigation project in Mali's Office du Niger area. Compensation in kind was found to be allowed in six countries studied by Cotula et al. (2009) (Sudan excluded). In all cases investigated, compensation was paid by the investor, not the government.

In the study by Cotula et al., assessment of the adequacy of compensation to restore livelihoods was made by in-country researchers for four countries: Ethiopia, Ghana, Madagascar and Mali. (No information was provided for Tanzania and Mozambique, but because they have state land ownership regimes, these countries are likely to fall into the same category as Ethiopia, for which inadequate compensation to restore rural livelihoods was reported. See also chapter 6 on Tanzania.) Even in Ghana, which has considerable private land ownership, compensation was found to be inadequate because the Land Evaluation Board usually inserted minimum land rates into the calculation for compensation. Only Mali and Madagascar reported adequate compensation, although in Mali indirect rights holders were excluded, while in Madagascar there were problems with resettlement (Cotula et al. 2009: 93).

The benefits to rural smallholders and communities also depend upon how investment projects, acquisitions and leases are designed and managed. According to IFPRI, projects that include contract farming and outgrower schemes and that involve existing smallholders and land users can generate benefits for both smallholders and communities (von Braun and Meinzen-Dick 2009: 3). The UN/SRRF recommends that the host government and investors should promote labour-intensive farming systems that can ensure employment creation (De Schutter 2009: 14). However, on the subject of employment creation, the Brazilian experience of labour-intensive and large-scale ethanol production from sugarcane shows that this is no guarantee of reasonable incomes and living standards, and no guarantee that environmental and health problems can be avoided (Comar and Gusman Ferraz 2007). SEKAB, in its planned biofuel investments in the Rufiji district of Tanzania, has included portions of smallholder contract farming adjacent to its large-scale operations.

Environmental sustainability issues

Environmental sustainability issues are important in the context of large-scale land acquisitions and leases for food and biofuel production. Intensive, large-scale agricultural production is often based on a transformation of complex and diversified smallholder farming systems to mono-cropping, based on high inputs of fertilizer and pesticides. The conversion of complex agricultural systems, rangelands and forests to mono-cropping leads to a reduction in the diversity of flora and fauna, a decline in agro-biodiversity, and a decrease in both above-ground and subsurface carbon stocks. Many tropical soils are unfit for intensive cultivation, or else they lack sufficient water for such cultivation. Although irrigation and fertilizers can compensate for some of these limitations, they often lead to sustainability problems linked to water-logging, salinity and soil erosion.

According to IFPRI, such problems are likely to emerge if external or domestic investors are driven by short-term profit motives or lack understanding of the agro-ecological environment in which their production takes place (von Braun and Meinzen-Dick 2009). There have been numerous large-scale agricultural projects in Africa (in both the colonial and the post-colonial periods) that have mined the soil and thus destroyed its future suitability for cultivation. However, the longer-term prospects of foreign (and domestic) land leases for food or energy over 33–99 years provide a possibility to plan and implement production sustainably over time. Both food and sugarcane production need proper access to water, which is often secured through the establishment of irrigation systems. The drawing of water for large-scale production does, however, often impinge on other water users, as well as on environmental flows, which secure and sustain finely tuned ecological systems (Havnevik 1993; Hoag 2003).

Drawing water from rivers or river basins for agriculture-related production may also conflict with hydroenergy projects that require continuous and predictable flows of water. In the 1960s and 1970s, Africa saw major hydropower projects develop without proper investigation of the ecological impacts. Because of critical energy shortages, such projects are again on the drawing board in many countries. The water needs and social and ecological impacts of large-scale agricultural and hydropower projects, and their possible competition, need to be carefully investigated before such projects are planned and implemented. IFPRI argues for the need to

> conduct careful environmental impact assessment that not only looks at the effects on the local area, but also considers off site impacts on soils, water, greenhouse gas emissions, and biodiversity. Land-lease contracts should also include safeguards to ensure that sustainable practices are employed. (von Braun and Meinzen-Dick 2009)

The UN/SRRF calls for even broader impact assessments prior to the completion of land acquisition and lease negotiations (De Schutter 2009: 15). These assessments would highlight the impact on the right to food from such perspectives as: (i) local employment and incomes; (ii) access to productive resources of local communities; (iii) arrival of new technologies and investments in infrastructure; (iv) various environmental impacts; and also (v) access, availability and adequacy of food. Although Cotula et al. (2009) cannot provide any insights into the environmental impact of the projects that were investigated (probably due to the short time span of their operation), they nevertheless recommend that host governments should conduct state-of-the-art assessments of the social and environmental impacts of proposed investments. In terms of the environmental aspects, these resemble the proposals of IFPRI. Environmental sustainability issues are strong in relation to the environmental and social impact assessment case study of SEKAB's planned activities in Tanzania (see chapter 6).

Food security

Since the rapid increase in food prices in 2007, the issue of food security has taken on a new importance. This is not a new issue, however, having been discussed and conceptualized in international fora since the 1970s.[11] The notion of food security has changed over time. In the 1970s, it was closely connected with production, on account of shortfalls in global production and rising prices. Later, Amartya Sen showed, using the experience of Ethiopia in the early 1980s, that food security was not necessarily connected with total production levels, but with the ability of people to access food, using their different entitlements. In addition, the question of nutritional adequacy of food takes the issue of food distribution all the way to the individual level. When assessing food security, we might consider that cultural acceptance of food also plays a role.

At present, global food production is sufficient to provide every human being with enough calories to lead a reasonable life, if distributed evenly. In sub-Saharan Africa, the number of undernourished people increased by 20 per cent from 1992 to 2002 (FAO 2006), while the absolute number of undernourished in global terms decreased. Undernourishment and hunger are, however, globally on the rise. After the global financial and economic crises, FAO estimates (19 June 2009) showed that 1.02 billion people were affected by hunger in 2009, an 11 per cent increase over 2008. Of these, 265 million people resided in sub-Saharan Africa. Recent estimates indicate that the number of people going hungry dropped somewhat in 2010, but not to the levels that existed before the crises. It is not far from the truth to claim that, in late 2010, about a billion people were going to bed hungry each night, despite the fact that sufficient food was available globally to feed everyone, if the distribution of food was equitable. This highlights the important issue of 'access' to food and the need to analyse global power relations in order to understand the forces that drive global injustices. In spite of the new global focus and priority related to food security issues, the necessary power analysis to drive understanding in the direction of food sovereignty is lacking in most institutional agencies, e.g. the FAO.[12]

This is the broader background to the sensitivity around the export of food and the conversion of agriculturally suitable land in poor countries of sub-Saharan Africa – whether or not in current use – to the production of energy (based on agricultural feedstocks) for export to investing countries. The sensitivity of the issue is also manifested in the widespread social unrest in at least 33 countries associated with the rise in food prices (World Bank 2007).

The production of agricultural food crops for export to the investor's home country is a main driving force for recent large-scale land acquisitions and leases. On the other hand, a number of African countries that host such investments are also food-importing countries or recipients of food aid. Kenya, for instance, was forced, on account of droughts and failed harvests, to declare a national food shortage emergency at the same time as a Qatar–Kenya deal came to public attention, involving the alienation of land for production and export of food crops – Ochieng-Oron, reported in Cotula et al. (2009: 87). The lease of 1.3 million hectares for maize and oil palm that was being negotiated by Daewoo in Madagascar was set against a similar background, and this played a major role in the political conflicts that overthrew the government in early 2009 (von Braun and Meinzen-Dick 2009). There have been a number of examples of insufficient protection of national food security by African governments and international and domestic investors. They draw attention to the need not only to address food security in the host country, but to reconcile food security concerns in both the host and the investing countries. Such concerns will require genuine benefit sharing or the creation of win-win arrangements, which many international investors claim they are developing.

The empirical material provided by research, NGOs and international institutions, however, indicates that, to bring about win-win outcomes, safeguards must be introduced in order to ensure that benefits accrue also to the weaker partner in the arrangements – the smallholder and local communities in the African rural areas. The ascent of food and energy security to the top of the political agenda of many states has led to major changes in the governance and investment systems related to food and energy. This new scenario has also provided a revalorization of land and opportunities for agriculture that, if handled competently, could generate potential benefits. Securing such benefits in a win-win context between rural African communities, host governments and non-African states and their associated companies and investors, represents a major challenge to all parties involved.

Revisiting the recommendations

Transparency in the negotiations IFPRI and UN/SRRF recommend that negotiations leading to investment agreements should be conducted transparently. This implies that local land holders should be informed of, and involved in, negotiations over land deals, and that free, prior and informed consent should be the standard to be upheld when land acquisitions and leases affect local land rights holders. The latter is also recommended by UN/SRRF and Cotula et al. (2009). UN/SRRF, however, qualifies transparency further, by adding 'full transparency', which also implies that local communities whose access to land and other productive resources may be affected by the investor should participate in the negotiations. There should be particular concern about protection of the rights of indigenous and marginalized ethnic groups. When deciding whether or not to conclude an investment agreement, host governments should, according to UN/SRRF, always balance the benefits of the agreement against the opportunity costs, especially if those costs are unconducive to the long-term needs of the local population and the realization of their human rights. Cotula et al. (2009) state that, whether or not it is legally required, local consultation is likely to be a key success factor in project implementation. But they also recommend that recipient governments should ask hard questions about the capacity of investors to manage large-scale agricultural investments effectively.

The findings presented above show that there is a long way to go to attain transparency in negotiations over land acquisitions and leases. This is particularly the case in countries where the state holds the ultimate title to land. Here, in many instances, the opposite scenario seems to be more common: local communities and affected rights holders are neither well informed, nor are they invited to participate in the negotiation processes. A further problem is that local communities and smallholders are often not well informed about their rights as stipulated in laws and regulations. Further problems related to transparency include lack of coordination among government agencies and various levels of government, which may cause confusion and uncertainty among both investors and communities. In many countries, policies and guidelines for providing a framework for large-scale investments in food or energy are unclear or lacking, or else those that exist are not implemented. Governments hosting large-scale land investments have much work to do before there is a 'one-stop' agency that can serve external investors well.

The rights of local communities, including customary land rights, should be protected Customary land rights are widespread in sub-Saharan Africa and respond to fundamental cultural features and the needs of African rural populations connected with access to food, belonging, status and meaning. Customary rights often exist as bundles or layers of rights relating to families, clans and communities that have developed over time, based on redistribution and reciprocity principles. Often they are not in writing. However, many countries with state land ownership regimes acknowledge customary land ownership systems, and even protect them by law. UN/SRRF recommends that states should adopt legislation to protect the rights of local communities at all times and to specify in detail the conditions under which shifts in land use, or evictions, may take place, as well as the procedure that should be followed. Both Cotula et al. (2009: 109) and De Schutter (2009: 14) recommend that states should also assist communities in obtaining collective registration of the land they use.

Currently, however, customary land ownership systems may be unable to identify clearly the rightful land holder who is to be entered in a contract. The process of freeing land for offer to investors for large-scale food and energy production often overlooks the fact that unused or underutilized land is important for communities or households. Lack of clarity – both within and between various laws – often makes it hard for smallholders and communities to understand their basic rights. The best way to protect local rights, including customary land rights, is to establish consultations and negotiations related to large-scale land acquisitions and leases that adhere to the principles of full transparency (see above). Otherwise, problems could later emerge that may reverse or undermine the investment, or else leave investors and local landholders frustrated.

The recommendations by IFPRI, UN/SRRF and Cotula et al. all place great emphasis on the sharing of benefits. According to IFPRI, the local community should benefit, and not lose, from foreign investment in agriculture. It states that leases are preferable to lump-sum compensation, since they will generate continuous revenue streams when land is taken away. Contract farming and outgrower schemes are considered even better, as they leave smallholders in control of their land, at the same time as they offer secure deliveries to the investor. IFPRI also underlines the need for explicit measures to enforce compensation if it is not forthcoming (von Braun and Meinzen-Dick 2009: 3). UN/SRRF goes a step further, recommending that investment contracts and investment agreement revenues should be used for the benefit and need of the local population. Contractual arrangements for provision by the investor of improved technologies, access to credit and pre-defined prices and volumes of crops may be preferable to long-term leases of land or land purchases (De Schutter 2009: 14).

Cotula et al. warn that local expectations of benefits may be beyond what is realistic. Unclear contractual conditions and over-optimistic promises by the investor may often result in frustration or conflict (see chapter 5). High priority should, therefore, be given to ensuring clarity about the costs and benefits of the land acquisition or leases from the very beginning. This includes realistic assessments, e.g. about the number and the types of jobs created, and honest communication of what the investment will generate (Cotula et al. 2009: 104). They also emphasize that long-term land leases of between 50 and 99 years are unsustainable unless there is some level of local satisfaction. Innovative business models and outgrower schemes could address some of these challenges. IFPRI recommends that the standards of the World Commission on Dams might serve as a specific example for compensation that restores to people their equivalent livelihood standard (von Braun and Meinzen-Dick 2009).

The empirical findings presented above show that the real situation as regards benefit sharing in the wake of land acquisitions and leases is a long way from what is being recommended. Where state land ownership prevails, the affected households normally get compensation only for crops and land improvements. Even where private land ownership is involved, there are often flaws in valuations and implementation of contracts. Stronger and binding regulations on an international level – regulations that can be enforced both in the host and in the investing countries – are required to ensure that local land rights holders receive real compensation. An issue not raised in any of the recommendations is compensation related to technological change, e.g. a breakthrough in second-generation biofuel technologies that could make current biofuel technology redundant.

Environmental sustainability All the recommendations are strong on environmental sustainability. Investments should include careful environmental and social impact assessment and monitoring to ensure sound and sustainable agricultural production practices (see chapter 6). The recommendations also aim at avoiding increases in greenhouse gas emissions. UN/SRRF recommends that host states should explore low-external-input farming practices to meet environmental challenges (von Braun and Meinzen-Dick 2009: 4; De Schutter 2009: 14). Cotula et al. recommend that recipient governments should place sustainable development at the centre of investment decision-making. Given the long-term nature of many of the recent land leases, strategic thinking, rather than ad hoc and short-term decision-making, is important if long-term rural development is to be secured. One element proposed by Cotula et al. (2009: 106) in this regard is for foreign investments to be combined with domestic resources, including smallholder farming, thereby creating long-term synergies.

The reporting so far on recent large-scale land acquisitions and leases for food and biofuel production does not include any substantial documentation on environmental impact. This is mainly due to the recent development of the process. However, many of the fears voiced are based on numerous past experiences of large-scale agricultural production, with documented and considerable negative impacts for the environment, including water-related impacts, loss of biodiversity, loss of soil fertility, negative effects of high levels of fertilizer and pesticide use, etc. In addition, social impacts related to the marginalization and exclusion of smallholders and pastoralists have been frequently reported in connection with large-scale agricultural schemes and investments. Although key aspects may vary, the issue of environmental sustainability related to large-scale production of food and biofuels is real and needs to be taken seriously by all parties concerned. The danger may arise, as in many past projects, that in the rush to maximize short-term profits, large-scale investors pay less attention to aspects of long-term production and sustainability. This fear is less pronounced if the large-scale land acquisitions and leases are for food production than if they are for biofuel (because of the technological uncertainty over biofuel mentioned above).

Food security in the African countries and communities should not be compromised The global rise in food prices since 2007 and the recent financial crisis (and its global economic impacts) have resulted in a setback for food security in sub-Saharan Africa, and indeed globally. Conversion of land to biofuels has also had an effect on rising food prices and increased food insecurity. As was mentioned above, the FAO estimated in 2009 that the number of hungry people globally had risen to 1.02 billion – a record high and an increase of 11 per cent over 2008. In 2009, 265 million of the world's hungry resided in Africa. The only regions to avoid an increase in hunger in 2009 were Latin America and the Caribbean. More recent estimates indicate, however, that the number of people going hungry in the world has declined somewhat since 2009. The Millennium Development Goals target of reducing hunger by 50 per cent by 2015 (based on the 1990 level of 800 million hungry globally) will be way beyond reach – indeed, the trend has been in the opposite direction. This development may underline the need in future to shift from a process of 'top-down' target setting for global development towards a more serious realization of the need to understand better the processes that generate poverty and hunger – including power relations.

The UN/SRRF is particularly concerned with recommendations that can address the human right to food and the attainment of food security (De Schutter 2009). In order to ensure that large-scale land acquisitions and leases do not lead to increased food insecurity for the local population (due to increased dependence on international markets or food aid in a context of higher prices for agricultural commodities), the UN/SRRF proposes that: 'Investment agreements should include a clause providing that a certain minimum percentage of the crops produced shall be sold on local markets' (De Schutter 2009: 3). IFPRI formulates its safeguard for food security in relation to adherence to national trade policies: 'When national food security is at risk, domestic supplies should have priority. Foreign investors should not have a right to export during an acute national food crisis' (von Braun and Meinzen-Dick 2009: 4). The recommendations of Cotula et al. do not specifically address food security. Nevertheless their wide-ranging recommendations for various stakeholders, including investors, recipient governments, development aid agencies and the organization of the rural poor, focus on the overarching perspective related to long-term sustainability and food security.

Some concluding remarks and questions

Technological change An important issue related to technological change is the possible breakthrough in second-generation technologies for biofuel production, which could utilize raw materials other than agricultural feedstocks. For instance, SEKAB of Sweden is heavily involved in such efforts and has received international acclaim for this part of its operations (see chapter 6). A commercial breakthrough in second-generation technologies is likely to undermine or make redundant the first-generation biofuel production technologies currently in use. When such a technological breakthrough occurs and new raw materials take the place of agricultural feedstocks, what will investors do? Will those who are now taking over large tracts of land in Africa remain with their production activities, employing first-generation biofuel technology, or will they withdraw? What will be the implications of the new technologies for the host countries' economies and the socio-economic welfare of the communities?

The implications of technological change related to biofuel production are real, but they may also relate to other types of production and products. Such issues need to be reflected upon because they have fundamental implications for Africa's long-term sustainable agricultural and rural development. African policies for agriculture and rural development seem to overlook such long-term strategic issues. The recommendations presented in this chapter for guiding large-scale acquisitions and leases of African land also seem unable to capture such issues. African development strategies have so far, and for understandable reasons, had to face mainly short-term, acute challenges. What is being done and who is taking responsibility for ensuring that long-term, strategic issues, such as those related to a breakthrough in biofuel production technology, are being properly addressed? A proper way forward to handle long-term strategic issues on the part of African governments and institutions will also help to protect the development space of African smallholders.

The role of smallholders In the discussion of the large-scale grabbing of African lands for food and energy, several trends and processes have been noted that are affecting African smallholders. In fact many of the recommendations proposed for regulating the grabbing of African land are specifically directed to protect rural people's rights and livelihoods. It seems that the dynamic global developments regarding food and energy securities are turning the

African agricultural agenda upside down. Rather than acknowledging that for generations African smallholders have been, and currently are, fundamental to African agriculture, the focus has shifted towards safeguarding their rights and conditions against large-scale investment projects driven by external states and international and domestic investors. Rather than a focus on the long-term potential contribution of smallholders and communities to broad-based African development, a welfarist approach has taken precedence in many quarters – how to ensure that the smallholders and communities survive. Even the *World Development Report 2008* is ambiguous about the role of African smallholders:[13]

> An emerging vision of agriculture for development redefines the roles of producers, the private sector, and the state. Production is mainly by smallholders, who often remain the most efficient producers, in particular when supported by their organizations. But when these organizations cannot capture economies of scale in production and marketing, labor-intensive commercial farming can be a better form of production, and efficient and fair labor markets are the key instruments to reducing rural poverty. (World Bank 2007: 8)

The editors of the *World Development Report 2008* did, however, later come out more clearly on the issue of large-scale versus smallholder agriculture in Africa:

> Although large-scale agriculture has a place in some land-abundant areas of Africa – if it is driven by markets rather than subsidies and if the rights of the current land users are adequately protected – it would be a grave mistake to forsake the proven power of smallholders to jump-start growth, reduce poverty, and solve the hunger crisis in Africa and beyond. Promoting smallholder farming is not 'romantic populism' but sound economic policy. (Byerlee and de Janvry 2009)

Other initiatives, such as the Alliance for the Green Revolution in Africa, are helping to strengthen the focus on African smallholders by providing research funding, capacity development and input support. The challenge is to base these new initiatives on a proper understanding of the complexities, constraints and possibilities in which African smallholder agriculture is embedded.

Institutional reflection related to promotion of smallholder agriculture In parallel with a strong push towards African land grabs for large-scale food and biofuel production, there is also a growing consciousness of the role of African agriculture and land, not only in production, but also in terms of belonging, of status, of solidarity, and, in the widest sense, of African culture. This opens up a wider understanding of rural production and livelihoods and their institutional foundation. The role of land ownership systems remains central to the discussion of African rural diversity and the conditions for improved agricultural productivity. The promotion of individual property rights to land has long been advocated by international financial institutions, donors and many economists as essential to generate agricultural productivity growth. This, it is claimed, would open a space for individual rational economic behaviour and provide security for long-term investments. It would also do away with gender-discriminating ownership systems.

However, from another perspective, a shift from existing customary land ownership systems based on redistribution and reciprocity principles, however weakening, to individual land ownership is likely to face numerous problems that may easily lead to conflict and unstable production conditions. In the context of overlapping and complex rights systems that have developed over generations, the land adjudication process may also undermine the future legitimacy of landowners. Another major hindrance to agricultural productivity enhancement is the fact that the state holds radical title to land ownership. This has led to continuous state-initiated institutional changes and interference, and has often undermined smallholder trust and created an underlying uncertainty regarding smallholders' and communities' land rights. It is also a major obstacle when it comes to compensation for local land rights holders and communities in connection with transfer-related large-scale land acquisitions and leases.

An alternative land ownership solution might be to prepare for the end of state land ownership systems and to transfer land ownership, as well as management, to rural smallholders and communities. This is not a new idea, and the change cannot be achieved without a protracted struggle. Nearly two decades ago, a similar recommendation came from the Presidential Commission on land in Tanzania (1992). The idea was, however, removed during the process of formulating the Tanzanian land policy of 1995, a process controlled by state agencies. The subsequent Land Act and Village Land Act of 1999 also retained a state land ownership regime.

Transfer of land rights to rural smallholders and communities would make it possible to develop rural production and livelihoods from below, using and building on existing institutions to adapt to internal and external pressures and opportunities. In parallel, individual ownership systems could be strengthened (where they exist, for instance in Ghana and Kenya). As I see it, long-term sustainable agricultural development that can induce growth and reduce poverty needs to emerge through the strengthening of local communities and institutions of rural Africa according to their own needs and perceived opportunities. This space for influencing one's own development is an important – perhaps *the* most important – impetus for change. Increased autonomy, local institutions and secure land rights and entitlements can, in my opinion, help create such a space. However, such a shift in perspective regarding African rural development can only come from increasing respect for, and changing power relations in favour of, smallholder and rural communities. Power is also bound up with the configuration of new governance, related to large-scale food acquisitions and leases.

Governance changes and the need for a widening of the analytical approaches
The emerging governance systems connected with food and energy security and related to large-scale land acquisitions and leases create challenges in understanding the driving forces and outcomes of the process. The rise of food security and energy security to primary political concerns may imply that economic aspects related to understanding the large-scale acquisitions and leases of African land have to give way to political considerations and aspects. Political considerations should not, however, be subsumed by, or be secondary to, economic aspects in the analysis, as is often the case in World Bank 'political economy', but should be given some autonomy in the explanatory models and perspectives (Olukoshi 1998). Such an approach may also provide a better basis for understanding the long-term strategic challenges facing Africa in the context of globalization.

A more comprehensive analysis could be attained by connecting the macro-oriented analytical approach to increased insights about micro-level institutional dynamics. This will require a broadening of the economic analysis with sociological and cultural aspects and perspectives, since African rural livelihoods seem to connect or integrate economic priorities and rationality with concerns about rural survival that encompass both redistributive and reciprocity aspects and relationships. The relevance of such broader analyses requires a genuine attempt to be made to include an investigation of power relations at the global, the national and the local levels, as well as of how they connect with one another.

2 | Biofuel governance: a matter of discursive and actor intermesh

Marie Widengård

Introduction

Today, biofuels are generally promoted as providing societal benefits of three kinds: energy security; rural development; and environmental protection. In this lies their political strength (Lawrence 2010). By combining these three main societal benefits, biofuels can attract the attention and support of just about anyone, provided it is done in the right way. As for what this 'right way' looks like, that is a difficult question. This chapter will look instead at how we are led to think that some ways are 'more right' than others.

The aim of this chapter is to provide a lens by which to read biofuel governance. The chapter takes a global point of departure to illustrate the origins of 'global biofuels' and the constructs of green biofuels and biofuels as 'win-win-win'. Following these green, neoliberal constructs, the chapter heads to the 'production site' of Africa, where 'governmentalities' start changing into something more 'local' or 'intermeshed' – literally. The text does not suggest that biofuel governance is linear or is directed in any way. Rather it provides a governance lens that allows an analysis of intermeshed governance, namely governmentality. The aim is to describe how biofuel governance *is* rather than how it should be.

The question of how biofuels are governed is particularly connected to a concern that biofuels might not be governable at all. There are concerns that the consequences are too large, too inconceivable, too unintentional, and too unexpected to be governed. Are biofuels out of control? To shed light on this question, this chapter takes stock of governance issues surrounding the oil-rich shrub jatropha. Jatropha generally receives a privileged position in biofuel discussions in Africa. In accordance with other studies, one might ask why, or rather how, jatropha has assumed this elevated status and what has kept it there. Hunsberger (2010) suggests that answering these questions involves delving into a tangle of actors, motivations and influences that operate across sectors and scales. This chapter introduces the reader to such intermesh, by giving illustrative cases from sub-Saharan Africa. The illustrations are based on literature review, personal conference notes and informal discussions with biofuel stakeholders across private, public and civil society sectors representing the global North and South. Draft government strategies and policies are brought in to illustrate how actors communicate around biofuels, but it should be acknowledged that such readings have not been adopted by government.

Biofuel and the imperative to go global

The increasing pressures to discover alternative sources of fuel and to control their production, processing and marketing constitute one of the fundamental drivers of economic and political behaviour on the global scale (Young et al. 2006). These pressures have led to 'a frenzy of activity across the world' (Borras et al. 2010), especially because of a global trend whereby countries adopt blending targets, mandates, tax exemptions, subsidies and other incentives for the production and use of alternative fuels (Lawrence 2010). EU energy policy, alongside most energy policies worldwide, signals a secure demand for large volumes of biofuels, which serves to incentivize biofuel development both in the EU and in the South (Franco et al. 2010). The new scramble for Africa is directly linked to the growing demand for the currently most 'viable' option for alternative fuel – liquid fuel derived from plant material, also referred to as 'first-generation' or 'agro-industrial' biofuels.

While biofuels started as national projects, there is today a clear tendency towards the development of a global biofuels network, in which production, trade investment, consumption, control and governance lie beyond the control of nation states (Mol 2007). The common understanding among economic and political elites is that, if biofuels are going to make a significant contribution to climate change mitigation, energy security and rural development, then their production and consumption need to globalize further (ibid.). This means that, although biofuels rely on government or state-like political mandates and support, they are in the process of becoming an item of global flow, indifferent to origin, destination or consequences, beyond the conditions set out in trade agreements or certification schemes.

In line with this, Kuchler (2010) indicates a convergence of understanding among major global actors[1] for international flows of biofuels: namely, for the production of biofuels in the South to be consumed in the North. The thought is simple. High energy demand calls for large biofuel volumes, which in turn assumes production on large areas of cultivable land. The logic assumes an international market based on production in the South and consumption in the North because of the favourable biophysical conditions and the low costs of land and labour in most developing countries. Kuchler also draws attention to how the International Energy Agency (IEA) bluntly suggests that 'since both greenhouse gas emissions and oil import dependence are essentially global problems, it makes sense to look at these problems from an international perspective' (IEA 2009). Developed countries could therefore invest in the production of biofuels 'in countries that can produce them more cheaply, if the benefits in terms of oil use and greenhouse gas emissions reductions are superior to what could be achieved domestically' (Kuchler 2010).

Governmentality: a lens on biofuel governance

This chapter looks at how such logic is made 'right', made dominant, and how it is resisted and transformed. Governmentality is a Foucauldian lens that tries to remove the 'naturalness' and 'taken-for-granted' character of how things are done, or, more specifically, how things are argued, calculated, measured and rendered governable (Dean 1999). 'Governmentality', or governing through mentalities, is a play on words that marks a shift in the use of power technologies towards 'soft' governing modes of modern societies, such as governing through thought and language, by invoking particular truths, by seeking to shape conduct, by working through our desires, aspirations, interests and beliefs, by giving responsibilities, and by self-regulation and self-discipline (Dean 1999; Foucault et al. 2003). Governmentality approaches governance as a rational and thoughtful activity, and asks questions surrounding the forms of thought, knowledge, expertise, strategies, means of calculation and rationality in various practices of governance (Dean 1999). It is a lens that tries to capture both the concrete (by describing the means, mechanisms, procedures, instruments, tactics, techniques, technologies and vocabularies that constitute authority), and the 'telos', or vision, that guides governance in certain directions, and the particular identities that are necessary to create a particular society (Dean 1999).

Governmentality studies go beyond government as controlled by the state. A governmentality is defined as a particular style of governance, which is shaped by an intermesh of various actors, discourses, forms of rationalization, logic and technologies of rule (Lockwood and Davidson 2010). As this chapter will demonstrate, the 'global' governmentality described in the opening section is but one form of the mentalities that govern biofuel developments. Such governmentality might prevail in a discourse of globalism. In a national and local context, however, biofuel governance is something different. The line of argument is that there is hybrid governance, in which 'green-washed' neoliberal mentalities mesh with localism, ecocentrism, and so on, to create regimes of practice surrounding the fuel in each particular case. An analysis of governmentality attempts to capture the actual or so-called 'real' governance. This means that it acknowledges that different ministries vary in rationales, technologies of rules and visions; that government positions shift depending on the audience; that transnational companies are more or less free to 'localize' their intervention or are concerned to address local rationales or national agendas; that the governmentality of NGOs transforms when the site of practice shifts from global headquarters to local offices; or that researchers use different frames or ask certain questions depending on where and who they are. The main explanation is that governance regimes or practices tend to evolve when different governmentalities intermesh. Lastly, governmentality also allows for an analysis of power that goes beyond the concept of sovereign territories.

Green governmentality Biofuels have been given a big push by what is sometimes referred to as a neoliberal 'green wash', which broadens the neoliberal governmentality to include matters that are green or that are made to *seem* green (Neumann 2004; Watts 2004). The vision of 'defossilizing' society has been key for global biofuels, especially in connection with the meta-discourse of ecological modernization that sets the agenda for much development strategy in the world. Within green or eco-governmentality, nature is made intelligible, measurable, assessable and thus governable. Green governmentality is important to biofuels on various counts. First, it refers to a governmentality that acknowledges environmental problems to be global, with climate change the most urgent. Secondly, it refers to a governmentality where biofuels become a logical solution to climate change – today most countries refer to the use of biofuels as a key strategy in their efforts to mitigate climate change (FAO 2008). Thirdly, it refers to a governmentality that legitimizes what has become known as 'land grab', which can be described as a government-sponsored strategy to secure food security and energy security through offshore production (McMichael 2010).

Biofuel and its changing rationales

When trying to grasp the mentality governing biofuels, it is important to take stock of the rationales underlying biofuel development. By reviewing the history of biofuels, it becomes clear that the rationale for promoting them changes over time (Ulmanen et al. 2009; Lawrence 2010; Obama 2010). While biofuels produced from agricultural products got started (to a large extent) as a way of addressing oil scarcity during the world wars of the twentieth century and the oil crises of the 1970s, they later became a way of dealing with agricultural surpluses, low agricultural prices and high farm subsidies, mainly in Brazil, the US and the EU. As such, the idea of producing oil from soil became linked to rural economic development and rural employment. Also, the issue of energy security, driven by high oil prices and volatile oil supplies, has spread out to include issues of energy sovereignty, national security concerns (especially in the US) and energy poverty (especially in Africa). Only lately have biofuels been promoted as a solution to environmental problems. While the green discourse started as a local strategy to deal with urban pollution, it soon became overshadowed by the rationale that biofuels can mitigate climate change on a global scale.

Biofuels and the imperative to save the planet

The construct of global environmental problems Once scientists became conscious of the problem of global warming, it became a problem that had to be measured and addressed. The original construction of climate change brought with it the conceptualization of a global environment, a 'planetary consciousness' and an interconnectedness usually spelt out as 'we are all in the same boat', or 'we share the same blame, fate and responsibility for the problems and for the solutions' (Barry 1999). Such a conceptualization was articulated in 1987, when the World Commission on Environment and Development presented evidence of the degradation of the environment on a planetary scale (WCED 1987). The Brundtland report concluded that the present pattern of development is environmentally unsustainable over the long term, and, as a response, the report presented and popularized the concept of 'sustainable development'.[2]

Regardless of the vagueness and ambiguity of the Brundtland definition, it was instrumental in developing a 'global view' with respect to the planet's future (Mebratu 1998; Garcez and Vianna 2009). At the centre of this particular green discourse stands 'the assumption that economic growth and the resolution of ecological problems can, in principle, be reconciled' (Hajer 2009: 82). This means that, rather than degrading the environment, modernization and economic growth offer the best option for escaping from the global ecological challenge, in particular through a decentralized liberal market order, where actors are free to choose their own optimal solutions or so-called 'greening strategies' (Hajer 1996; York and Rosa 2003; Bäackstrand and Lövbrand 2007). The notion of mutually reinforcing links between economic growth and environmental protection proposed by the Brundtland report reinforces the discourse on ecological modernization as a win-win strategy, as well as the compatibility of a liberal market order and sustainable development (Bäackstrand and Lövbrand 2007). The key idea is that society can reach a sustainable state without any major structural adjustments or value changes. The idea is for society to use the potential from within the prevailing market system, or simply 'green wash' business as usual (York and Rosa 2003: 274). This discourse emphasizes the role of 'green' technology and instrumental measures as pathways away from environmental problems (Hajer 1996; Huber 2008). This belief denies the need for solutions that call for social change. It rather favours solutions that have a weak connection to time and place (Böhler 2004).

The construct of biofuels as a solution In 1991, the Intergovernmental Panel on Climate Change (IPCC) declared that climate change was a global problem caused by fossil fuel burning. This offered a scientifically substantiated rationale for the 'global politics of the climate' and for the subsequent global policy advice to adopt 'climate-neutral fuel'. [For more on climate change and its discourse, see Bäackstrand and Lövbrand (2007).] It is into this ecological modernization discourse that the 'clean, carbon- and guilt-free' fuels fit perfectly. Numerous accounts 'proved' that biofuels were climate friendly by using lifecycle analysis and other modelling techniques. Biofuels also imply that vehicles can continue to use liquid fuels, a type of fuel that the transport system is built around. In particular, global biofuels – as in global sourcing and international markets – could provide fuels with a fuzzy sense of origin, meaning that fuel could be produced 'elsewhere' and 'out of sight'.

The implications of green governmentality For the sake of saving the planet, a new set of administrative truths and knowledges (plural) emerged that stretched beyond the administration of life into nature, the entire planet and the very biosphere in which people live (Bäackstrand and Lövbrand 2007). If 'society must be defended' as Foucault et al. (2003) suggest, biofuels become a weapon to combat climate change, no matter what (Kanter 2008). It is within such governmentality that we may say that, while biofuels are not an innovation, their newness lies in their proclaimed ability to solve problems of a global dimension for the 'good of society'. According to White and Dasgupta (2010), the green discourse offered distinct opportunities for biofuel advocates to make corporate land acquisitions, forest conversion and the introduction of contested biotechnologies more publicly acceptable. It is also in light of the green governmentality that biofuels make a particular case, distinct from the governance of other cash crops in Africa. When biofuels were promoted as green, they gained a global momentum that had seldom been seen. Biofuels were supported not only by actors who believed in economic development through markets, but also by enthusiastic environmentalists, who initially jumped on the bandwagon in support of agro-industrial biofuels.

Being green, biofuels moved into the realm of governance by technocrats and scientists: Bäackstrand and Lövbrand (2007) note that the governmentality of green matters is a science-driven and centralized multilateral negotiation order, associated with top-down monitoring and mitigation techniques implemented on global scales. Such governmentality reflects the notion that 'global experts' should assist Africa in setting environmental criteria for sustainable fuels, because environmental criteria are 'global' and can be handled by 'expertise' (Widengård 2009a; Widengård 2010b). Pro-biofuel arguments especially elaborated the notion that biofuels can be produced on so-called marginal, degraded or otherwise idle land. The inclusion of land in the discourse invited new governing authorities, such as ministries dealing with land, but also experts dealing with maps. Command of technology, including satellite imagery, gave experts the 'right' to govern land through desk-top studies, or, as Franco et al. (2010: 674) say, 'experts can regulate-govern by choosing whether to protect the best agricultural land for local food uses or to protect the most biodiverse or most "high carbon stocked" land for environmental purposes'. Today, land for biofuel production can be identified for the consumption of others by means of satellite imagery, through a 'global gaze' that is ignorant of what is taking place on the ground, in the local social context (Cotula et al. 2009). Resolutions of 1 km² might be used to identify areas available for biofuels, but when viewed at the finer resolution provided by Google Earth, such areas may be found to be extensively utilized and inhabited (Shut et al. 2010). Mathews (2007) exemplifies such discourse with an assertion that global transport demands can be secured sustainably by creating eighteen Brazils in 'marginal' parts of the world, such as Africa.

The concept of 'degraded' or 'marginal' land can also be a means of normalizing past degradation, so that agro-industrial biofuel monocultures become an 'improvement' (Franco et al. 2010). Such reasoning is found in the Zambian draft policy (2009), where it is also argued that, once it has been rehabilitated, it may be possible to return some of the land to food production. Franco et al. (2010: 673) argue that the marginalization of land has arisen mainly in response to the food versus fuel debate.

The discursive shift in 2008

To invite new actors and subjects means to invite new logics, rationales and visions into biofuel governance. Aaron Leopold writes that, by allowing the environmental storyline to be added to the discourse surrounding biofuels, the pro-biofuels coalition had opened up its doors to a new set of civil society actors, 'who by their very nature are generally critical of environmental exploitation' (2009: 8). He argues that environmental concerns over biofuels were not enough to convince governments to withdraw their significant financial and political support for the biofuel industry. It was only the dramatic rise in food commodity prices in 2007 and 2008, and the subsequent critique by NGOs and intergovernmental organizations, that managed to create space for a more critical discussion around biofuels. Franco et al. (2010: 674) also write that the more palatable the narrative of environmentally and socially sustainable biofuels is, the more potentially vulnerable that narrative becomes. The reason being that the narrative then depends on conditions that can be changed through strategic research and public action.

According to Mol (2010: 65) there have been two particularly bitter controversies around biofuels: these have been associated with its environmental sustainability and its effects on food security, especially among the poor in developing countries. The UK's Gallagher Report also emphasizes growing concern about the role of biofuels in rising food prices, accelerating deforestation and doubts about the benefits to the climate (Gallagher 2008). In 2008, these controversies turned into a discursive shift, as biofuels were accused of being the major culprit for the global food price hikes. This shift in discourse meant that biofuels moved from being promoted as a clean, green, sustainable and guilt-free fuel to being a technology that did more harm than good (ActionAid International 2008; FAO 2008; Leopold 2009; Ulmanen et al. 2009). Or, in more conservative terms, there was a shift in discourse during which biofuels became less of a sustainable fuel by default, and more of a potentially low-carbon energy source. Such a shift was also prompted by new knowledge, which was spearheaded by scientific reports (e.g. Fargione et al. 2008; Searchinger et al. 2008). Proper accounting skills in relation to carbon savings became more detailed. They started to include qualifications on how biofuels were to be produced, especially if land had to be converted and cleared. It was agreed that biofuels implied not only carbon savings, but also carbon costs if forests were cleared. Indirect land use change, carbon debt, carbon cost, carbon storage, sequestration, annual carbon repayment rate, and the years it would take to repay biofuel carbon debt after land use change became part of the biofuels dictionary.

The Gallagher Report also contributed to biofuel discourse in 2008 by proposing continued biofuel production – but only on non-agricultural land, so as to avoid risking the displacement of food crops. The message was that feedstock production must avoid agricultural land that would otherwise be used for food production. The issue was politicized and spread further through the critique by, for example, the global farmer network Via Campesina, which questions the justness of producing food to feed cars while so many people are starving (Via Campesina 2007). These debates opened up the biofuel discourse to issues of land and social and environmental equity. Biofuels became more publicly known as land-based fuels, agro-industrial fuels, or 'agrofuel' for short. McMichael (2010) argues that renaming biofuels 'agrofuels' is part of this discursive shift that stems from the crisis in the food regime. The next section will argue that such a shift can be seen to aid actors promoting biofuels in Africa.

The construct of win–win–win

When trying to grasp the mentality governing biofuels, it is important to take stock of the rapid changes that are occurring in the global discourse on biofuels – because, as the critique against the production of biofuels in developing countries grows, so the dominant governmentality is transformed to accommodate (or strategically resist or silence) the rising concerns. The current rationale for biofuels is a discursive alliance that bundles most of the former benefits together. Biofuels are generally promoted as a package solution to energy security, environmental protection and rural development. As such, biofuel discourses must be considered to have scored a political success (Lawrence 2010). The three assumed societal benefits of biofuels have diffused into much of the rhetoric of public, private and civil society actors, even in Africa.

Today, most strategies, policies, business plans, aid programmes and development projects related to biofuels chorus these three 'win-win-wins' (or 'win-win', as the narrative is more generally known), albeit with slight differences in emphasis. Borras, McMichael and Scoones (2010) note that it is the 'win-win' narrative that dominates the framing of the biofuel debate globally. For Africa, win-win-win includes agricultural development, technological progress, poverty reduction and social and economic justice (COMPETE 2009). The logic is that biofuels will 'bring development to Africa', in terms of rural development, job creation and cash incomes for small-scale farmers, or through so-called 'spill-over effects' in terms of infrastructure, rural electricity, schools, clinics and side-businesses from plantations and processing plants. As regards Africa, global biofuels are especially promoted for their proclaimed ability to bring agricul-tural development. Agricultural investments seem logical to many stakeholders, especially African governments and agricultural ministries. In governmental terms, biofuels are therefore mainly discussed as a vehicle for modernizing agriculture, and as a way of increasing export incomes from agricultural products (Republic of Mozambique 2009; Republic of Zambia 2009).

There is also an argument that biofuels are pro-poor, or, as the Mozambique minister of energy writes in the preface to the National Biofuels Policy and Strategy, 'we cannot simply deny our communities the unique opportunity they have today to help themselves fight poverty through their participation in the production and use of biofuels' (Republic of Mozambique 2009). In Zambia, the smallholder horticulture production is taken as an example in which large agro-industries can bring benefits to local communities by offer-ing smallholders access to international markets, professional know-how and private investment (Republic of Zambia 2009). At a macro level, employment benefits are often highlighted by politicians as the key benefit of bioenergy production. The Zambian biofuels policy draft refers to an analysis by the World Bank that suggests that many millions of jobs in Africa could be generated if only money earmarked for conventional energy investment could be diverted to bioenergy. Such logic needs to be scrutinized. The draft emphasizes that job quality and worker welfare are important developmental issues, and it points towards a quality assurance through labelling or certification schemes for 'sustainable products', using social criteria derived from the International Social Accountability Standards. Personal comments in relation to Chinese biofuel initiatives often boil down to the lack of development opportunities for rural areas. A district commissioner in Northern Zambia argued, for instance, that local chiefs would not hand over huge tracts of land to the Chinese, because Chinese investments signalled few opportunities for local people.

In Africa, biofuel production also becomes a proclaimed opportunity to source foreign direct investments. The chapters in this book on FDI, Ethiopia and Tanzania exemplify measures that have been taken to facilitate the flow of foreign direct investments, and especially the need for the private sector to access land. The rationale of reducing climate change takes a back-seat role in driving biofuel development in African discussions. The rationale for reduced use of fossil fuels is mentioned rather as a strategy to mitigate the high import costs of fossil fuels (Republic of Mozambique 2009). According to the Zambian biofuel policy draft of 2009, there is a growing realization in Africa that high dependency on imported petroleum fuels is having a negative impact on the continent's economic development. The draft argues that the economies of countries in sub-Saharan Africa are oil intensive and therefore vulnerable to the adverse macro-economic of high oil prices. Climate change is sometimes even discussed as an opportunity, meaning an opportunity to source carbon funds through, for instance, the Clean Development Mechanism (Widengård 2010b).

The conditionalities of the social win

Dauvergne and Neville (2010) note that the rhetoric of win-win has come to dominate the sustainability discourse, so that it is difficult for critics of biofuels to challenge its appeal. Much of the critique is, in other words, held *within* the win-win paradigm, which is held to work across the globe – yet it remains silent on issues of developmental or distributional differences (Langhelle 2009). Win-win and ecological modernization connect to a discourse that pivots on a globalism that assumes the inevitability of a boundless flow of finance and neoliberalism – on a belief in the efficiency of free competitive markets and in the notion that this efficiency will maximize benefits for the greatest number of people in the long run (Hoogvelt 2001: 155). This is where the discourse of ecological modernization fits: sustainable development is to come naturally, over time, through markets and technologies.

A parallel assumption is that a neoliberal state, through the facilitation and stimulation of business interests, will foster growth and innovation, and that this is 'the only way to eradicate poverty and to deliver, in the long run, higher living standards to the mass of the population' (Harvey 2006: 25). In terms of biofuels, such stimuli include tax breaks, generous land leases, and the privatization or deregulation of public services or assets such as natural resources. Primitive accumulation and the radical transformation of nature nestle within this belief system 'as necessary evils, a stage to be gone through in order to break with tradition, superstition, religion, etc. en route to a better kind of society' (Harvey 2006: 74). Africa becomes once more a continent of 'backwardness', as a result of its 'unwillingness' (or 'inability' in its racist version) to 'catch up'. Africa in this perspective has but one option (or perhaps rhetorically two) as regards its development: it can leapfrog into green technology (or wait for history to take its turn). This is where we can place arguments such as those voiced by the Swedish company SEKAB and associated consultants: 'biofuels might not be ideal but they are the only development opportunity that is likely to ever come this way'.

In this discourse, biofuels are a cure. Biofuels are to bring agricultural modernization and investments through fair North–South biopacts (Mathews 2007). The biofuel market is said to represent an opportunity for Africa 'provided sustainability criteria are met', and any risks are to 'be managed' (FARA 2008). In this sense, the ecological modernization discourse silences issues of global social and environmental justice. It does not historicize the unequal causes of social or environmental conditions. It diverts calls for less energy-consuming lifestyles or fair trade towards discussions of improved energy efficiency and cost-efficient solutions. The social win claimed within the ecological modernization discourse is, therefore, confined mainly to the (internal) context of the South for a number of reasons: social issues, such as development and poverty, are higher on the political agenda in the South; it is assumed that markets and business-friendly regulation and deregulation will do the trick; the discourse was born in the context of Western countries and industrialized societies that are taken as the epitome of the modern and progressive; and development and distributional issues are silenced so as to preserve the status quo between North and South (Langhelle 2009).

In an African context, the social win focuses on agricultural growth, rural development, poverty reduction, rural electricity, local opportunities, technology transfers and 'fair' markets (Mathews 2007; Achten et al. 2010). This is where we find outgrower, cash-cropping or contract schemes, promoted as environmentally friendly, wealth-generating and ensuring corporate security. The third win (or the winner) can be illustrated through the case of the Swedish biofuel company SEKAB and its attempt to set up responsible business in Tanzania (see chapter 6). In addition to developing its own sugarcane estates, SEKAB explored the prospect of complementary production in a sugarcane smallholder and outgrower scheme. Of interest here is the advice that SEKAB received in relation to the benefits of asserting a win-win-win identity, within which strategic local political, social and economic interests and aspirations could meet on the basis of 'enlightened self-interest' (CSDI et al. 2008). To the consultant hired for advice, a franchise network would be ideal, since such developments 'by their very nature require a co-operative win/win/win relationship between the partners'. Win-win-win was conceptualized as sharing both the benefits and the risks. The company's assets were to join farmers' own finances and 'sweat-equity' (2008: 23–4). Another rationale is to provide for a code of conduct or a 'surrogate rule of law':

> In the developing world, the rule of law is frequently irrelevant or highly compromised, particularly in the informal economy where most low-income people live and work. A franchise system establishes a surrogate rule of law that provides the framework for business success. Franchisees who disregard the rules risk losing their investment, so it is in their self-interest to be 'law-abiding citizens' within their franchise community. (2008: 27)

Such an argumentation resonates with Beyene's analysis in this book, drawing on the work of Ellis (1993: 146–7), whereby the espoused purpose of agrarian contracts is 'to reduce transaction costs in the context of the unevenly developed markets and scarce information found in the rural societies of many developing countries'. The rationale for pulling in the social discourse could be read as an institutional response to imperfections in markets for credit, insurance, information or factors of production, as mentioned by Beyene, as well as a strategy to draw low-income growers into the modern and industrial agricultural sectors, that will make them better placed to benefit from economies of scale and regional and global markets.

An intermesh of actors

Agrawal (2005) suggests that to understand any form of rule, it is necessary to understand those who are subject to it. Biofuel governance becomes particularly messy if actors want different things from biofuels. We may think of actors, individuals and their organizations as both potentially governable through the agency of their responses to direction, and capable of thinking and acting in a manner contrary to that being sought by the dominant actors (Dean 1999; Lockwood and Davidson 2010). From this perspective, small-scale farmers in Africa can act as 'governors of biofuels', because they add their own logics, rationales and vision to biofuel governance. The governmentality of a small-scale farmer can be said to intermesh with that of a biofuel company, NGO, local leader, government, scientist, consultant, media and so on. This can be thought of as a regime of practice that constitutes multiple governmentalities, in a hybridizing governance assemblage. Different groups representing different governmentalities thus coexist 'in reality', in a particular policy, national agenda, or local community. Being land-based, biofuels make a particular case where sectors and actors are forced to intermesh.

Because the issue of biofuels is 'cross-sectoral' – and because biofuels can be justified in so many ways – they attract attention from a wide set of actors, in unexpected ways. Biofuels have been seen to join actors across public, private, civil society and ideological divides, often in slick, unholy and ambiguous alliances (Borras et al. 2010; Pye 2010). There are numerous accounts to describe this process – e.g. how jatropha joined British Petroleum with small-scale farmers in Africa (*Wall Street Journal* 2009); how jatropha joins General Motors with the US and Indian governments in a programme meant to show that jatropha was viable (General Motors 2010); how jatropha joins biofuel companies with life technologies and oil multinationals (Lane 2010); or how charities and NGOs join with universities, local energy champions and biofuel associations and outgrower schemes, such as in the district of Mungwi in Northern Zambia, where I conduct fieldwork.

There is much blurring of the public and the private, the local, national and global, and the implementers and regulators of biofuel investments (Dauvergne and Neville 2010). It is, in other words, difficult to assess who is governing whom and for the purpose of what. Biofuel players are often far removed from each other, but are linked through fragile and tenuous connections (ibid.). In this picture, capitalist and post-colonial relations between North and South remain, but are supplemented by new configurations, including South–South relations and North–South–South formations, where transnational capital based in the North allies with South–South collaborations (ibid.). This means that biofuel development is driven by multiple and sometimes competing rationales.

An intermesh of rationales

There is a frequent mismatch between global campaigns organized by civil society (often addressing biodiversity conservation, climate justice and food security from subsistence farming) and rural social movements and local concerns (focusing on land rights, cash incomes from feedstock sales, employment conditions and food security based on a diversity of livelihood strategies) (Borras et al. 2010; Pye 2010). Farmers may want to focus on household use and income generation from biofuels. Project leaders may prioritize value addition, and donors the potential for emissions reduction and carbon offsets. Different objectives may, to some degree, converge, but they may also lead to conflict. Land deals and contracts are particularly conflict loaded.

The rationale for private agents using contracts to secure investments may mesh with a smallholder's rationale in signing as many contracts as possible to secure a market. This also means that it may seem logical to some that production of a non-edible agrofuel does not threaten food security. To a smallholder, however, it may seem more logical to plant crops that represent multiple uses and alternative markets. To some, it may also seem logical to minimize risk by clearing additional land for biofuels, instead of shifting from food to fuel production. Local discourses from places such as Swaziland, Kenya and Mozambique, however, refer to a preference, or a need, on the part of smallholders to exchange one row of food for one row of biofuels, either because land is scarce or because the risk of investing in land clearance for a new and unknown crop appears greater than the risk of planting it on land that has already been prepared (Burley and Griffiths 2009; UNAC&JA 2009; Hunsberger 2010). There is a disconnect between rationales that might be said to resonate with a general political ecology rule:

> Macro discourses implicitly assume a priority for economic values and the need to have new 'clean' energy supplies for national economic growth, whereas local discourses place a value on household or community reproduction and employ a diverse and more plural set of values. (Ariza-Montobbio et al. 2010)

Can biofuels achieve 'everything', or would a single objective (not to mention three) be easier to achieve if actors shared the same thought or vision? Who is to accommodate whom in this power game? Is there one code of conduct that is more 'right' than others?

The formation of smallholder identity

The neoliberal vision is articulated in the 2008 *World Development Report* on agriculture. The 'new agriculture' is to be led by private entrepreneurs in extensive value chains linking producers to consumers (World Bank 2007: 8). In this vision, smallholders are law-abiding and economic rational entrepreneurs. If smallholders cannot 'upgrade themselves technologically to be able to integrate into niche markets of high value production through the fast developing global agri-supply chains', the World Bank suggests that they will have to find a way out of agriculture to the rural non-farm sector, or else migrate to the urban sector (White and Dasgupta 2010: 597). The global biofuel discourse also allows smallholders to become farm workers. In the extreme neoliberal vision of agro-export platforms providing food and fuel security in global space, by outsourcing food and agrofuel production to foreign territories smallholders will be compensated in various ways (McMichael 2010). Neoliberal structural market-based reforms generally create conditions by which global private interests strategically acquire and manage natural resource assets as part of large portfolios that are largely insensitive to the particularities of local geography (Lockwood and Davidson 2010). Within this vision, biofuels are produced by smallholders who have adopted a transnational code of conduct, or else within large-scale systems 'without farmers'. In contrast, the 'local' vision can be described as motivated by an ethic of maintaining the integrity of local places, as this is understood by the local communities (Lockwood and Davidson 2010: 393). In biofuels, the 'local' discourse refers to actors as 'traditional users' who privilege local control over resources, are faced with restricted capital mobility and respect traditional modes (ibid.). Such a vision often pivots on a smallholder identity that is to provide food and energy sovereignty at the community level, often at subsistence levels. These are the small-scale farmers who feed the world and cool the earth (Via Campesina 2007). In the real intermesh, a smallholder identity is likely to be something in between.

Intermeshed directions

How biofuels are governed differs from country to country, and the difference is tangible for small-scale biofuel producers. The Zambian jatropha case is, for instance, described by a group from civil society as initially led by market actors for the purpose of producing biodiesel (Widengård 2010b). When the price of fossil fuels decreased, many biofuel companies had either to phase out or suspend their purchase of seed. For instance, in Zambia the Australian Oval Biofuel company has abandoned its contract farmers in Western Province; Marli Investments failed to fulfil its purchase agreement; and British Petroleum left its joint venture with D1 Oils in 2009 (personal communication 2010; D1 Oils 2009). The result was a lack of market for jatropha seed in Zambia. International NGOs initially stepped in to mitigate the situation, creating what is described as an artificial market, with high prices for jatropha seed. When international funding or momentum ran out, local civil society actors stepped in to build capacity around the jatropha seed for local use in cooking, lighting and floor polish and soap making. From this perspective, biofuel development can be said to have changed direction from the global to the local.

The literature suggests that this is a global trend; that is, the global jatropha hype has turned into a local opportunity (Achten et al. 2010). This means that biofuel governance should by no means be viewed as static. Borras et al. (2010: 580) emphasize that there is no a priori reason why the biofuel complex 'should be constructed around nodes which are Northern and metropolitan and controlled by global capital'. The authors argue that it is rather the 'terms of incorporation' or the way in which politics intersects with economic processes and ecological conditions that shape how a biofuel intervention plays out (ibid.: 588). It is therefore no coincidence that analysts trying to grasp biofuel development reach out for concepts such as alliances, chains, networks, assemblages, frictions and hybrids to describe how biofuels evolve in the global–local dynamics (e.g. Hollander 2010; Hunsberger 2010). Though these concepts do have different connotations, they share the notion that biofuel as a commodity is constructed through social, political and economic relations, in ways that must be understood as a whole, and located within wider, often global, processes (Borras et al. 2010).

Conclusion

This chapter has mapped out the leading discourses around biofuels, and the issues of governance associated with the differing 'governmentalities' of shifting coalitions of actors and interests. Today, biofuels can be said to be governed through a complex web of global private actors, state (or state-like) governments, international bodies, transnational NGOs, local groups and smallholder visions. Governmentalities meet by necessity, but they do not meet on a level playing field. And neither do they communicate perfectly. Governing through mentalities is not a play on words but a power game. To govern how actors think about biofuels and themselves is partly to rule what biofuels and society are to become. If large-scale plantations in Africa seem rational, clear, systematic and explicit about how things are and how they ought to be, then that mode may start to dominate.

I should like to close with the thought that, while biofuels are nothing new, global biofuels are. And so any prescription as to how to govern global biofuels is based on (more or less valid) assumptions. I suggest that these should be taken for what they are: assumptions, not *the* truth.

3 | Peak oil and climate change: triggers of the drive for biofuel production

Rune Skarstein

Peak oil

The term 'peak oil' was coined by the geologist Marion King Hubbert (1903–89). Hubbert, who had also studied mathematics and physics, worked at the research centre of the oil company Shell for more than 20 years. After he retired from Shell in 1964, he became senior research geophysicist at the US Geological Survey (1964–76), and held positions as professor of geology and geophysics at Stanford University (1963–68), and at the University of California, Berkeley (1973–76).

In 1956, Hubbert first presented the now well-known bell-shaped curve of oil production (the Hubbert Curve), which is assumed to apply to individual wells as well as to whole fields and whole countries. In 1956, Hubbert used his model to predict that US oil production would peak in one of the years between 1965 and 1970. Actually, the US reached peak oil, of 9.5 million barrels per day, in 1970.

In most cases, the Hubbert Curve is steeper on the left than on the right, indicating that, because of high well pressure, oil production increases quite rapidly up to the 'peak', and then declines more slowly, with the falling pressure in the wells causing a gradual slowing of production. Production in Alaska, which peaked in 1988, typically follows such a pattern. However, there are important exceptions to this rule. One case in point is petroleum production in Mexico, which increased relatively slowly, peaking at almost 3.4 million barrels per day in 2004, and then declined steeply to less than 2.8 million barrels per day in mid-2008.

In 1974, Hubbert projected that global oil production would peak between 1995 and 2000 'if current trends continue' (Hubbert 1974). That prediction was obviously wrong. The IEA reports that world oil production increased steadily from about 65 million barrels per day in the late 1970s to 83 million barrels per day in 2008 (IEA 2009: 84). However, Hubbert was not entirely wrong. Of the 48 greatest oil-producing countries in the world, 33 have passed peak oil, and some of those countries have experienced a rapid decline in production. Among them are the USA (peak oil in 1970), Indonesia (1997), Australia (2000), the UK (1999), Norway (2001) and Mexico (2004). Also, the sultanate of Oman has passed peak oil, and there are strong indications that the same has happened in Kuwait (Follath and Jung 2006: 87–9). Another significant point is that, since 1984 the annual discoveries of new 'proved' reserves of oil have been smaller than annual production – a gap that has been increasing over time. In the period 1958–66, discovered new reserves of oil averaged 48 billion barrels per year. In the period 1994–2004, new discoveries declined to less than 10 billion barrels per year, which represents only a third of the average annual production of 27.5 billion barrels in that period. In other words, since the mid-1980s, the oil companies have been finding less oil than the world has been consuming.[1] This development indicates that the costs of oil extraction will rise strongly in the coming decades, and as a consequence so will oil prices.

Some studies, especially those made by the Association for the Study of Peak Oil and Gas (ASPO), argue that the world as a whole has now arrived at the point of peak oil. On the other hand, the IEA estimates that world oil production will increase to 86.6 million barrels per day in 2015 and to 103 million barrels per day in 2030, while the US Energy Information Administration (EIA) is even more optimistic, forecasting a world oil production of almost 107 million barrels per day in 2030. Moreover, the IEA forecasts that the share of OPEC (Organization of the Petroleum Exporting Countries) in world oil production will jump from 44 per cent in 2008 to 52 per cent in 2030 (IEA 2009: 84–5; cf. also EIA 2009: 22).

Possibly more important than production forecasts are the estimates of 'proved reserves'.[2] For crude oil, these estimates vary from ASPO's 800 billion barrels to the estimate of the US EIA of 1,342 billion barrels.[3] Based on the present annual production, this implies a reserves-to-production ratio (RPR) that ranges from 26 years (ASPO) to 44 years (EIA). In other words, even the most optimistic estimates indicate that the world's oil reserves will be depleted around the middle of the present century.

Among fossil fuels, natural gas can quite easily replace oil in permanent installations (households, factories, thermal electricity plants, etc.), as well as in large parts of the transport sector, except (so far) in air transport. Based on the EIA's estimate of the world's proved reserves of natural gas of 6,250 trillion cubic feet, the RPR at present production levels is 57 years (EIA 2009: 39, 45). However, if gas should replace most of the present production of oil, the production of gas would have to be more than doubled, which implies that the RPR would decline correspondingly.[4]

We may conclude that, as far as oil and natural gas are concerned, the end of the fossil age is not more than about half a century away, simply because these resources are being depleted. Moreover, especially the extraction costs for oil will escalate dramatically within the coming decades (Campbell and Laherrère 1998). At present agricultural costs, biofuel production with 'first-generation technology', based on food crops such as maize, soya beans, rape, sugarcane and sugar beet, becomes economically viable in the United States at an oil price of about $80 per barrel, and in Europe at about $115 per barrel (Sexton and Zilberman 2010).[5] An oil price permanently above $115 per barrel will most probably be the reality in the near future. Therefore there is good reason to assume that the pressure to increase 'first-generation' biofuel production will be greater in the coming decade.

The only fossil fuel of which there are still abundant reserves is coal. In the last two decades, the estimates of world exploitable reserves of coal have declined gradually, from 1,145 billion tonnes in 1991 to 929 billion tonnes in 2006. However, with the production level of 2006, the RPR is still as much as 137 years (EIA 2009: 59).[6] But the combustion of all this coal would cause incalculable damage to the global natural environment.

CO_2 emissions and climate change

From the actual start around 1885 until 2004, the world's total oil production amounted to about 945 billion barrels, leading to total CO_2 emissions of about 330 billion tonnes (Campbell 2005: 6). We have seen that information on proved remaining reserves varies from ASPO's 800 billion barrels to the EIA's 1,340 billion barrels. In any event, not much more than half of total world oil reserves have been burnt so far, implying that – with present technology – there is scope for doubling the world's oil-related CO_2 emissions from today's level. The combustion of 1,340 billion barrels of oil will result in about 470 billion tonnes of CO_2, while the combustion of the exploitable coal reserves of 929 billion tonnes would lead to CO_2 emissions of more than 3,000 billion tonnes.[7]

It is important to note that most of the CO_2 emissions have taken place since the Second World War and have been concentrated in the industrialized countries (United States, Western Europe and Japan). They have more than quadrupled – from an annual average of 6 billion tonnes in 1946–55, to 26.2 billion tonnes per year in 1997–2006.[8] In its reference scenario, assuming that the present policies and technologies continue, the IEA assumes that global energy-related CO_2 emissions will rise to 34.5 billion tonnes in 2020 and 40.2 billion tonnes in 2030, which will be almost seven times the annual figure in 1946–55 (IEA 2009: 185).

In the last 20 years, the so-called emerging economies (especially China, Russia, Brazil and India) have joined the West in raising CO_2 emissions. This is due to rapidly increasing combustion of coal, as well as of oil, and is related to rapid industrialization and accelerating development of private motoring.[9] China is the lead country in this trend. In the 1980s, it was the greatest oil exporter in Asia, and was self-sufficient in oil up to 1993. Since then, consumption has been rising rapidly, as have the country's net imports of oil. Consumption more than doubled, from 3.3 million barrels per day in 1995 to 7.2 million in 2006, which means an annual average growth of 7.3

TABLE 3.1 The share of different countries and regions of total world population and the world's total CO_2 emissions, 2004

Country/region	1. Per cent of population	2. Per cent of CO_2 emissions	2/1 = CO_2 emissions per capita as a factor of global average
USA	4.6	20.9	4.54
China	20.2	17.3	0.86
Russia	2.2	5.3	2.41
India	17.4	4.6	0.26
Japan	2.0	4.3	2.15
Germany	1.3	2.8	2.15
Canada	0.5	2.2	4.40
Great Britain	0.9	2.0	2.22
All (137) underdeveloped economies (u-countries)	80.1	42.5	0.53
54 u-countries with lowest GDP per capita	37.2	7.2	0.19
24 richest OECD countries	14.3	41.9	2.93

Source: UNDP (2007: 243–6, 310–13).

per cent. In 2003, China became the world's second-largest consumer of oil, surpassed only by the USA. China's share of the total world oil consumption almost doubled, from 4.7 per cent in 1995 to 8.6 per cent in 2006, and in 2006 it imported 47.2 per cent of its total oil consumption (Downs 2006: 8–11).[10] The IEA forecasts that China will account for 30 per cent of the growth in world oil consumption between 2006 and 2020. Moreover, it estimates that China's net oil imports in 2030 will represent 80 per cent of the country's total oil consumption (IEA 2002; see also *Petroleum Economist* 2006).

In 2003, the USA (20.9 per cent) and China (17.3 per cent) together accounted for over 38 per cent of the total emissions in the world. If the trend in the period 1997–2003 continues, those two countries will account for half of the global CO_2 emissions in 2030. However, there is an important difference, not only between the USA and China but also between developed and underdeveloped economies, generally. Whereas the CO_2 emissions per capita in the US are more than 4.5 times greater than the global average, the emissions per capita in China are still much lower than average. For all 'developed' economies shown in Table 3.1, CO_2 emissions per capita are more than double the global average. For the 24 richest (OECD) countries, the ratio is 2.93. On the other hand, for the 54 poorest economies, it is as low as 0.19. In other words, CO_2 emissions per capita are more than 15 times greater in the 24 richest countries than in the 54 poorest. This implies that the scope for the richest countries to buy CO_2 quotas from the poorest ones is severely limited.

Table 3.2 shows data published by the IPCC on global CO_2 emissions in 2001 related to different activities. Public electricity and heat production for industries and households (34.8 per cent, the main part from coal burning), manufacturing and construction (18.1 per cent) and all types of transport (23.9 per cent) account for 78 per cent of total CO_2 emissions.[11] Combustion of oil and oil products accounts for 60 per cent of total emissions, while burning of coal, which is strongly on the increase globally, accounts for 33.7 per cent (Table 3.2).

TABLE 3.2 Activities with CO_2 emissions from burning of fossil fuels and CO_2 emissions according to type of fuel: global figures for 2001

CO_2 emissions created by	Emissions in million tonnes	Per cent
Public electricity and heat production	8,236	34.8
Car production	963	4.1
Energy extraction*	1,228	5.2
Manufacturing and construction	4,294	18.1
Road transport	4,208	17.8
Other transport	1,448	6.1
Use of fossil fuel in private households	1,902	8.0
Other sectors	1,405	5.9
TOTAL	23,684	100.0
Burning of coal	7,984	33.7
Burning of natural gas	1,511	6.4
Burning of oil and oil products	14,189	59.9
TOTAL	23,684	100.0

Note: * Includes extraction of coal, oil and natural gas, including flaring, as well as oil refining and other activities related to energy extraction.
Source: IPCC (2005: 56, 81).

Data from the IPCC show that the CO_2 content of the atmosphere was some 37 per cent higher in 2005 than before the industrial revolution, in 1750 (IPCC 2007a: 138–40). Only from 1995 to 2005 the atmospheric CO_2 content rose by 20 per cent, mainly from the increasing use of petroleum. This is the greatest increase during any decade in the last 200 years (IPCC 2007a: 131; 2007b: 5). The IPCC estimates that CO_2 emissions from fossil fuels and cement production have contributed about 75 per cent to the increase in the greenhouse effect since 1850, while the remaining 25 per cent stems from, among other things, deforestation, anthropogenic emissions of methane gas (CH_4) and nitrogen compounds. CO_2 from the burning of fossil fuels increased its share of the total annual contribution to the greenhouse effect from around 50 per cent in 1970 to 57 per cent in 2005 (IPCC 2007b: 2).

Much independent research confirms the IPCC's conclusions, as shown, for example, in a very careful review study by Jones and Mann (2004). Part of the conclusion of that study is worth quoting:

> Our review reaffirms that the warmth of the late 20th century has been unprecedented at the Northern Hemisphere and, likely, at global scales in at least a roughly two millennium (1800 years) context. The 20th century has seen the greatest temperature change within any century in the past two millennia (0.6°–0.9°C compared to less than approximately ± 0.2°C for any other century) ... solar and volcanic forcing have likely played the dominant roles among the potential natural causes of climate variability. Neither can explain, however, the dramatic warming of the late 20th century; indeed natural factors would favor a slight cooling over this period. Only anthropogenic influences (principally, the increases in greenhouse gas concentrations) are able to explain, from a causal point of view, the recent record high level of global temperatures during the late 20th century. (Jones and Mann 2004: 31)

It is important that the IEA has now joined the IPCC in emphasizing the disastrous climatic effects of continued high emissions of CO_2. As already noted, the IEA's 'reference scenario' implies that policies and technologies remain approximately as today. In its 2009 report, the IEA concludes that:

> the Reference Scenario ... leaves the world on course for a concentration of greenhouse gases in the atmosphere of around 1000 parts per million [up from about 400 parts per million at present], implying a global temperature rise of about 6°C [towards the end of this century]. (IEA 2009: 167)

The expected impacts of a global temperature rise of around 6°C are summarized as follows:

- Sea level rise of up to 3.7 metres, with 50 per cent loss of coastal wetlands, the loss of several islands and millions of people experiencing flooding each year.
- Increased malnutrition, cardio-respiratory and infectious diseases, and increased mortality from heat waves, droughts and floods.
- Damage to ecosystems, with extinction of over 40 per cent of the world's species and widespread coral mortality.
- Water droughts in mid-to-low latitudes and disappearance of glaciers.
- Food shortages and decreased productivity of all cereal crops.
- High risk of dangerous feedbacks and an irreversible vicious cycle of environmental destruction. (IEA 2009: 192; IPCC 2007a: 344–410)

Biofuels development: part of the solution or a cul-de-sac?

The drive for biofuel production comes from two groupings, which quite often represent contradictory interests: states that are concerned about their energy security and environmentalists who are concerned about the destruction of the environment due to CO_2 emissions. As for the first grouping, there can be little doubt that peak oil, the approach of the end of the oil era and expectations of escalating oil prices over the next two decades have led to increased interest in biofuels.[12] This is not least the case in those states with high oil consumption and rising net imports as a share of total consumption. The strong support for biofuels in the USA is, to a large extent, premised on the fear of an imminent rise in the price of oil, as well as on the national security advantages of reduced dependence on imported oil. The US Energy Independence and Security Act, which was revised in 2007, calls for the use of 36 billion gallons of biofuels by 2022, up from about 7 billion gallons in 2007 (Earley and McKeown 2009: 3). Likewise, for the Chinese authorities, the prospect of having to import more than 80 per cent of all their oil in the near future is not particularly attractive (Kreft 2007).

Biofuel production can certainly contribute to damping down the rise in oil prices and can marginally improve national energy security. On the other hand, it is – to say the least – highly questionable whether biofuels can contribute at all to abating the climate crisis. A considerable increase in biofuel production on already cultivated land will soon come into conflict with food production and will drive up food prices to levels that will be extremely harmful to a large share of the world's population, and especially to those living in the so-called developing countries.[13] It is telling that, by some estimates, the annual displacement of only 10 per cent of US fossil fuel demand by biofuels would require 43 per cent of the total US maize harvest (Sexton and Zilberman 2010: 7). Another study concludes that diverting 12.8 million hectares of land, otherwise generating 10 per cent of the world's feed grain by weight, 'would reduce world consumption of meat 0.9% by weight and dairy products [by] 0.6% (fluid milk equivalents)' (Searchinger et al. 2008: 1240).

There seems now to be general agreement among agricultural researchers that a significant increase in biofuel production would be possible only if forests and grassland were converted to new cropland to replace grain or cropland diverted to biofuels. However, regional and global studies of different biofuel crops show that land use change will lead to large net increases in CO_2 emissions because of the decomposition of organic carbon stored in plant biomass, including roots and soil. 'Soils and plant biomass are the two largest biologically active stores of terrestrial carbon, together containing ca. 2.7 times more carbon than the atmosphere' (Fargione et al. 2008: 1236). Part of a study of biofuel production in the USA and Brazil deserves to be quoted:

> Our method yielded an average GHG [greenhouse gas] emission of 351 metric tons per converted hectare (CO_2 equivalent) ... We calculated that GHG savings from corn ethanol would equalize and therefore 'pay back' carbon emissions

from land use change in 167 years, meaning GHGs increase until the end of that period. Over a thirty year period, counting land-use change, GHG emissions from corn ethanol nearly double those from gasoline for each km driven. (Searchinger et al. 2008: 1239)

In other words, the greenhouse gas emissions per hectare of formerly uncultivated land converted to food crop production greatly exceed the annual reductions per hectare resulting from former cropland devoted to biofuels. This is also the conclusion of a global study of biofuel production and CO_2 emissions. One of the premises of that study is that:

After a rapid release [of CO_2] from fire used to clear land or from the decomposition of leaves and fine roots, there is a prolonged period of GHG release as coarse roots and branches decay and as wood products decay or burn. We call the amount of CO_2 released during the first 50 years of this process the 'carbon debt' of land conversion. (Fargione et al. 2008: 1236)

The main conclusion of the study was that:

Converting rainforests, peat lands, savannas, or grasslands to produce food crop based biofuels in Brazil, Southeast Asia and the United States creates a 'biofuel carbon debt' by releasing 17 to 420 times more CO_2 than the annual greenhouse gas reductions that these biofuels would provide by displacing fossil fuels ... Our results demonstrate that the net effect of biofuel production via clearing of carbon-rich habitats is to increase CO_2 emissions for decades or centuries relative to the emissions caused by fossil fuel use. (Fargione et al. 2008: 1235, 1237)

It is an illusion that the climate crisis can be averted by converting natural forest or grassland to cropland in order to replace grain and cropland diverted to biofuels. This illusion, which is nurtured by corporations hunting for profits, can lead to serious damage and suffering for millions of people in developing countries. The 'first generation' of biofuel technologies, based on agricultural crops as raw materials, represents a cul-de-sac in the history of energy development. It remains to be seen whether a 'second generation' of biofuel technology, based on other types of plant material, such as trees and agricultural waste, will succeed in terms of cost (compared to oil), as well as in terms of environmental and social sustainability.

4 | Attracting foreign direct investment in Africa in the context of land grabbing for biofuels and food security

Prosper B. Matondi and Patience Mutopo[1]

Introduction

In light of a new wave of investment in Africa's development, foreign direct investments (FDIs) associated with biofuel and food production have generated political, economic and ethical questions.[2] As governments in Africa compete for FDIs, policy safeguards to protect their own people have either been set aside or are only vaguely considered. Apart from the official development assistance, Africa needs foreign investments to help its people extricate themselves from poverty and underdevelopment. However, it requires growth that is based on equity, because it is a continent that lags far behind others in terms of economic growth and standards of living for the majority. Yet, when carefully examined, biofuel investments seem to come with growth skewed towards certain areas, and with benefits that largely flow to the sources of capital investment. A real danger is that 'prosperous islands' may grow up around areas where biofuel investments are targeted, and these may create skewed growth and imbalanced wealth distribution, which may exacerbate conflicts.

A key resource requirement for biofuels is land, which has traditionally been a much-contested subject in Africa. In this chapter we argue that the positive economic rationality for introducing biofuels sounds laudable. However, given their requirement for large tracts of land, there is a risk that biofuels may ignite land conflicts, with far-reaching implications for trade relationships. In the first place, while land is one of Africa's treasured resources, most countries in Africa do not have sound land policies and land tenure is insecure. Secondly, most African countries have weak or nonexistent legal and administrative frameworks for land and resources rights. There are growing fears that multinational corporations (MNCs)[3] may take advantage of the weak legal and administrative arrangements to appropriate land and, in the process, undermine the rights of locals as they secure their tenure. Thirdly, land in Africa is the main source of livelihood and food security, and forms a basis for social identity. In this chapter we critically explore these issues by examining the position of African countries in the competition to access foreign investments through biofuels.

Globalization and FDI in Africa

Investment relationships of the North–South and South–South The relationship between North and South has, over the past decade, been enhanced by processes of globalization. In the last two or three years, change has been taking place in the African agrarian landscape in response to globalization within the context of biofuel investments. The broader character of the change process is a move from local production systems to large-scale, complex production systems in some of the remotest parts of Africa. This has been made possible through new financing in the area of biofuels – from sovereign funds, to private sector and government finances. We have seen the development of large-scale farms and the rapid transformation of indigenous agrarian societies. Despite the unprecedented expansion of trade, not all African countries have reaped the benefits. Some countries curse globalization for having made them worse off.[4] In addition, globalization, as expressed through FDIs, has been skewed towards certain countries and certain segments of the population.

The majority of African countries continue to rely on exports of low value-added primary commodities. According to UNCTAD (2007), the least developed countries have suffered from worsening terms of trade, highly volatile world prices and a decline in their share of world trade. The export share of the 50 least developed countries, most of which are in sub-Saharan Africa and are dependent on commodities, fell from 2.5 per cent in 1960 to about 0.5 per cent in 1995. Since then they have hovered around that level, though the improvement in commodity prices helped raise their share to 0.8 per cent in 2006 (UNCTAD 2007).

Africa is in perpetual search for financial resources in an international system dominated by competition for investors. This competition has triggered a debate on how to balance the need for 'effective' or meaningful development against the impact of export-led economic growth through biofuel investments. In addition, there are questions about whether Africa should continue to depend on the trickle-down development that comes with FDIs in such forms as biofuels. It should be recognized that, despite extensive trade liberalization, African countries have not achieved significant poverty reduction, and some have experienced negative economic growth. The belief in the benefits of globalization may be weak, because many countries are still struggling to grow their economies. There is a school of thought that when investments are mobilized, the benefits that are reaped come at the expense of the poor, environmental degradation and workers' rights. This has created the foundation for protest movements in civil society, largely against biofuels.

Africa traditionally receives much of its investment from developed countries; however, in the last few years, economic recession and the financial crisis have created major instabilities in the flow of FDIs. The major sources of FDI coming to Africa in recent years have been quite diverse, with emerging countries such as China, South Korea, Brazil, Saudi Arabia, Malaysia, Qatar and the United Arab Emirates playing a prominent role. A 'second generation' of globalization is emerging in complex ways, dominated by two forces. First, the new globalization is a process mediated according to corporate interests dominating their governments. This has raised the possibility of alternative global institutions and policies that at times penetrate developing nations. Second, a distinctive characteristic of this phase is economic multipolarity, in which the South plays a significant role. A 'second generation' of globalization is emerging. China, India, Brazil and South Africa are now major forces in international agreements and economic cooperation, pushing the stakes for themselves and other countries. The economic growth of the South and the rise of the BRICS group of Brazil, Russia, India, China and South Africa mean there is a bloc of countries resisting unilateralism, in a way that used to be done by the Group of 20 (G20) and Group of 8 (G8) countries. The global democratic space has been opened up for the possible formulation of balanced policies. While the new economic weight of some developing countries provides significant opportunities for the rest of the developing world, it will also need to be kept in check, as it may create negative relationships. For instance, the fact that some of the countries are acquiring land at the expense of the poor and are flooding African markets with cheap, less durable goods creates grounds for animosity. This means that there is a need for policy diversity rather than uniformity.

Africa's strategies for attracting FDI The creation of investment vehicles in the form of investment centres, one-stop investment portfolios, investment authorities, etc. signifies the importance that Africa attaches to (and its eagerness to take advantage of) the business opportunities presented. Most African countries have designed investment agencies as a basis for creating an enabling environment for external investors, because they did not have regulatory frameworks. Difficulties were encountered when investors were faced with a series of hurdles, such as unclear policies, delays in investments approval (in some countries of more than a year), restrictions in the granting of permits to external technical experts, unclear rules on the remittances of profits, limitations on exports, etc. Most governments now provide fast-tracking of investment, tax breaks, ease of profit repatriation, suspension of worker rights to strike, ready access to permits for workers from the investing companies, etc. Much of the negotiating occurs within the foreign affairs ministries, which also have a special desk for outside investors. Yet the foreign ministry does not control activities that are of concern to other ministries – e.g. in Zimbabwe the Ministry of Lands could be against bilateral promotion and protection agreements (BIPPAs) on land ownership matters, whereas the negotiating ministry could be in favour of them. The question is how much capacity do such offices have to deal adequately with investment of such magnitude.

In most cases, BIPPAs are signed to protect the external investors. Coordination between the various stakeholders at the ministerial level is crucial if appropriate policies are to be adopted. There are few countries that put the rights of their citizens ahead of those of investors. Some countries, such as Zimbabwe and South Africa, have indigenization policies or affirmative action, under which foreign investors have to partner locals in any investment. However, such policies have tended to be exploited by the elites and the powerful. The smallholders are usually the losers, yet they have more to give in terms of their land, on which they depend for their livelihood. Once a government has decided to use FDI as a basis for economic development, there is a tendency for the protection of foreign investors to be prioritized over that of the locals.

Biofuel investment, economic growth and development

Economic growth promises of biofuel investments in Africa Biofuels are seen as potential sources of economic growth and as an alternative source of 'clean' energy (compared to fossil fuels). The need to reduce oil imports by diversifying energy sources and technologies has provided the motivation for increased investment in biofuel production. The instability in world oil prices and the increased threat of global warming caused by excessive use of fossil fuels have contributed to the demand for ethanol. World production of ethanol is projected to rise substantially over the next 10–20 years in response to economic growth, especially in the emerging and developing countries (EIA 2009). Increased biofuel production is considered to have the potential to strengthen African national economies and energy balances, and at the same time reduce greenhouse gas emissions.

The promises held out for biofuels by their proponents are potentially very great for African countries, where 70 per cent of the population live in rural areas and subsist on agriculture. It is said that biofuel investments in Africa could potentially lead to the creation of jobs and stronger rural economies, as biomass conversion (which would take place in large-scale bio-refineries) will need to occur near the production zone. Chapters 1 and 6 of this book show that the projected benefits are not as straightforward as promised, however. A few rural-based Africans will be incorporated into the companies as wage labourers, but the better jobs will be reserved for foreign technical experts. On balance, the types of shop-floor jobs that will be created do not make up for the loss of land. However, growth promoted by FDI can have both positive and adverse effects on economic growth, as Box 4.1 shows.

New agricultural markets, income generation in rural areas and the reduction of greenhouse gas emissions and air pollution are viewed as part of a package within the search for alternative, cleaner energy. Since 2004, there has been significant and continued channelling of vast financial resources towards the development, processing, storage, distribution and marketing of biofuel products. Energy crops are often regarded as a 'cash crop' and represent a significant diversification of income sources for subsistence farmers. UN (2007) believes that biofuels will 'create higher-value co-products (and thus greater wealth generation)'. On introduction, these crops can create value for rural economies through infrastructure and associated developments. Non-food crops for biofuels can contribute to a diversification of farmers' production with 'cash crops' and can provide them with an income, even on a very small scale, in the way crops grown for fibres used to. UN (2007) notes that there is an incentive for governments to support small-scale bioenergy producers because

> governments tend to get higher returns on investments by fostering small scale production due to the lowered demand for social welfare spending and the great economic multiplier effects incurred where money is earned and spent by community members who obtain new or higher paying jobs or businesses.

The employment promises of biofuel investments There is an assumption that employment will be created through FDI. FDI will indeed generate new jobs; however, they tend not to be of a quantity or quality that would warrant the wholesale displacement of communities. Agriculture provided jobs for 1.3 billion smallholders and landless workers worldwide in 2007, but in rural areas there was severe underemployment (World Bank 2007). The problem of unemployment in rural Africa continues to this day, and thus it becomes a central issue in the budgeting processes of all African governments. To this end, massive investment in agriculture often leads to infrastructural developments, as well as to employment creation on farms.

In many instances where foreigners invest in farms, these tend to be highly commercialized and on a larger scale. This means that high-level technical farming skills are required, and in Africa these take time to develop because of a weak capacity for training. Usually, the technical skills are imported, and so African countries do not benefit from the creation of highly skilled jobs, as those who argue for biofuel investments promise. Investors argue that they need the quality of the produce to be very high to ensure products' competitiveness on the world market. This in turn is assumed to translate to a higher income return on the investment. In some labour-intensive industries like floriculture or tea production, employment generation by foreign affiliates has been significant in countries such as Colombia, Ecuador, Ethiopia, Kenya and Mexico. For example, in Kenya, the cut-flower industry, in which transnational corporations (TNCs) are major players, provides direct employment to about 55,000 people (OECD 2008). Much of the promised employment is non-skilled; however, requirements for skilled labour often increase, meaning the import of skilled people. Thus, in the new arrangements, indigenous people are limited to lower-paying jobs because of their lack of skills. The domestic elites partnering in the projects usually do not have the finance, technology or management skills, and this sometimes substantially reduces their ability to negotiate, because biofuel investments on a large scale require significant resources upfront.

When the local people are dispossessed of their land, they are expected to provide wage labour to the large-scale farms; yet the issue of monitoring wages so that they improve the welfare of the farm employee is something that is always overlooked.[5] Sometimes the working conditions and the remuneration will make the local people more vulnerable than before the introduction of the biofuel enterprise. In some cases, there are forced evictions, which are led by the military protecting the harvests of the large-scale biofuel farms. This may result in arrests or even violence against unarmed locals, as has been the case in Paraguay. Moreover the rural poor are often forced to migrate to urban areas, putting pressure on the already crumbling urban systems in the cities and towns of developing countries.

Agricultural technological change through biofuels It is also argued that African agriculture needs technological revolution and finance, which can potentially come with biofuel investments. Some researchers argue that the increased demand for land for biofuel can partly be offset by technical improvements in production, more efficient processing and higher yields of feedstock per unit area. This calls for intensive cultivation of the land, with the use of improved crop varieties (meaning genetically modified), fertilizers, chemicals and irrigation.[6] However, the susceptibility of rural communities to extreme weather events, such as droughts and floods, makes things less hopeful for Africa. In addition, Africa is the continent at greatest risk of climate change, largely because the majority of the people are dependent on nature. Proponents of biofuels argue, on the other hand, that Africa could benefit from mitigating the effects of climate change through economic growth via commercial agriculture. However, the reality of massive land clearance will have a far more catastrophic environmental impact (Rajagopal et al. 2007). Fossil fuel-driven global warming is said to be a far greater threat than that posed by biofuels. But biofuels have a specific and localized negative impact on biodiversity, with the potential extinction of some species.

The intensive production of feedstock entails use of improved varieties, agrochemicals and fertilizers to increase productivity. Intensification will mean a rise in the use of toxic pesticides, which are destructive to flora and fauna. Intensification will mean that ground and surface water will be overused, to the detriment of wildlife and food crops. For the majority, their livelihoods are likely to be impacted negatively. Plants such as *Jatropha curcas* can proliferate in dry and marginal lands, and this also makes them a potential invasive species when they are introduced into a new environment. Traditional perennial and annual crops cannot compete with such invasive plant species. In addition, research has shown that native biofuel species (such as *Panicum virgatum*, also known as 'switchgrass') can become invasive when they encroach upon habitats in which they are not endemic.

Land grabbing for biofuels and food security under the banner of FDI

Land acquisition and conflicts over the reclaiming of rights The major requirements for biofuel production are land and a constant water supply for irrigation purposes (Cotula et al. 2008b). In addition, it is generally assumed that sub-Saharan African countries such as Angola, DRC, Sudan, Mozambique, Ghana, Tanzania, Zambia and Zimbabwe have vast reservoirs of unused or underutilized land that could potentially be converted into large-scale biofuel production. The FAO, IIED and IFAD (2009) note that, due to Africa's resource endowments, natural resources are at the heart of FDI flows to the continent. In an analysis of nine African countries that was carried out by IFPRI, more than 10 million hectares of land were provided to foreign investors (including governments and the private sector) for agricultural development, targeting biofuels and food (von Braun and Meinzen-Dick 2009).

The last couple of years have seen an increased drive by foreign investors for large-scale land acquisitions in Africa, as the world progressively shifts to a new order that promotes biofuels rather than petroleum-based fuels. Many land acquisitions have come under the media spotlight in recent years, with the failed bid to take over 1.3 million hectares in Madagascar attracting world coverage. However, there are numerous land deals that have not been reported in the media. African governments have even gone as far as formulating policies that attract foreign investment into their countries, but there is considerable debate on whether these FDIs benefit Africa's poor majority or just the vested interests of a few elites in government and the private sector.

According to the IPCC (2000), land availability for the production of biofuels is influenced by a number of factors, including the value of the land and the variety of services that the land provides, from wilderness, to food production, to urban occupation, as well as its overall biomass productivity levels. Giampietro et al. (1997) estimated the land demand for large-scale biofuel production, based on the commercial energy used per citizen per year. They found that, in a number of developed countries, there is not enough land to produce all their energy needs from biomass and biofuels. It is not possible to devote enough land to biofuels in the developed countries without affecting their food production. Developed and emerging nations have, therefore, focused their attention on sub-Saharan Africa as a land source for biofuel production.

The large-scale purchase of land and the long-term leases by investors (dubbed 'land grabbing') stoke up emotions on a continent that saw an end to colonialism in the period from the 1950s to the 1990s. Anger is still felt in Africa over the lost opportunities for Africans under colonialism, demonstrated by land reforms that aim to reverse colonial land grabs in countries such as Zimbabwe, South Africa and Namibia. However, the current land acquisitions seem to mirror the displacement of Africans in the colonial era, albeit in a different form, involving the exchange of money, and sometimes through dialogue rather than by force. The perception of 'unused' land in Africa is historical, because it was the basis for the colonization of the continent, as powerful nations used violence to displace Africans. There is now an assumption by foreign investors – an assumption generated by images of a food and an agricultural crisis in Africa – that the continent needs foreign investments in agriculture. The key role in communicating the African agricultural crisis has been played by the media. The governments of developed countries have sometimes defended land grabs by noting that there is adequate land in Africa. Cotula et al. (2008b) identify a range of potential socio-economic risks to African countries if they adopt wholesale biofuel production. Conflict over land might increase relocation or displacement of local populations to pave the way for investors. In the long term, such trends will compromise food security, as land is taken for commercial production of feedstock. Conflicts are likely to emerge when smallholders resist relocations and forced evictions.

The weakness of indigenous land ownership in the context of biofuel-led FDI The rights over land vary across Africa; however, there is a generally convoluted and complex land ownership arrangement for the majority, who depend on land management either by government or by traditional chiefs. As government owns much of the land, the land users have no rights ascribed to them, since usually such rights are vested in the president as a trustee on behalf of communities. User rights are weaker in situations where the land remains outside the control of families and communities. In turn, communities, as represented by the local authorities and traditional chiefs, exist at the whim of central government in terms of usufruct rights to land. In this case, central government can transfer large tracts of land used by villagers to private ownership by companies. A key area of contestation is the amount of compensation, the period within which it must be paid, the valuation methods, and a tendency to compensate for current use without including components of loss of future use and livelihood. In some cases, benefits are promised by companies but are not incorporated into written contracts.

Land management and the role of communities provide legal uncertainty, because central government controls land through local institutions, which are vested with powers over it. It is at this level that MNCs have used various means to approach the local authorities and negotiate for access to land for biofuel production. This implies that land users have limited or no access to legal redress if they are pushed off their land. Moreover, the possibility of receiving adequate and fair compensation if they are evicted from the land they use is just as limited. Therefore, when a government agrees that foreign investors can take possession of the land, the land users have very little chance of success even if they contest the decision in a court of law. Furthermore, rural land users tend not to have adequate representation by attorneys, who are usually urban based, whereas the private MNCs have the capacity to hire attorneys to represent them in land disputes. Therefore communities are most likely to lose their rights to land they have used for generations.

In the quest for FDI, governments have had a softer stance towards MNCs with money and that promise economic development of marginalized areas. In the majority of cases, the government – through local proxies (chiefs and councils) – expropriates land being used by smallholder farmers for direct allocation to the MNCs.

Cotula et al. (2009) identify a more complex type of direct linkage caused by market forces in countries with weak market systems. The spread of biofuels to meet growing international demand tends to increase the value of land. However, in most of Africa, the market in land is limited or informal, meaning that the opportunities for small farmers to participate are limited. The poor in Africa live on less than US$1 per day, and their livelihood options are based on the use of natural resources found on the land. If small farmers are priced out of the market in land (whether sale or rental), they will remain vulnerable. This factor may also foster changes in land access along gender lines, as control over increasingly high-value land may shift from women to men.

In most of Africa, the procedural mechanisms to protect local rights and take account of local interests, livelihoods and welfare are absent. Even in the minority of countries where the legal requirements for community consultation are in place, the processes for negotiating land access with communities remain unsatisfactory. Lack of transparency and of checks and balances in contract negotiations creates a breeding ground for corruption and for deals that do not maximize the public interest. Insecure usage rights on state-owned land, inaccessible registration procedures, vaguely defined productive use requirements, legislative gaps and compensation that is limited to loss of improvements, such as crops and trees (thus excluding loss of land), all undermine the position of local people.

A common feature of most contracts is that they are strikingly short and simple, unlike the economic reality of the transactions involved. Key issues like strengthening the mechanisms to monitor or enforce compliance with investor commitments, sanctions, maximization of government revenues and clarification of their distribution, promotion of business models that maximize local benefit, and balancing food security concerns in both the home and the host countries are dealt with by vague provisions (Cotula et al. 2009). In many countries the policy mechanisms to guide decision-makers in brokering the land deals are absent (ibid.).

Elite-led land deals The greatest threats surrounding land grabbing are the lack of proper guidelines on land acquisition and the elitist nature of the deals involving governments and the private sector. In most cases, African governments struggle to negotiate deals that favour their own people, because of the competition for FDI.[7] MNCs take full advantage of the fact that governments are desperate for finance by negotiating deals that favour them throughout the duration of the project. In most instances, this means unfettered leaseholds of long duration or outright freehold titles to the land. Such leases are also provided in areas where indigenous people are farming (Cotula et al. 2009 Arndt et al. 2008; Toulmin 2008). World Bank (2010) calls for a rethink over land grabbing within the context of the global governance system and international law. Land is at the core of the livelihoods of the people in Africa. At the local level, land rights may be hotly contested, which is the case in most developing countries. What results is a situation where local tenure may be very complex and where local communities are sidelined, despite knowing their rights.

There is a need for careful assessment of local African contexts, as well as for long-term engagement with local interests, beyond the elites, to foster an understanding of the issues and impact of biofuel land deals. Elites usually negotiate deals that largely favour a minority for the utilization of key agricultural resources, such as land and water (Greenpeace 2007). In most cases, they act as the intermediary agencies responsible for the local deal-making. They tend to weave through government bureaucracies in such negotiations, so that official bureaucrats deal with agencies rather than directly with the foreign investors. This is because capital shares are promised to the local elites, who then take responsibility for the land deal negotiations. In such deal-making, it then follows that local people's resource rights may be suspended as elites jostle to attract FDI through biofuel deals for personal gain. Usually political transparency and accountability are lacking in Africa, where the dominant elites use their literacy to override illiterate and semi-literate people in negotiating for foreign investments.

During the negotiations, local people are promised the best opportunities that biofuel production can offer. The benefits range from employment opportunities for poor people, access to services and better infrastructure (roads, electricity, water, etc.), revenue for the local authorities, etc. Very little is about the limitations of biofuels, and it is emphasized that the costs are outweighed by the benefits. Given the way money is dangled and the opportunities are pushed by the MNCs, the local authorities have little bargaining power and hence end up conceding land to the MNCs. In the background, central government officials – who are also eyeing the same revenue – tend to manipulate local authorities to agree to the land concessions, based on spurious arguments that it is not land takeover but the leasing out of land for economic development for the greater public good. Yet the large-scale land deals throughout Africa threaten to have a massive negative impact on local people in the immediate future. It is therefore imperative that a balance should be struck between public, individual and acquired rights, so as to create a win-win situation that ensures respect for the interests of all stakeholders.

Distortion of effects of FDI-led large-scale production systems The demand for land for feedstock production will increase the value of land in the long term. This in turn will transform land tenure, giving smallholder farmers less security. According to Amanor (1999), an argument also supported by Cotula and Neves (2007), historically the spread of cash crops and the associated increase in land value led to greater individualization of land rights previously held in common. It also led to the greater commercialization of land rights, where these previously operated outside market logic. In essence, those with better access to financial resources are likely to be better able to gain or secure access to land, while poorer and more marginalized groups may see their access to land eroded. The risks are particularly high where land title and use rights are inadequately documented, which is the case in numerous African countries.[8] In some countries with no formal land laws to provide protection to the poor, such land grabbing will further impoverish them even as they are promised that biofuels will benefit them.

In many of the biofuel investments to date, the MNCs have preferred large-scale production models that allow economies of scale. The large-scale systems based on sugar plantations depend on high technology to increase yields, in order to offset any pricing instability for inputs and outputs. Such production is associated with negative environmental impacts, such as decreased soil fertility and increased water pollution. Downstream effects, such as those that arise from the draining of wetlands, pose long-term threats to common sources of livelihood.

There is an assumption that biofuels will contribute to total agricultural growth through such innovations as contract farming. Contract farming does provide a potential benefit in terms of the mobilization of skills, finance and inputs. In most African countries, the production and supply of agricultural inputs is erratic because of a weak manufacturing base. In such cases, inputs could be purchased by the money raised through FDI for the benefit of the small producers, who may be outgrowers of the main estates. Small farmers will thus have inputs readily available from the contracting MNC, and this will have a positive impact on their food security status and also on the overall development of an area. On the other hand, these links run the risk, for instance, of making farmers highly dependent on large and powerful companies: if (or when) the investment is pulled out, farmers will lack self-reliance and growth will be undermined.

The assumption that foreign currency will be generated for the benefit of the poor may not hold true. The problem of the generation of insufficient foreign exchange is widespread throughout Africa. How and to what extent FDI will contribute to the generation of foreign currency is therefore important to a developing country's growth prospects. In most cases, FDI has positive implications in terms of the balance of payments, since most of the products are for export. However, because most economies do not have the capacity to supply large-scale operations with inputs, such as fertilizers, agro-chemicals and hybrid seeds, these have to be imported. Such input imports mean that the net amount of foreign currency that is gained is reduced and, at the end of the day, does not benefit local industrial growth. A country's policy framework will also determine the level of foreign currency that is generated by the companies that operate within it. According to UNCTAD (2009), there is scant evidence for the contribution of FDI to fiscal revenue, which makes it difficult to conclude whether a contribution is sizeable enough to affect economic growth and development through fiscal growth.

Inducing smallholders to participate in distorted markets There is an increasing inclination to compel the poor to participate in the market, through what has been popularized in donor circles as market linkages for poverty reduction (DfID forthcoming; DANIDA 2010; Weidemann Associates 2010). The poor are increasingly being encouraged to participate in the market via biofuels. It is assumed that the markets can work for communities in the same way as they work for private entrepreneurs. There is no doubt that the market economy does provide new opportunities, but from the very outset rural and communal enterprises face a big hurdle. Nor can we assume that the free market is cognizant of the inherently unequal terms on which poor communities must participate in this market. The encouragement for them to participate in the market stems from a residue of naivety, or else from the fear that, if a greater proportion of the poor do not see the benefits of the market, they will revolt against it. The participation of the poor in the formal economy always takes place from a position of asymmetry.

The main challenge is that the poor are estranged from the market because of the lack of information and unfamiliarity with the rules of the market. Lacking direct access to the market, they can only operate through intermediaries. Since such indirect access comes at a price, their profits are whittled away. Moreover, in societies that have traditionally been reliant on agriculture as the primary (or only) form of economic activity, the poor often lack the entrepreneurial and management skills that allow greater agility and responsiveness to the market. Therefore the biofuel investors come with their own skilled people, because they have no time to grow local entrepreneurship – they need a quick turn-around time to recoup their investments while demand for the product is high on the global market.

Since formal banks will not lend without the backing of a credible guarantor, local community entrepreneurs find their access to credit limited. This is largely because their assets are inadmissible. Out of desperation, they are forced to pawn their belongings to the highest and most available private bidder, or subject themselves to the unequal, rapacious free market. The evidence would suggest that such pawning is a result of economic duress, rather than voluntary participation in the 'free market'. The familiar assumptions that biofuels are a panacea for market participation may be resting on weak ground.

Biofuels and smallholders

Biofuel investments and the impact on smallholder food security Concerns about the expansion of biofuel production and the impact this will have on smallholders centre mainly on the diversion of agricultural land from food production to biofuel production (IFAD 2009; Sulle and Nelson 2009a). A common objection is that this occurs on a continent that faces recurring hunger, especially in sub-Saharan Africa. Biofuel investments have a direct bearing on world and domestic food availability and pricing. Land grabbing by MNCs for biofuels has a correlation with food insecurity, because land used for food production is taken over to grow agro-feedstocks. The demand for biofuels the world over is largely influenced by policy, with feedstock producer countries concerned about FDI, and the investors more concerned with securing their energy sources. OFID (2009) notes that the interest in biofuels has been accelerated by governments' adoption of policies and support measures, including time-bound targets for biofuel consumption. For this reason, commercial agriculture has embraced the opportunity of assured long-term government support and has responded with investments and efforts to increase production to meet the market demand for biofuel feedstocks. This has resulted in increased national and world market prices for current first-generation biofuel feedstocks, which are also important food and feed crops. The impact of biofuels on food security is twofold: first, they contribute significantly to the increase in food prices; and second, they encourage land concentration for plantation-type production, producing feedstock at the expense of food crops. This second impact will lead to the eviction or marginalization of vulnerable groups and individuals, and will thus bring about food insecurity.

Increased biofuel production from first-generation feedstock production will compete with agricultural land needed for food and wood production, unless surplus land is available. Studies to date have, however, shown that only three countries – Burundi, Uganda and Bangladesh – have enough land to produce biofuels without negatively affecting food production (Giampietro et al. 1997). The global expansion of biofuel production from maize, oilseed and sugar crops will have a negative impact on food security. According to the Council for Agricultural Science and Technology (2006) the price of these commodities will be determined by their value as feedstock for biofuels, rather than by their importance as human food or livestock feed. Farmers in countries that account for the bulk of the world's biofuel crop production (sub-Saharan Africa) will be enticed to continue to produce not food crops, but crops for biofuel production because of the rising global price of oil, which means that their commodities will fetch markedly higher prices and they will receive higher incomes. Yet the urban and rural poor in most of these selfsame food-importing countries will pay much higher prices for basic food staples, since there will be less grain. The question is: in what ways will biofuel-induced changes in agricultural commodity markets affect net consumers of food?

Those at risk include over 800 million food-insecure people, who live mostly in rural areas and are dependent to some extent on agriculture for their incomes, who live on less than US$1 per day and spend most of their income on food (Ziegler 2007). In addition, the authors observe that a further 2–2.5 billion people who live on US$1–2 per day are also at risk, as rising commodity prices could pull them swiftly into a food-insecure state. Increased use of food and feed crops for fuel has altered (and will continue to do so) the fundamental economic dynamics that have governed global agricultural markets (Elobeid and Hart 2007).

The basic argument is that energy-crop programmes compete with food crops in a number of ways (agricultural, rural investment, infrastructure, water, fertilizers, skilled labour, etc.) and thus cause food shortages and price increases. Food security involves four major dimensions: availability of enough food; access; stability of the food supply over time; and utilization (meaning people's ability to use the nutrients in the available food). It follows that if land, water and other resources are used to produce biofuels rather than food, then *availability* of the food could decline. In addition, if the use of food crops such as maize, soya, etc. for biofuels, increases, so the prices of these commodities will increase, making the crops less *accessible* to the poor. Instead of increasing the area under cultivation, there is a drive to increase investment in agricultural research aimed at improving productivity, conserving water and building soil fertility, which could reduce the tension between food, feed and fuel production by increasing overall agricultural output in a sustainable manner.

Despite these arguments, there is a need to balance food security policies with policies that promote biofuel production. Studies commissioned by OFID (2009) concluded that accelerated growth of first-generation biofuel production is threatening the availability of adequate food supplies for humans by diverting land, water and other resources away from food and feed crops. According to OFID (2009), between 2002 and 2007, world food prices increased by some 140 per cent, due to a number of factors, including increased demand for biofuel feedstocks and rising agricultural fuel and fertilizer prices. Higher food prices as a result of expanding biofuel production would consequently reduce food consumption (reduced access to food) in developing countries, which in turn would result in increased undernourishment. It remains the responsibility of each individual government to ensure that its populace is food secure. Thus each government should consider seriously the implications of any policy it makes regarding the expansion of biofuels.

Impact of biofuels on the livelihoods of smallholder farmers As reflected earlier in this chapter, biofuels have been widely seen as an opportunity for some poor rural people to secure their livelihood and ensure food security. For these opportunities to become a reality, then, as well as ensuring food security, all strategic priorities should be pro-poor, pro-nature, pro-livelihood and pro-women. The greatest question that remains, however, is how biofuel investments can satisfy these requirements, given that the investments are intended to yield a profit and that they essentially involve the transfer of rights to profit-oriented multinational companies (Box 4.2).

In a study that investigates and describes patterns of biofuel development in Tanzania, Sulle and Nelson (2009b) report that some land acquisitions for biofuels are targeting land that is used for forest-based economic activities, and on which villagers depend heavily. It is highlighted that large-scale biofuel investments that require such land are likely to create the most frequent negative local impacts and grievances. Wolde-Georgis and Glantz (2008) concur that a national biofuel strategy based on large commercial farms might not lead to a realization of rural development, energy security and increased rural income. Such a strategy might instead lead to landlessness, increased rural poverty and the transformation of African farmers from being smallholders to being wage earners on the new biofuel commercial farms. Peskett et al. (2007) note that there are some challenges that smallholders face both at the farm level and off the farm if they are to be involved in large-scale biofuel production. These often lead to them losing their rights to large multinational investors, who are perfectly in tune with the nature of investment in biofuel production.

Agriculture in most countries is shifting from subsistence to commercial farming. This is part of a process of modernization to make agriculture competitive on the world market. It should be noted that this process of commercialization goes ahead with or without FDI; but by helping to expand production and introduce new and efficient technologies, FDI helps to accelerate the process. A surge in FDI has seen an increase in infrastructural development in host countries, including improvements to water resources and availability. These large-scale operations may have negative effects: they may drive farmers out of business, for instance, with adverse consequences for employment and rural society. They may thereby negate economic growth and development in economies in which the greater part of the population resides in rural areas.

Land use change may involve conversion from one crop to another, from grazing land to cropland, from unutilized to utilized farmland, or from low-intensity management (e.g. shifting cultivation) to high intensity. As the economic opportunities linked to biofuel production improve, so agricultural producers may shift from food or cash crops to feedstock, and from forest and conservation areas to biofuel crops (Cotula et al. 2008b). This is usually done on the basis that such land is not being fully utilized. It is also done on the assumption that biofuel crop production is more economically viable than existing forms of land use. However, the history of ethanol production provides pointers as to the negative impacts of land use change towards commodity commercialization. Such a history provides a basis upon which to question the role and impact of biofuel production.

According to Aide (2008):

The history of Brazil is one of enormous land holdings for individual owners (latifundia) resulting in earlier centuries from evictions and outright killings

83

Box 4.2 The short story of land loss in Ghana

This is the story of how a Norwegian biofuel company took advantage of Africa's traditional system of communal land ownership, using current climate and economic pressure to claim and deforest large tracts of land in Kusawgu, Northern Ghana, with the intention of creating 'the largest jatropha plantation in the world'. Bypassing official development authorization and using methods that hark back to the darkest days of colonialism, this investor claimed legal ownership of these lands by convincing an illiterate chief to sign away 38,000 hectares with his thumb print.

This is also the story of how the community affected came to realize that, while the promised jobs and incomes were unlikely to materialize, the plantation would mean extensive deforestation and the loss of incomes from gathering forest products, such as sheanuts. When given all the information, the community successfully fought to send the investors packing, but not before 2,600 hectares of land had been deforested. Many have now lost their incomes from the forest and face a bleak future.

In November 2007, a team from Ghana's Regional Advisory and Information Network Systems (RAINS) discovered massive destruction of vegetation cover over a large stretch of land near a village called Alipe within the White Volta River basin, about 30 kilometres from Tamale, the capital town of the Northern Region of Ghana. Heavy agricultural machinery was systematically pulling down trees and degrading the area a few metres south of the village. The land had been stripped bare of all its vegetation cover. Enquiry revealed that the site was to be the beginning of a large jatropha plantation developed by a Norwegian biofuel company called BioFuel Africa – a subsidiary of Biofuel Norway (www.biofuel.no). At a public meeting in Kusawgu, the traditional capital of the Kusawgu Division of the Gonja Traditional Council, Mr Finn Byberg, Director of Land Acquisition for BioFuel Africa, said that he could not state categorically what commitments the company would make: 'Commitments are

of large parts of the indigenous populations, then followed by extensive use of slavery for the plantations, later the use of highly exploited cheap labour. Without the latifundia structure, the Brazilian sugar cane production would not have evolved in the way it has.

Such a history provides a basis upon which to question the role and impact of biofuel production. Whereas today there may be 'efficient' technological production systems that may not require the use of cheap labour, there are not very easy and so when I am required to make these, I need to be very careful. I do not want to be caught for not keeping my word.'

The discovery of the cleared land brought a realization that the battle against land grabbing and community disempowerment was no longer just happening in other countries, but also in Ghana. In collaboration with the Central Gonja District Assembly and the Environmental Protection Agency, work was suspended on the development site. Rural communities, desperate for income, are enticed by developers, who promise them a 'better future' under the guise of jobs, with the argument that they are currently only just surviving from the 'unproductive land' and that they stand to earn a regular income if they give up the land for development. This argument fails to appreciate the African view of the meaning of the land to the community. While the initial temptation to give up the land to earn a wage is great, it portends an ominous future, where the community's sovereignty, identity and sense of self is lost because of the fragmentation that it will suffer.

The strategy for the acquisition of land often takes the following course. The imaginations of a few influential leaders in the community are captured. They are told of the prospects for the community held out by the project, and are swayed with promises of positions in the company or monetary inducements. The idea is that these people do the necessary 'footwork' in the villages, where they spread the word about job opportunities. A document is then prepared, essentially a contract, to lease the land to the company. In the event of problems, the developer can press its claim by enforcing the 'contract' or agreement. When the legality of the process is not adequately scrutinized, the developers have their way; but if proper scrutiny takes place, it emerges that these contracts are not legally binding, as they have not gone through the correct legal channels. This is what happened in this particular case in the Alipe area.

Source: Bakari Nyari, Vice-Chairman of RAINS, Ghana, and member of the African Biodiversity Network Steering Committee.

still concerns when the majority of smallholder farmers are turned into outgrowers for big companies. They will not be able to acquire the technology and may put aside issues of safety and environmental concerns, as they turn their traditional lands over to the production of biofuel crops. Smallholders will have a limited role in this production, which requires an integrated agro-industrial organization structure of production, factory processing, transport and distribution. In this vein, plantation-type production is also much more attractive than smallholder agricultural activities. It is usually those with adequate financial resources who will venture and benefit most from large-scale production.

Protecting the land space and livelihoods of smallholder farmers in Africa

The issue of protecting the rights of smallholder farmers in the face of investment in biofuel production can be tackled using a wide range of actions. However, the most important actors are the governments, as the onus is on them to refuse, accept or set conditions within which investment in biofuel production can take place. In cases where governments and authorities do not see communities benefiting, governments have a duty to refuse investments that compromise the rights of the poor. Typically, investment should first be subject to a social and environmental impact assessment if the rights of the local communities are to be protected, and governments should play an active part in such assessment. Governments can also influence the outcome of negotiation between landowners and investors by establishing the institutions that guide this process. International authoritative institutions and regional groupings also have a role to play, since they can dictate and limit the room within which individual governments can manoeuvre in terms of allowing or disallowing investment.

Large-scale biofuel investments that require the transfer of village lands to privately owned companies are inherently subject to problems of equity, transparency and difficulty in evaluating the distribution of costs and benefits. These types of biofuel investments are likely to engender the most frequent negative local impacts and grievances. While there may be many positive local economic opportunities from biofuels, the risks of large-scale projects need to be more clearly understood, especially with regard to the loss of rights by smallholders. Investment plays a key role because it simultaneously generates income, expands productive capacity and carries strong complementarities with other factors in the growth process, such as technological progress, skills acquisition and institutional deepening. However, the occurrence of innovative investment is not automatic; it can encounter structural and institutional impediments.

While the prospects of competitive returns from FDI in biofuel production remain a huge and a tempting attraction, Africa must be prepared to negotiate win-win policy frameworks. This means a set of regulatory frameworks (such as sustainable production certification schemes) that promote sustainable economic growth and that support (rather than alienate) smallholder farmers. The respective governments ought to monitor influx of FDI into biofuel production to guard against adverse consequences for the rights and livelihoods of smallholder farmers, ecological systems and the environment.

Efforts to improve the investment climate in order to attract FDI with favourable benefits for Africa include a reduction in tax rates and royalty payments on investment earnings. An effort should be made to formulate regional and multilateral policies in order to sustain the flow of FDI. Promotion of regional and inter-regional FDI (as opposed to FDI moving into a single country) could provide leeway for regional responses that are more effective. This could create and improve opportunities for FDI that does not harm local people. At the same time, removal of the barriers to investments, the promotion of joint ventures and the harmonization of national investment codes are critical elements for getting investments into Africa (UNCTAD 2006). It is the responsibility of governments to ensure that biofuel policies guard against the discrimination of local companies in benefiting from land resources. In cases where communities lose their land rights there should be fair compensation, with clear capital-transfer and dispute-settlement mechanisms.

As biofuels are introduced, so win-win outcomes are possible with greater collaboration and awareness of the issues and risks. Therefore there is a need to improve the awareness of rural villagers and schemes of the issues surrounding biofuels. This requires innovation and collaboration between villagers, district councils, investors and civil society organizations, as well as flexibility from central government and financial institutions. To ensure that the rights of smallholder farmers are protected, there should be (as a minimum) policy guidelines on land acquisition, with clear provision for the compensation of those affected, as well as guarantees for their long-term livelihood.

In this context, the promotion of outgrower and contract biofuel production seems to have minimal direct negative impact on land access and presents a compromise model for local livelihoods. In this case, the indigenous people remain in control of their environment and have the chance to opt out when their livelihoods are negatively affected. Sulle and Nelson (2009b) conclude that companies which have engaged entirely in outgrower and contracted smallholder production of biofuel crops in Tanzania have had no negative impact on local land tenure, and generally represent the most positive biofuel production model from the perspective of local livelihoods. It is argued that these companies offer rural communities opportunities for agricultural diversification, including communities on relatively marginal land. Against this background, such models should be widely supported and promoted.

It is, however, worth noting that the suitability of different models depends on local contexts, such as population density or the local capacity for agricultural production. Some models can foster collective innovation among private, public, local and civil society groups on ways to stimulate private investment in biofuels. Therefore, the organization of smallholder farmers into cooperatives or commodity associations to increase their access to markets and to take advantage of economies of scale should be promoted. Crops such as jatropha can provide new opportunities for local farmers to improve their income from unproductive or infertile lands, and the formation of farmers' cooperatives can improve access to markets. Villages can form equity-based joint ventures, which can potentially stimulate private investment and allow greater collaboration between investors and local communities.

With commodity associations, it becomes convenient to provide technical support to smallholder farmers. If the outgrower farmers are technically competent and are producing quality products, that increases their power to negotiate favourable terms. Accordingly, governments should take responsibility for training poor farmers in production techniques that increase their competence and viability. Governments should invest in institutions that empower local communities to make decisions about their own resources, including land. As they build producer associations, the smallholders should develop a stake in the management of the MNCs. Smallholder farmer representatives should be included on the boards and management as active decision-makers who are accountable to their own people. In this way, they can ensure that benefits trickle down to the previous landowners. Such arrangements are, however, very difficult, as they are likely to be captured by the elite and politicians, so that smallholders lose out in the end.

Conclusion

The introduction of biofuels and the targeting of land in Africa tests the relationship between the North and the South, and indeed South–South relationships. Africa may seem to be in a powerful position of having the important resource of land, but there is a real possibility that Africans could lose their livelihoods on account of biofuel investments. In the broader international discourse, ways must be found to reconcile the needs of multiple stakeholders if biofuel production is to have a secure future. Foreign investors seek security for their investment; while the Africans' stake is not monetary but lies in the social systems now under threat from biofuel investments.

Consideration of issues of participation, consultation and consent in the negotiating processes is paramount. The evidence would suggest that, as the biofuel investments are biased in favour of private property and commercialization through the markets, there is an increased propensity to neglect and ignore the interests of those who could be exploited and made more vulnerable by these processes. In order to correct this imbalance, active state intervention is required, so that overall economic growth and development is directed towards the interests of the poor. Such interventions may mean ensuring security of rights. There are major concerns in some countries about the weakness of provisions within national law for local people to steer development options and defend their own land rights. In other countries, such rights are, in theory, substantially more secure, but concerns remain about implementation of the law and voluntary good practice on the part of investor companies (Cotula et al. 2009, citing the observations of Colchester and Ferrari 2007).

Biofuel investments are anchored in global tendencies, because the benefits are not largely meant for Africa. It would seem, therefore, that the recolonization of Africa by conglomerates of various shades through biofuels could be a reality, as they seek product supply chains for non-African markets. Through FDI, unbridled marketization is being introduced to vulnerable societies, as if African livelihoods do not matter. Moreover, the profound inequality between the different economic classes in Africa serves to ensure that the privileged are absorbed, leaving the majority vulnerable. In general, when FDI is pushed without any form of regulation or supervision, it distorts local markets and, in the process, creates social chaos, which governments may not be able to control.[9] Therefore state intervention is necessary to shepherd FDI-led biofuel investments towards benefiting the poor and vulnerable.

5 | Smallholder-led transformation towards biofuel production in Ethiopia

Atakilte Beyene

Introduction

Production of first-generation liquid biofuels (hereafter referring to ethanol and biodiesel produced principally from sugarcane and jatropha/castor, respectively) is a growing sector of the world agriculture market (FAO 2007; UN 2007).[1] The sector ranked third in investment within the renewable energy sector, after wind and solar power (Wamukonya 2007; Biofuels Digest 2009). The key drivers are global energy insecurity and demand, the need to reduce dependency on fossil fuels, the climate objective of reducing greenhouse gases, and perceived opportunities for rural development in biofuel-producing countries, especially developing ones. In addition to this, other processes, such as globalization and mobility of national and transnational agro-industries, have accelerated the development of biofuel production and the interactions of different actors. External interest in biofuel production in African countries is driven largely by the low cost of land and labour in rural Africa (Cotula et al. 2008a; 2008b).

These processes have resulted in different forms of biofuel production models emerging across Africa and elsewhere. Such models include: large-scale plantations – where biofuel companies control all aspects of production and processing; contract farmers, outgrowers and independent suppliers – where biofuel companies enter into contracts with local farmers; and hybrid models – which combine production from large plantations and small-scale farmers (Sulle and Nelson 2009a).

This chapter focuses on contract biofuel production by smallholder farmers in Ethiopia. Contract biofuel production is expected to be the dominant form of production relationship in biofuels (particularly biodiesel) for various reasons. First, contract farming is potentially the most feasible way of engaging the vast rural land and labour resources in the production of feedstock for biofuel-processing agro-industries. Secondly, in regions where the population density is high and the availability of land is limited (as in the Ethiopian highlands), contract farming is probably the only way for new agricultural products such as biofuels to develop. Last, but not least, contract farming is seen as a means of achieving development goals. The expansion of biofuels has generated high expectations that the development needs of millions of smallholder farmers can be facilitated. New initiatives in Africa, such as the Comprehensive Africa Agriculture Development Programme (CAADP 2002), emphasize contract farming as a priority area of investment that has the potential to enable smallholder farmers to practise high-value agriculture and to reach markets at all levels (see also Eaton and Shepherd 2001).

However, the outcomes of contract farming depend on a mix of conditions that involve labour (skills, wages), agrarian structure (e.g. property rights regimes, rural entrepreneurship, etc.), political economy (e.g. labour rights and protection and enforcement codes), technology (e.g. availability and access to appropriate technologies) and trade relations (Kirsten and Sartorius 2002; White 1997; Buch-Hansen and Marcussen 1982). Alongside these general conditions of contract farming, biofuel feedstock contract farming has further layers of issues, such as politics of energy, discourses on green or clean development, climate change, and the urgency of reducing greenhouse gases.

The push for biofuels in Ethiopia: an overview

The drive for biofuel production originated primarily with global demand and the private sector, and not with local or rural needs (Amigun et al. 2008; this volume, chapters 1 and 2). Economic liberalization, globalization and foreign direct investments, and the increasing role of sovereign funds and state companies have all become global processes whose priority is to increase the return on capital invested, and also to enhance their respective countries' energy and food security. Many African governments have also seen biofuel production as a vehicle to modernize their agriculture and to increase export incomes; their concern for the welfare of smallholders in their countries varies.

In Ethiopia, biofuel production is a new development initiative. For the first time, in August 2007, a Biofuels Development and Utilization Strategy was introduced by the federal government Ministry of Mines and Energy (MME 2008). By any standards, then, biofuels are at a very early stage, and most of the activity so far has centred on land allocation and plantation. Exceptions to this are the state-owned sugar industries, especially the Fincha sugar factory, which has been producing 8 million litres of ethanol from molasses each year since 1999. The other factories are the Methara and Wonji sugar factories, which are pursuing a similar process to produce ethanol.

In general, the Biofuels Development and Utilization Strategy is brief and falls short of addressing such crucial dimensions as the legal and institutional aspects of small-scale biofuel production, labour policies, localization of biofuels, environmental impact assessment mechanisms, etc. It does, though, include plans to extract biodiesel from jatropha, palm oil and castor seed, and ethanol from sugarcane. The strategy principally focuses on attracting foreign and domestic investments, the provision of incentives and information for biofuel investors and the allocation of land resources. Large-scale

TABLE 5.1 Major agricultural land leases in Ethiopia

Company	Ownership	Granted (ha)	Under negotiation (ha)	Total (ha)
Karuturi Global Ltd	India	300,000		300,000
Saudi Star Agricultural Development Plc	Ethiopia	139,000	361,000	500,000
Sannati Agro Farm Enterprise	India	10,000		10,000
Afro Power Initiative Renewable Energy	Uganda	50,000		50,000
Agro Peace Bio Ethiopia	Ethiopia	49,000		49,000
Sub Biofuel	UK	80,000	245,000	325,000
Becco Biofuels	USA & Israel	35,000		35,000
Hovev Agriculture Ltd	Israel	40,000	400,000	440,000
Flora Ecopower	Germany	13,700	200,000	213,700
National Biodiesel Corporation (NBC)	Germany & USA		90,000	90,000
LHB	Israel	100,000		100,000
Ambassel	Ethiopia	10,000	20,000	30,000
Horizon Plantation Plc	Ethiopia	250,000		250,000
Fri El Green Power	Italy	30,000		30,000
Malaysian Company	Malaysia	31,000		31,000

Sources: Anderson and Belay (2008); www.bloomberg.com/news/2010-10-26/ethiopia-plans-to-rent-out-belgium-sized-land-area-to-produce-cash-crops.html; www.ena.gov.et/EnglishNews/2009/May/09Mayo9/86699.htm; www.grain.org/seedling_files/seed-07-07-en.pdf; Beflkadu Walelign, 'A synthesis report on the status of biofuel investments in Ethiopia', unpublished field assessment report, September 2010, Stockholm.

commercial productions of biofuels by investors are mentioned as key energy projects. It also aims at involving farmers in planting biofuel crops around their homestead, on their farms (intercropping with food crops) and on marginal (degraded and unused) land. The strategy emphasizes the importance of *Jatropha curcas* and castor bean as a principal feedstock for biodiesel production. Sugarcane is also indicated as the principal feedstock for ethanol production. The strategy also sets targets for ethanol blending with gasoline: 5 per cent by 2007, 10 per cent by 2012, 15 per cent by 2013, 20 per cent by 2014 and 25 per cent by 2015 (Anderson and Belay 2008; All Africa News 2010).

The country's total available potential land for production of feedstock for biodiesel is estimated at about 23,305,890 hectares. These areas include pockets of 'unused' and degraded land in the smallholder farming systems, areas of low population density and the lowlands. The total irrigable land for sugarcane production for ethanol is about 700,000 hectares. This area is mainly located along the major river basins, such as the Awash River of the Afar region, where water supply is abundant. Annual ethanol production was projected to increase from 8 million litres in 2007 to 130 million litres by 2010/11, and the potential to produce ethanol alone is estimated at 1 billion litres per annum (Meskir 2007).

Over the past few years, Ethiopia has seen a large increase in the demand for land for agro-industrial development. It has attracted sizeable stocks of foreign investment (UNCTAD 2009), and the country is one of the few key recipients of FDI in land in Africa. According to the state minister at the Mines and Energy State Ministry, as of August 2010 there were 82 registered biofuel investors, of which 16 were operational (Table 5.1 shows some of them). The total land area assigned for biofuels (cultivation, assigned or under negotiation) is 1.5–2 million hectares. Recently, the Ministry of Agriculture indicated that the country planned to lease out 3 million hectares of farmland over the next five years for agricultural purposes, including for biofuels.

Plantations for sugarcane and oil seeds, such as castor beans and jatropha, vary in scale and organization. Large-scale plantation monocultures are run by companies, and land is made available by the government direct to the companies through land lease arrangements based on the cost of plots. The annual cost ranges from 111 Ethiopian birr ($6.89) per hectare in peripheral areas to 2,000 birr per hectare in the fertile Ethiopian Rift Valley adjacent to Addis Ababa. On the other hand, there are various types of small-scale plantations of biofuels, such as hedges, patches or intercrops. The small-scale plantations are undertaken by those smallholder farmers who possess extensive land and labour resources. Biodiesel crops, in particular, are expected to be produced by the smallholder farming sector. It is in this area that outgrower schemes and contract farming are being encouraged.

The government policy also explicitly supports the promotion of biofuels from an economic and development perspective. Energy security and the partial substitution of imported petroleum (with a concomitant saving of hard currency) are primary policy goals (MME 2008). Petroleum accounts for only 7.4 per cent of total energy consumption. However, Ethiopia is a net importer of petroleum, and demand increased from 1.1 million tonnes in 2001 to 1.9 million in 2008. The value of the imported petroleum increased by over 500 per cent, from US$0.27 billion to US$1.6 billion in the same period. In 2008, for the first time, the cost of importing petroleum fuel exceeded annual export earnings, resulting in a negative trade balance (Lakew and Shiferaw 2008). This currency imbalance is one of the major driving forces behind biofuels.

Another potential for biofuel development in Ethiopia is household energy consumption. The energy system in Ethiopia is highly dependent on solid biomass (wood, crop residue, etc.), which accounts for 91 per cent of total energy consumption (Mebratu and Tamire 2002). This dependence on solid biomass has been a major cause of deforestation and other environmental impacts. Using up dung and crop residues as fuel for fires has a negative impact on the level of soil nutrients, and that affects agricultural productivity. Replacing solid biomass with biofuels can greatly help to reduce such negative impacts. However, current trends in biofuels do not address this issue seriously.

In general, the main attraction for the private sector to invest in Ethiopia's energy sector is the country's favourable investment policies (such as access to land, tax exemptions, fuel blending policies) and the environmental conditions, which are suited to biofuel crops. The country is also perceived as having abundant 'unused' land and water, and 'cheap' and 'abundant' labour resources. The extensive government support systems, however, may have created an artificial push for biofuels and may have raised expectations too high. Viable and sustainable commercial biofuel production systems need to be proved successful over the coming years. To facilitate this, biofuels need far greater policy engagement. This will be discussed in the following sections.

Uncertainties and promises of biofuels

In recent years, the implications of biofuels for development and for environmental objectives have been debated intensively. Some argue that biofuel production competes with food production, exacerbating hunger and undermining the social and political stability of developing nations (e.g. von Braun and Meinzen-Dick 2009; IFPRI 2008). In late 2007, the prices of food crops spiralled upward. This was partly caused by an expansion of biofuels in many developing countries, while many developed countries, severely affected by the fossil fuel crisis, subsidized biofuel production heavily and converted food crops into biofuels. As Pimentel and his research colleagues indicate, some 10–30 per cent of the increase in the price of food (the price of US beef, chicken, pork, eggs, bread, cereals and milk) could be linked to the expansion of biofuel (Pimentel et al. 2009). In Ethiopia, following the sharp rise in grain prices in 2007, the government imposed an export ban on such major cereals as maize, sorghum, wheat and 'teff' (an indigenous staple grain) to ease the food shortage. This ban was lifted in July 2010 (IRIN 2010).

This double-edged crisis has been interpreted as a causal relationship: the energy crisis has brought about a food crisis. Both the conversion of food crops and the allocation of rural resources to biofuels were regarded as counterproductive and politically unjust, and were seen to have had severe consequences for developing countries, where most of the global poor and food-insecure people live. Many realize the links between food insecurity, energy insecurity and the wider social and political instability, although this relationship is complicated and may not necessarily be direct or causal.

Beyond the immediate pressure of reducing poverty, many countries in Africa have outstanding political and moral questions of food sovereignty and rights to quality food that they need to address. These questions have increasingly become issues for the international 'framework' (WTO, IMF, World Bank, etc.), and studies have been undertaken into the international causes of hunger and malnutrition (Windfuhr and Jonsén 2005; Via Campesina 2003). To address these questions, the views of the studies are that national policies also need to target the right to adequate food all the time. Whether biofuel production directly addresses these political questions is an open question. In light of the current underlying trends in biofuel development in Africa (such as dependency on external resources and markets, grabbing of natural resources, and the fact that biofuels are primarily designed to meet global and urban demands and not local needs), the risks are high that Africa may fail to meet its broader social and economic objectives.

While the above (more political) questions have been inadequately addressed, there are arguments in favour of biofuel production: it opens up opportunities for much-needed cash flows to small farmers, for diversification of those farmers' sources of income, and for the governments of developing countries to save hard currency. Rural job opportunities are another potential benefit: biofuel production could add an estimated 1.1 million jobs by 2012 in sub-Saharan Africa (De Keiser and Hongo 2005), and in Ethiopia it is expected that there will be 111,000 new job opportunities (ENA 2010).

Biofuels are also seen as a means of mitigating environmental problems, such as greenhouse gas emissions. Biodiesel produced from jatropha is said to deliver carbon savings of over 66 per cent compared to fossil fuel diesel (Dehue and Hettinga 2008). Some countries, such as South Africa and India, try to account for environmental damage through the systematic measurement of carbon emissions. As a strategy towards environmental mitigation, the carbon savings and credits are monitored and the findings shared. Some authors, however, warn that environmental and development goals may not be achieved simultaneously. Policies need to clearly prioritize which goals to promote. Matinga, for instance, indicates that, for developing countries, the starting point for biofuel development should not be environmental goals (such as greenhouse gas reduction targets), but rather policies should maximize sustainable development benefits for the poor (Matinga 2008). In general, the current initiatives involving carbon trading are faced with a number of challenges, including: the risk that existing inequalities will be strengthened and vulnerable people further marginalized; uncertainty as to the various actors' political and institutional commitments; and even doubts whether carbon trading works at all, given the current asymmetrical climate policies across countries.

In the case of contract farming, where small farmers are involved, biofuel production is labour intensive. The farmers have insufficient funds to buy fertilizers that emit greenhouse gases, and they rarely use mechanized farm equipment that consumes polluting fossil fuels. Consequently, small farmers in developing countries are more environmentally friendly than large-scale, commercial, mono-cropping operations (Bolwing et al. 2009). In this respect, biofuels in developing countries should be seen primarily as an opportunity for development, as rural areas that are abundant in land and labour can benefit from domestic and global biofuel demand. The impact of biofuels on land use (water, nutrient, vegetation cover, etc.) needs to be considered within the sustainable natural resources development framework. Depending on the land resources, type of feedstock, cultivation methods, conversion technologies and energy efficiency, the impact of biofuels could vary significantly (Hazell 2007).

Much of this discussion reflects a high level of uncertainty as to how biofuels are going to develop in the future. Alongside the general scenarios (negative and positive) described above, there are critical issues that need to be addressed: such as the prospects for smallholder farmers in biofuels. This is a particularly critical issue in Ethiopia, where the majority of the rural population survive on smallholder agricultural systems. The following sections explore the political, institutional and economic aspects of contract biofuel production, where the crucial resources of smallholder farmers – labour and land – are involved.

Contract biofuel farming schemes

Contract farming is an organizational and institutional form of production relations that directly targets smallholders. It is an intermediate institutional arrangement that allows agricultural companies to participate in, and exert control over, the production process, without owning or operating the farms. Studies in contract farming often focus on understanding why agro-industrial companies and smallholders choose contract farming over other organizational strategies. Contract farming itself may have different arrangements, depending on duration, price guarantee for produce, share of product, etc. As Little and Watts (1994: 9) indicate, contracting is a form of institution that guides production coordination 'between growers and buyers-processors' and allows the actors to

> directly shape production decisions through contractually specifying market obligations (by volume, value, quality and, at times, advanced price determination); provide specific inputs; and exercise some control at the point of production (i.e. a division of management functions between contactor and contractee).

Another market-based conceptualization of contract farming is described by Ellis. He sees the primary purpose of agrarian contracts as being able 'to reduce transaction costs in the context of the unevenly developed markets and scarce information found in the rural societies of many developing countries' (Ellis 1993: 146–7). In other words, contract farming is an institutional response to imperfections in *markets* for credit, insurance, information and factors of production; and in *transaction costs* associated with search, screening, transfer of goods, bargaining, litigation and enforcement. From this perspective, contract farming has the potential, in the long run, to incorporate low-income growers into the modern and industrial agricultural sectors and to create economies of scale, access to regional and global markets, and dissemination of skills and techniques. What is not addressed is the question of which conditions are required for such forms of production to generate any of the perceived positive outcomes.

Empirical evidence suggests that contract farming needs to be looked at beyond the operational and market boundaries. Case studies on major African export crops show that contract farming, which started to be popular in the 1980s, is not necessarily an institutional panacea for smallholder involvement in agro-industrialization (Porter and Phillips-Howard 1997; Gibbon and Ponte 2005; Reardon and Barrett 2000; Carney 1994). Africa has been losing out on international markets, its share of world agricultural trade has declined for nine out of ten major exports, and most of the export systems have been extractive (Kofi and Desta 2008). Other recent studies have also stressed the difficulties that African smallholders face in trying to compete on the global market (World Bank 2007; Havnevik et al. 2007). The outcome of contract farming thus hinges on broader national and international political and economic structures, as well as on local conditions (the figure below summarizes the major dimensions).

Challenges in biofuel contracts

Institutional questions of the land Land tenure has been a key challenge in Ethiopia. Historically, rural areas have faced strong interventions from the state. The redistribution of rural land, the lack of clear ownership and in-secure tenure terms have been challenges facing the smallholder farmers of Ethiopia (Joireman 2000; Young 1997; Dessalegn 1996; McCann 1995; Cohen and Weintraub 1975). According to the current constitution, land is owned by the state. Farmers have user rights over the land. Permanent transfer of land (such as land sale) is prohibited (Proclamation No. 1/1995, Article 40, No. 3). A major drawback of the current land tenure policy is its weak incentive for long-term land investment, especially by indigenous people (Atakilte 2003). Yet, government has allowed foreign investment as a priority without examining how best land tenure can be secured for the indigenous people. Studies are required to further examine land tenure in view of such external investments and what they imply for indigenous people.

On the other hand, state land ownership has protective features. It has safeguarded farmers from the risks of liberal land markets. Accordingly, there is little risk that contract farming in Ethiopia will lead to the gradual transfer of land from smallholders to bigger landholders, which might result in a concentration of land ownership and displacement of the rural poor.

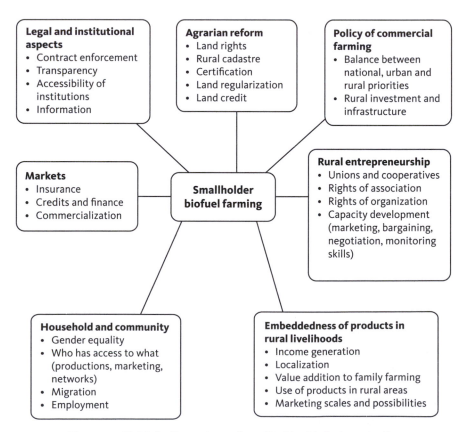

Legal and institutional aspects
- Contract enforcement
- Transparency
- Accessibility of institutions
- Information

Agrarian reform
- Land rights
- Rural cadastre
- Certification
- Land regularization
- Land credit

Policy of commercial farming
- Balance between national, urban and rural priorities
- Rural investment and infrastructure

Markets
- Insurance
- Credits and finance
- Commercialization

Smallholder biofuel farming

Rural entrepreneurship
- Unions and cooperatives
- Rights of association
- Rights of organization
- Capacity development (marketing, bargaining, negotiation, monitoring skills)

Household and community
- Gender equality
- Who has access to what (productions, marketing, networks)
- Migration
- Employment

Embeddedness of products in rural livelihoods
- Income generation
- Localization
- Value addition to family farming
- Use of products in rural areas
- Marketing scales and possibilities

Figure 5.1 Multiple dimensions of smallholder biofuel production

However, two processes are taking place that have direct implications on the use, access and 'control' of rural land. First, the state itself has become an active economic agent in allocating land for the private sector (both domestic and multinational agro-industries). The general policy emphasizes that commercial land allocations should not alienate the rural people from the land. The exceptions are intensive commercial farms, such as floriculture, horticulture and dairy farms in the densely populated highlands. It has been claimed that farmers have been compensated for their displacement. Otherwise, the argument is that the land being allocated for biofuels is 'unused' and is located in the lowlands, where population density is low. The vast land areas being allocated for food and biofuel production are primarily located in such areas. However, there are various aspects to the dependence of rural people on the land, including shifting and long-term rotational grazing and farming, and use of forest and wildlife products. These forms of customary land uses are less well recognized and are undefined. As a result, rural communities can risk losing their communal lands.

The second process is the increasing role of urban people and of the private sector in contract and sharecropping arrangements with smallholders. These practices were illegal between 1974 and 1991. The 1974 land reform officially prohibited any form of sharecropping and rural waged employment, in a drive to abolish the land-based production relations of that time. The engagement of urban dwellers in agriculture was discouraged and controlled. The government that came to power in 1991 scrapped these restrictive policies (Hamza and Azanaw 1995). As a result, urban people have increasingly come to participate in contract and sharecropping practices, particularly in areas near towns and in high-potential agricultural areas. Smallholder contract biofuel production (for biofuel companies) is another example taking place.

These processes are making increasing headway in the rural areas, and particularly the smallholder farming systems. Hence they are also coming to affect the issue of property rights. Contract enforcement, ownership of the plants grown, duration of contract and other aspects of contract farming and outgrower schemes need clear and institutionalized policies and guidelines for the different actors involved. Lack of clarity in terms of these land-related institutions has often been a source of confusion and conflict between industrial and agricultural expectations in the expansion of biofuels. Both domestic and foreign biofuel companies have clear expectations as regards the processing plants and the large-scale plantations they establish. However, the realities of African land tenure and agricultural production are issues that are oversimplified by investing companies. Many financing agencies want a clear distinction between what is agriculture and what is industry.

The impact of biofuels on local social and economic processes is also crucial. Rural communities embrace many legitimate and accepted ways of accessing and using resources. These are described as 'customary' or 'informal' systems operating and coexisting with formal state institutions. These informal institutions are generated by people's active 'investment' in them (Berry 1993) and are upheld by mutual agreements between actors. Yet rural communities are also heterogeneous, and their relations are characterized by power and authority (Moe 2005). As a result, informal or customary institutions over time and space may not necessarily have a collective purpose, as people reform them under the influence of social and economic changes.

As rural people constitute heterogeneous groups, reflecting varied and even conflicting interests (along status, wealth, gender, age and social or professional lines), how the different groups respond to biofuels is an important internal process. For instance, depending on assets and capabilities, the members of rural communities have different access to and use of rural land resources (Atakilte 2003). Well-off households (such as households with livestock) have greater use of, and a stronger claim on, communal lands. Women and poorer households are dependent on such areas, but their claims are weaker and of a temporary or seasonal nature. Landless, poor and young people may not have access to such lands (or may have no means of using them, such as to graze livestock), but may still constitute a strong potential claimant on community lands. These processes may be self-organizing if the systems of local land tenure are well developed and function properly. But in contexts where state institutions are active, people may resort to different institutions, depending on their access to them. In the context of competing tenure systems, the institutions may not only undermine one another, but they may also be sources of conflict and mismanagement of natural resources.

In general, the introduction of biofuels in rural areas will have an impact on local social and economic processes. As cash and perennial crops, biofuels will primarily benefit rural people who have relatively large land areas, as they will be able to accommodate the planting of biofuels. Landless people will resort to claiming communal and degraded land. In parts of northern Ethiopia, local administrators have taken the initiative to allocate hilly and 'unused' land to landless people, for them to plant trees and grasses. Biofuels can fit into such initiatives. In the Ethiopian smallholder context, households headed by women are the main group that rents land for sharecropping, and the opportunities for them to enter into contract biofuel production can be very limited.

Entrepreneurial and organizational conditions Rural entrepreneurship development in Ethiopia has been neglected for many years. State intervention in the 1980s was politically and ideologically driven (Alemayehu 1992; Alemneh 1987). State interference in the marketing and distribution of agricultural products left rural people with a deep distrust of government (Franzel et al. 1992). The state forced rural people to create rural agricultural cooperatives and service associations, which in essence ran government programmes (Teketel 1998). With regime change in 1991, such rural organizations disintegrated. The process initiated by the government of building new confidence and goodwill among farmers has been very slow. Over the past few years, producer associations of major cash and export crops, such as coffee, oil seeds, fruits and vegetables, have been established in many regions. However, the traditional, subsistence-oriented and smallholder cereal-producing farmers are not organized. The Ethiopian Commodity Exchange Centre in Addis Ababa was opened in 2008 principally to help the major farm producers with marketing their agricultural commodities. The Centre assists farmers in obtaining better prices by providing information on international market prices, providing storage and distribution, and credit facilities for traders. It helps reduce the number of links in the trading chain and also provides a reliable system for handling, grading and storing agricultural products. Traders will be able to match offers and bids for commodity transactions, and there is a risk-free payment and goods delivery system to settle transactions. Despite these improved conditions, dynamic rural entrepreneurships and producer associations have not emerged. In their absence, the overall negotiating capacity of the rural people vis-à-vis the biofuel companies is weak and fragmented.

Institutionalized and informal social practices also determine how individuals organize themselves to form social capital. This applies at different levels of social and economic structures: the household, the community and other economic groupings. Far from being orderly, adaptive structures, rural households are founded on conflicting relationships. Individual members of households have different decision-making powers. Control and access to resources, social networking and marketing can be significantly different among the members of households, depending on gender, age and education. Female-headed households often tend to lack farm implements and labour. They tend to be subsistence oriented, while male-headed households are better at cultivating cash crops. How contract biofuel farming will impact on gender and power relations in rural areas, and how it will influence household labour and income, are key questions.

At the village and community levels, social relations are partly shaped by patronage and kinship relations. They are crucial to accessing resources in rural settings. Existing authority and roles (formal or traditional) can easily be expanded to capture new advantages. The way in which local power and local relations are negotiated has an impact on the decision of households to participate in biofuel production. In any case, such relationships will shape the long-term social and economic sustainability of smallholder biofuel farming.

In general, current policies on biofuels assume that smallholders will respond to the opportunity presented by biofuels: income generation from supplying their products (biofuel feedstock) to the processing industries. However, local institutions, organizations and existing systems of production may not respond smoothly. Any shift in production objectives and any accommodation of new production systems involves changes in institutional and organizational arrangements, which are essentially endogenous processes. How such processes will take shape and evolve is exogenous to current biofuel policies in Ethiopia.

To facilitate reorganization processes, biofuel policies need to address organizational needs, ways of acquiring capacities (learning and skills) and the incorporation of these skills into the production systems. Similarly, institutionalized skills related to entrepreneurship and organizational competence are critical for capturing the benefits of the processes of globalization and for expanding the networks of actors at different levels in biofuels. Organizational arrangements that can concentrate the technical and management know-how, capital and financing, labour, and connections to local and international markets are critical for smallholder development (Jayne et al. 2006). Risk-minimization strategies and support systems in biofuel farming are also crucial components in smallholder biofuel development. In the current global chain of production and trading, among the many actors, smallholders are perhaps the least well informed and least organized category in relation to the political and economic imperatives of biofuels.

Embeddedness of biofuels in rural livelihoods As indicated above, the current expansion in biofuel production in rural Ethiopia emerged in response to global and national (or more specifically urban) interests, and not primarily to meet the development needs of rural areas and people. The different government strategies developed for commercial biofuel and food production, the investments and the incentive structures aim to facilitate the flow of FDI and the needs of the private sector. The government strategies, however, also try to remedy (or to mitigate) the unintended social, economic and environmental consequences.

The important question, however, is whether the rural community will be central to the production, marketing and consumption of biofuels. Will production and consumption of biofuels be part of the social and economic life of the rural people who produce them? How can biofuels be integrated into the local and regional markets? These key issues require balanced, broad-based, sustained, long-term policies and strategies. Table 5.2 summarizes these issues. In this regard, mainstream policies need to expand their goals. In the current biofuel strategy, the development and role of biofuels are mainly justified in terms of the hard-currency earning potential. The substitution of petroleum is also offered as a major goal. Alongside these, the contract production of biofuels by smallholders should also be scrutinized, to make sure that it delivers real opportunities for the rural people who produce the crops.

One way in which biofuels might be of benefit to people in rural Ethiopia is through localization – not only of the feedstock but also of the processing and use of biofuels. Clearly, to avoid the risk of biofuels becoming yet another extractive industry, the current mainstream, export-oriented development path of biofuels needs to be balanced with robust and broad-based strategies that put energy as a developmental goal of the rural people. The expansion of the skills and capacities of rural people and the promotion of locally relevant, small-scale and affordable biofuel processing technologies are critical in encouraging the localization of biofuels.

Support for the local biofuel market and promotion of the domestic use of biofuel products can secure broad-based demand for biofuels. In this regard, there are some positive initiatives taking place in Ethiopia. The municipality of Addis Ababa, in collaboration with the government, local and foreign companies, is introducing modern, affordable and clean-cooking bio-ethanol stoves. The initiative includes the supply, distribution and installation of the whole package of fuel and stoves in the apartments that are springing up across the city. Ethanol is purchased locally from the Fincha sugar factory. By way of creating a suitably 'enabling' environment, the government decided that the ethanol produced by the factory is to be used only within Ethiopia. This has created a win-win situation for the residents (clean energy supply) and

TABLE 5.2 Balancing policy focuses for biofuel and the desired policy goals in the rural development context of Ethiopia

Focus of mainstream biofuel policies	Desirable policy goals for the broad-based development and sustainable production of biofuels
Saving hard currency by exporting biofuels	Deliver social return and real opportunities for rural people
Consolidate corporate and TNC interest and privileges	Promote locally accountable, socially and environmentally responsible policies
Promote commercialization and commoditization of rural land and labour	Create conditions for decent and secure rural livelihoods and for social orientation
How to bring capital- and resource-intensive technologies to the poor or to the country to increase the production of biofuels	Embed investments or integrate them with the existing livelihood systems without creating dramatic loss of or disruption to livelihood, ownership and indigenous knowledge systems
Rural areas as sources of land and labour in biofuels that companies can directly contract	Empower rural producers and facilitate renewable energy technologies Build and share models of innovation rooted in locally developed innovation

for the sugar factory (secure local market) (Practical Action Consulting 2009). Replicating such initiatives across towns alone would create a tremendous potential for the localization of biofuels in Ethiopia.

In summary, in order to promote the localization of biofuels, biofuel policies need to be designed from the perspective of how they can improve local livelihood systems. Rural energy security can be improved through the use of liquid biofuels. Other energy-related rural problems – such as the health implications of using wood biomass – can also be addressed. The liquid fuel can also benefit rural women, who expend large amounts of time and energy looking for firewood. In addition, rural people's dependence on wood fuel, crop residues and cow dung negatively impacts on the environment. In fact, local biofuel production means there is the possibility of cleaner energy in rural areas, and this has environmental benefits. In this respect, biofuel production may provide opportunities for tackling such problems, if it is properly designed and also has a focus on smallholder welfare.

Conclusion

Liberalization and globalization processes and national food and energy insecurity are changing the state–rural relationships in Ethiopia – relationships that are defined along the dimensions of 'private sector', 'investment', 'export-oriented productions' and 'foreign investment'. The outcome is a new and stronger focus on commercial farming in Ethiopia. The government has set up a special office to allocate up to 3 million hectares of land to investors. A major aim of the Biofuels Development and Utilization Strategy is to encourage an export-oriented production system. In many cases, dependency on major export-oriented agricultural schemes, including biofuels, raises the question of whether these address the development needs of the country itself and of its rural population. To address these concerns, the current biofuel strategy needs to go beyond its current goals. Biofuel strategies and policies need to be situated within rural livelihoods. They also need to tackle the ways in which biofuels – their production, their use and the marketing of them – can bring about rural transformation and change.

Ethiopia needs to be better prepared strategically to handle the globalization and monetization processes taking place. There is considerable interest today in getting the private sector more involved in rural development. There needs to be institutional and organizational support to link biofuel processors up with small farmers through production contracts, and to create conditions that are conducive to exchanging agricultural inputs and services for biofuels.

Smallholder contract biofuel farming can potentially suit small farmers, and there is very little risk that farmers will lose their land. However, the introduction of biofuels does imply changes and adjustments to existing production systems. The cost and risks of such changes need to be recognized in biofuel strategies. Contracted smallholders may face serious problems in dealing with firms. To help with this, the establishment of overarching legal and other institutional frameworks for contract farming would be an important area of intervention by government and/or farmers' organizations. Finally, contract farming involves multiple actors, including investors, industrialists, local administrative people, urban middle men and rural land holders. In order to ensure sustainability of the production systems, the various arrangements between the different actors should create an engaging and long-term partnership. This requires longer-term planning and regulation if small-scale bioenergy projects are to develop.

As the biofuel sector expands, there needs to be clear definition and categorization of land resources for different purposes, as well as sustainability and impact assessments of the investments on the physical environment. A physical inventory of land resources also needs to take into consideration the rights to natural resources of people across various social categories. The rights of different and vulnerable sections of society and livelihood systems – women, nomads, herders, shifting cultivators, forest-dependent people, communal/ traditional natural resources management systems, etc. – should be carefully considered and taken into account.

6 | Biofuel, land and environmental issues: the case of SEKAB's biofuel plans in Tanzania

Kjell Havnevik and Hanne Haaland[1]

Introduction

Since investments in biofuel expansion in most sub-Saharan countries are fairly recent, empirical investigations into the implications for land grabbing, environmental aspects and food security are still in their infancy. Access to data about the establishment of facilities and about how concessions are gained is difficult, and methodologies are mostly unproven. To address this gap, this chapter investigates the plans for, and implementation of, biofuel production in Tanzania by a Swedish municipal company, SEKAB International AB (henceforth SEKAB) and its subsidiaries, with the aim of attaining a more empirically based knowledge on the ground. The findings from this research may complement other findings presented in this book and elsewhere, and help us reflect on how realistic are the recommendations for large-scale land acquisitions and leasing of African land for biofuel and food production. Concerns have been raised by international research institutions, the UN Special Rapporteur on the right to food and other UN organizations about the implications of such acquisitions for the livelihood of African people. Those recommendations of the institutions on which there seems to be agreement are:

1 There should be transparency in the negotiations.
2 The rights of local communities, including customary land rights, should be protected.
3 There should be a sharing of benefits between local communities and investors.
4 Environmental sustainability should be ensured.
5 Food security in the African countries and communities should not be compromised.[2]

In the following text, we present the two interlinked projects that SEKAB initiated in Tanzania in 2005, focusing particularly on the environmental and social impact assessment (ESIA) process of the Bagamoyo project. We carried out investigations, including interviews with various stakeholders involved in the ESIA process or with knowledge of it, in Tanzania and Sweden in the period 2008 to 2010. This chapter is part of a broader research project that will also focus on suggestions as to how to improve ESIA processes and procedures in relation to biofuel projects.

The choice of a case study involving a Swedish municipally owned company, SEKAB (70 per cent municipally owned and 30 per cent privately owned by EcoDevelopment in Europe), which has long experience in the energy sector, was made on the basis of the fact that the company has a reputation to uphold, since it is directly accountable to Swedish taxpayers. SEKAB is also heavily involved in the promotion of certification processes for biofuels globally and in developing second-generation technologies for bioenergy production.[3] SEKAB was founded in 1906, and the core business of the present company, SEKAB Group (established in 1985), is to develop second-generation ethanol and green chemicals from ligno-cellulose biomass. However, it has taken longer than expected to achieve commercially feasible production of these technologies, and SEKAB therefore decided to venture into first-generation ethanol production globally where 'land is available'. SEKAB's vision, formulated by its previous chief executive, Per Carstedt, was based on the idea that the production and use of non-fossil fuels in the transport sector has to increase in order to address climate change before second-generation ethanol becomes commercially available.[4] SEKAB subsequently decided to internationalize its production and trade in first-generation biofuels with Brazil, Ghana, Poland, Hungary, Tanzania and Mozambique. During the first years of the twenty-first century, SEKAB became the largest importer of biofuel to the EU market.[5]

In its biofuel promotion in Tanzania, then, SEKAB might be expected to stand out as a 'good case' in addressing the recommendations proposed by research institutions and UN agencies.[6] To implement its vision, SEKAB established the subsidiary companies SEKAB Bioenergy Tanzania Ltd (henceforth SEKAB T) and Ecoenergia de Mocambique. SEKAB T was 98.5 per cent owned by SEKAB, Sweden, and 1.5 per cent by the Tanzanian Community Finance Company. SEKAB's total investment in the two companies from 2005 to October 2009 was 170 million Swedish krona (SEK) (about US$25 million).

Another reason for focusing on SEKAB's project was that the discussions and debate about SEKAB T's Bagamoyo project and the process around its ESIA have been particularly heated. The polarized discussions about the environmental and social impacts of SEKAB T's planned projects relate to the potential competition between food and fuel, as well as to reports of increased insecurity for smallholders' land rights due to the large-scale investments. Against this background, there is thus a need to investigate the current procedures and standards for ESIAs connected with applications for investment licences for large-scale projects with potential environmental and social impacts. There is reason to ask whether such projects are radically different from other large-scale land-demanding projects, and whether they therefore require different procedures for preparation and planning. What can be learned from a more empirically oriented study and from interviews with the major stakeholders? How could this generate proposals for improvement of the ESIA process in general?

Another important objective of this research was to gain some insights into the role of the state, donors and investors, including SEKAB, in promoting a broader framework (i.e. policy and guidelines for the sector) that goes beyond strategic environmental analysis (SEA) and ESIA. The Tanzanian government was unprepared for the rapid influx of international investors/companies into this sector.

Background and key developments

SEKAB's choice of Tanzania as a production country was based on the assumed existence of available and suitable land for large-scale biofuel production. Tanzania also has a strong Swedish and Nordic aid relationship, dating back to the 1960s. During the last decade, Swedish development assistance has widened its perspective through the Policy for Global Development (PGU, abbreviation in Swedish for Politik för Global Utveckling) and has made commercial and business relations between Sweden and developing countries a more integral part of it (Odén 2006). To this end, a new department was established in the Swedish International Development Cooperation Agency (Sida) to deal with tripartite initiatives between governments, development assistance and commercial companies (Department of Partnership Development, Aktörssamverkan, or AKTSAM). This approach can be seen as a response to the PGU, and it also makes it possible for Sweden to continue cooperation with countries where development assistance has been phased out (such as Vietnam, India and Namibia) on more commercial terms.

In addition, the UN initiative to engage the business world in global development (the Global Compact) has been concretized in the guidelines for corporate social responsibility (CSR), which emphasize the ethical, environmental and social responsibilities of business companies and investors. SEKAB has made elements of the CSR guidelines central to its activities and, in particular, to issues of sustainability. According to Anders Fredriksson, chief executive of SEKAB Biofuels and Chemicals (part of the SEKAB Group), SEKAB 'works actively towards promoting sustainability criteria in a globally accepted system'. The Sustainable Bioethanol Award, bestowed on SEKAB in March 2009 by Green Power Conferences, a British company, is seen by SEKAB as recognition that its work in this direction has yielded results (SEKAB 2009a).

As for developments in Tanzania, SEKAB T's objective was to set up an office in Dar es Salaam, to recruit competent personnel to plan the projects, start land acquisitions and conduct an initial risk assessment and ESIA. SEKAB T gained access to land after discussions with the Revolutionary Government of Zanzibar to lease part of its Razaba cattle ranch in Bagamoyo district, Coast Region, which had not been operational since 1994. The ranch is located adjacent to the Wami River, from which it was planned to draw water for sugarcane cultivation. SEKAB T requested the lease of 24,200 hectares of the ranch. However, only 22,000 hectares were granted to it by the Tanzania Investment Centre (TIC – the investment-licensing government agency) and derivative rights were being processed during 2009 (Sulle and Nelson 2009b: 56).

An ESIA can be defined as a systematic process that examines in advance the environmental consequences of development action. Normally, project ESIAs have to be based on a project investment feasibility study, in order to identify potential impacts and how they can be mitigated. A fundamental problem that affected the planning of the Bagamoyo project was that SEKAB T did not develop an investment feasibility study as an input to the ESIA. The lead consultant for the Bagamoyo ESIA was the Swedish consultant company ORGUT, in cooperation with Ardhi University (ARU) in Dar es Salaam. ORGUT was contracted directly by SEKAB T. The environmental and social impact study for the project was conducted in 2008 and resulted in the Tanzanian National Environmental Management Council (NEMC) awarding a licence in April 2009. As for the Rufiji project, the Stockholm Environment Institute (SEI) and the Institute of Resource Assessment (IRA) at the University of Dar es Salaam conducted a risk assessment study of the planned project (SEI/IRA 2009). This study was strongly criticized for various weaknesses.[7] In addition, the process of acquiring land from villages in Rufiji district turned out to be much more complex than had been anticipated by SEKAB T.

The Bagamoyo project was seen as a forerunner and pilot project (to gain experience and produce seedlings) for the much larger biofuel project in Rufiji district, which was originally planned for 400,000 hectares. Rufiji district is located to the south of Coast Region, and its nature, ecology and flood-plain agricultural production are intimately tied to the variable flow of the Rufiji River, whose catchment area covers about 30 per cent of Tanzania's land area (Havnevik 1993: chs 3 and 4; Hoag 2003; Öhman 2007; Duvail and Hamerlynck 2007). Analysis of the plan for the Rufiji project showed an emphasis on the land-acquisition process, environmental and climate issues related to the plans for the project. SEKAB's planned sugarcane production was not to be located on the flood plain itself, but on higher ground to the north and south of it. Hence, water for sugarcane cultivation needed to be drawn from the Rufiji River.

In order to fund its development costs in Bagamoyo and Rufiji, on 28 July 2009 SEKAB T applied to Sida, Stockholm, for a Credit Enhancement Guarantee that would allow the company to borrow money from Tanzanian banks (SEKAB Bioenergy Tanzania 2009). This move was necessary because the board of SEKAB had refused to inject more money into SEKAB T. The processes surrounding the Tanzanian projects were, in addition, becoming increasingly contested by many stakeholders and concerned observers, including NGOs and researchers, both in Sweden and Tanzania (Roberntz et al. 2009; Benjaminsen et al. 2009; Benjaminsen and Bryceson 2009; ActionAid 2009; also Widengård 2009b). *Development Today* is a journal, published in Oslo, which focuses on development assistance. It had followed SEKAB T's involvement in Tanzania closely and it published an article reporting that SEKAB T had tampered with the conclusions of the Bagamoyo project's ESIA, which was carried out by ORGUT and ARU. The journal's conclusion was that SEKAB T had received permission from the Tanzanian NEMC to proceed with the Bagamoyo investment under false pretences (*Development Today*, April 2009). This threatened the reputation of SEKAB, which had furthermore been hard hit by the financial crisis and had accumulated losses amounting to SEK 317 million in 2008.[8]

On 29 October 2009, Sida decided, after a thorough analysis, to reject SEKAB T's application for a Credit Enhancement Guarantee on various grounds (to be taken up later). A week earlier, however, on 21 October, SEKAB International AB and EcoDevelopment in Europe AB had entered into an agreement, by which EcoDevelopment took over 100 per cent of the shares in the two subsidiaries in Tanzania and Mozambique at practically no cost – SEK 400. Three of the owners of EcoDevelopment were also on the board of SEKAB, but were said not to have taken part in the board's decision on the issue. With this agreement, SEKAB 'extracted itself from its African projects except for the four potential off-take contracts, one for its Ghana efforts and three for EcoDevelopment in Tanzania and Mozambique respectively'. The agreement between SEKAB and EcoDevelopment also stated that, in case EcoDevelopment 'is able to find financial backers for the African ethanol projects and is able to implement its plans, the contract includes a pledge for an off-take contract and a repayment clause, with which SEKAB can regain the entire amount it invested in Africa between 2005 and 2008, approximately SEK 170 million' (SEKAB 2009c).

Hence, over a period of four years, a highly respected energy company, SEKAB, had run up losses of SEK 170 million, of which 70 per cent had come from the pockets of Swedish taxpayers, in its attempt to develop biofuel production based on sugarcane production in Tanzania and Mozambique. How was this possible and why did the processes related to the development of these projects become so contested?[9] These are questions to which we will return throughout this chapter.

The Tanzanian context

SEKAB T was established at a time when development assistance fatigue had taken hold of the many Swedish and Nordic development practitioners who had long experience of working in Tanzania. With its vision and dynamic leadership, SEKAB T promised employment opportunities, increasing investments and incomes, and the modernization of agriculture in Tanzania. For many years, development assistance had generally failed to deliver such modernization. SEKAB T was, therefore, considered dynamic and development oriented by important sections of the donor community, by many Tanzanian government officials, and by development practitioners, who longed for action and concrete results.

Alongside experienced Tanzanian professionals, SEKAB T was thus able to recruit competent and committed Nordic project managers and advisers with long Tanzanian experience.[10] SEKAB also organized meetings and seminars in Sweden, in order to inform the relevant authorities, particularly Sida and the foreign ministry in Sweden. Professionals with long experience and with high positions in Swedish development assistance, including former ambassadors and senior government officials, likewise made their services and knowledge available to SEKAB and SEKAB T. SEKAB T also put a lot of effort into informing the appropriate Tanzanian authorities and international agencies and donors, not least the Swedish and Norwegian embassies in the country.

When SEKAB announced its Tanzanian biofuel plans, the ideas found support among many development assistance officials and diplomats. Even the Swedish ambassador to Tanzania in the middle of the decade took a keen interest in the project. Tanzania had neither guidelines nor policies that could assist government agencies at all levels in coordinating and guiding the proposed biofuel projects, some of which were expected to comprise hundreds of thousands of hectares. The Swedish embassy, with active support from SEKAB T, created a forum for discussion of how a biofuel sector framework could be developed.[11] The pressure from potential biofuel investors was enormous, and a representative from the Ministry of Agriculture claimed that, by mid-2008, 30 foreign investors were preparing the ground for biofuel projects.[12]

In March 2006, the Tanzanian government established a National Biofuel Task Force, coordinated by the Ministry of Energy and based on a recommendation in a German Technical Cooperation study from 2005 (GTZ 2005).[13] This was the first study to address biofuel development in Tanzania. In January 2009, the Norwegian and Swedish development agencies, Norad and Sida, gave the Tanzanian government US$3 million to develop guidelines for the biofuel sector. The two donor agencies are currently also contributing financially to the process of establishing biofuel policies (interview with Sandvand Dahlen, 3 November 2009). Guidelines, not policy, had to come first, due to the urgency of the situation. Various draft guidelines were circulated in the relevant Tanzanian ministries. A problem with the guideline process is that biofuel development was primarily conceived as an energy issue, and was insufficiently connected with agricultural, land and food security aspects. It took until November 2010 before draft guidelines for the biofuel sector were produced and officially approved (URT 2010).

Although development of SEKAB T's biofuel projects took place in a context without guidelines and policies for the sector, the Tanzanian government and parliament had earlier passed laws and regulations of relevance to its development. These included the Tanzanian Investment Policy of 1997 and the Land Act and the Village Land Act of 1999 (with subsequent amendments). The TIC was established in 2005 to identify suitable land for investors and a Land Bank was to be created that could act as a 'one-stop agency' to attract and serve external investors.

Regarding the land situation in Tanzania,[14] the FAO estimated that 4.5 per cent of the total land area was arable and 1.3 per cent was under permanent crops (FAO 2006). The World Bank's World Development Indicators Database, on the other hand, claims that as much as 10 per cent of Tanzania's land area is arable (about 90,000 km^2) while 1 per cent of the land is under permanent crops.[15] Thus, there are discrepancies in the land statistics that amount to almost 50 million hectares. The situation with arable land availability becomes even more confused when the TIC's Investors Guide (2008) states that 58.3 million hectares of land are available for biofuel development. Other sources mention 55 million hectares as available for such development, but without any critical reflection on the numbers (Sawe et al. 2008; Mwamila et al. 2008; Benjaminsen et al. 2008). This latter figure amounts to 62 per cent of the total land area of Tanzania. However, we also know that about 70 per cent of the land in Tanzania is under the jurisdiction of 11,000 registered villages. In addition, 39.6 per cent of Tanzania's total land area lies in 'protected areas', mostly under the International Union for the Conservation of Nature category of 'Managed Resources Protected Area' (World Resources Institute 2003). Hence, land conflicts are bound to occur when TIC tries to earmark land for investment and seeks to transfer it, via the Commissioner of Land, to itself, according to the 1997 Investment Act. Even the 2 million hectares of land that TIC claimed in late 2008 to have identified and targeted for biofuel production cannot be offered to investors on account of the complex land legislation. One source of the land conflict with villages lies in the fact that the Land Act and the Village Land Act (both of 1999) define 'unused village land' differently, thus offering TIC the scope to appropriate 'unused' village land.

The idea of establishing a Land Bank under the auspices of TIC has not materialized because of lack of funds for land compensation. International donors are reluctant to provide assistance to a TIC-administered Land Bank for fear of marginalizing smallholders with weak land rights (personal communication between representative of TIC and Havnevik, November 2008). Thus, potential foreign investors are recommended by TIC to visit areas where land might be available for biofuel production. Such visits should start with a call on the District Land Officer, who would guide the investors to villages for discussion about possible leases of village land and what could be offered by the investor in return.

The SEKAB Bagamoyo project

The ESIA – content and process Environmental impact assessments (EIAs) have existed in some form since the 1960s, when the US Environmental Protection Agency developed them for investment projects in the US. The use of EIAs to predict the environmental impacts of investments and as an essential tool in the permit-issuing process for new investments has since spread. It is now a basic requirement in most countries for all new, large-scale investment projects that bring with them a potential for environmental and social impacts. Impact assessments can be a policy instrument, a tool for planning, or a way of ensuring public involvement, and they can treat environmental aspects and social aspects as distinct units (Barrow 1997). However, according to Graham Smith (1993), the social, economic, physical and biological aspects of the environment are so integrated that impact assessments should not treat them as separate units, but rather should integrate them. We will return to this, because it provides context and justification for the use of the term 'ESIA'.

In Tanzania, the National Environmental Management Act of 2004 and its associated regulations explicitly prohibit implementation of any projects 'likely to have a negative environmental impact'. When it comes to *micro* project activities, the law allows for a 'trading, commercial or development permit or license' to be issued in the absence of a 'certificate of environmental impact assessment issued by the Minister' (Kamanga 2008: 10). However, an ESIA has to be conducted for medium- and large-scale projects, whether they are related to biofuel production, the establishment of fish farms or tourist enterprises.

In the late 1980s, the EIA requirement for new investments was adopted by many multilateral development agencies – such as the UN Environment Programme (UNEP) in 1988 and the World Bank in 1989 – that assumed a role of guidance and supervision, while the actual EIA was to be carried out in the country concerned.[16] In 1991, the OECD recommended that member governments adopt EIA procedures and methods as part of the process for granting aid to developing countries. The 1992 Earth Summit provided additional momentum through Principle 17 of the Rio Declaration, which stated that:

> Environmental Impact Assessment, as a national instrument, shall be undertaken for proposed activities that are likely to have a significant adverse impact on the environment and are subject to a decision of a competent national authority.

Generally, the EIA procedures adopted in many developing countries are based on international standards, and thus build on several years of experience and adjustments. However, a review by Wood (2003) of developing countries' EIAs found that their quality generally fell far below that of EIAs in developed countries. Wood felt that it was crucial for this performance be improved, in order to protect (or better balance) the environmental concerns of three-quarters of the world's land area. He reviewed developing countries' EIAs against the following set of robust evaluation criteria, in order to determine their strengths and weaknesses: legal basis; coverage; consideration of alternatives; screening; scoping; EIA report preparation; EIA report review; decision-making; impact monitoring; mitigation; consultation and participation; system monitoring; costs and benefits; and strategic environmental assessment.

Because developing countries' EIAs met so few of the 14 evaluation criteria established, several urgent generic issues were identified that needed to be addressed if EIAs were to fulfil their potential. These included legislation, organizational capacity, training, environmental information, participation and dissemination of experience, donor policy and political will for implementation. Gradually the social impacts of investments also came to be given an important place in the EIA, and therefore the name was changed to 'environmental and *social* impact assessment'. General procedures today are such that an ESIA is carried out on a geographically limited investment project and is *microeconomic* in nature. It is also carried out after project investment pre-feasibility and feasibility studies are done, so that the nature of the investment project is known in some detail.

Since the introduction of ESIA as a tool for analysis and investment clearance, limited research has been conducted on how ESIAs have been carried out in practice. The question of whether different types of project require different ESIA routines or processes has not been raised. One possible reason for the limited research and attention devoted by the academic community is that only the final ESIA study is made available to the public. Consultants involved in the process of negotiating terms of reference and actually carrying out the ESIAs do not have funding to carry out methodological reviews or deeper analysis of the process with the aim of generating proposals for improvement. Another important point is that, even when funds have been available for such purposes, ethical questions would surface as to the role of academics and their proximity to investors, governments and the process.[17] The lack of research-oriented reviews or critical analyses of the process means that few lessons have been learned as to how ESIA processes are carried out and how they can be improved (Fones-Sundell n.d.).

The autonomy of the team involved in the ESIA is an obvious factor when ESIA teams are identified and recruited. Otherwise the investors (or other groups interested in biasing the findings one way or the other) can manipulate the study and its results, which can lead to faulty grounds for issuing licences. But even though independent consultants are selected to carry out the ESIA, the question still remains of just how independent they can be. And more importantly, there is reason to ask whether the independence of the ESIA team of the project proponent can guarantee impartial results, given the institutional routines currently governing the issuance of investment permits.

Current practice is that ESIAs are carried out by an independent consultant contracted by the proponent or the investor. However, when he applies for an investment licence or permit, the project proponent generally hands the final ESIA document or report to the relevant government agency. Criticism of the ESIA processes has come about because of changes made to the independent consultant's ESIA report and its conclusions before they are presented in the final ESIA report that is handed over to government agencies. The potential discrepancy in results and conclusions has been one of the core topics of discussion with reference to SEKAB T's ESIA process in Bagamoyo district.

An ESIA process is usually divided into several stages. But before the launch of the ESIA, a feasibility study and the technical planning exercise for the project or investment in question should be finalized.[18] The formal procedure in Tanzania involves registration of the project at the NEMC, before a project brief is submitted. The content of this brief was described in the 2005 regulations for ESIAs. Based on the brief, the NEMC decides whether or not a project requires a full ESIA. A full ESIA process involves a scoping process, on which terms of reference (ToRs) for the ESIA are based. Assuming that the ToRs are approved by the NEMC, the ESIA process can subsequently continue with baseline studies.[19] The baseline studies are the first stage of the ESIA, covering the physical and social environment. A second part is a summary document, founded on the baseline studies. The summary document sets out detailed recommendations and suggestions for mitigating measures under the proposed project or investment. This final ESIA and the baseline studies are then submitted by the proponent or investor to the relevant government agency for assessment. According to informants at the NEMC, it is important that the ESIA is submitted by the proponent, as the ESIA is also regarded as an environmental impact statement, which reflects the proponent's commitment to the environment.[20] However, lack of clarity about who does what throughout the process may compromise the transparency of the ESIA. In Tanzania, the National Environmental Management Act, which stipulates the role and structure of EIAs and guidelines, was prepared by the Vice President's Office (Fones-Sundell n.d.).

Generally, for all levels of the ESIA, questions of access to information and information sharing are pertinent and significant to the process and outcome. As in most processes, information may be withheld from those stakeholders who are likely to suffer from the investment project. In the discussion of biofuel investments, smallholders and poor people are those most likely to suffer from a lack of information sharing, as land rights (formal and customary) and irrigation impacts and needs may not be taken properly into consideration. Land and water are critical resources for smallholders, large-scale biofuel projects and ecological systems. Within formal political structures and the bureaucracy, lack of information can lead to decisions being made that are based on wrong assumptions. In a developing context, land grabbing by foreign investors in connection with large-scale projects is a recurring theme (see chapter 1). Hence it is crucial to clarify the laws, rules and regulations related to land access as a basis for respect by all stakeholders involved and for enforcement by the relevant government authorities. This is one important reason why the NEMC sends a Technical Advisory Committee (TAC) team to conduct a review of the ESIA submitted. Through a field visit, the team checks the validity of the information presented in the ESIA. The proponent pays the costs, and the duration of a field visit is normally three to four days.[21] However, the length of the visit is likely to be insufficient in the case of some of the larger, more cross-cutting projects that involve a range of different stakeholders.

The structure and table of contents of the summary ESIA to be handed to the government agency are explicitly spelled out in Tanzanian government guidelines. On the other hand, the content and structure of the baseline studies will vary, depending on the location and nature of the project. What is to be included is specified in the ToRs for the ESIA, and those are stipulated in the contract between the consultant conducting the ESIA and the proponent. However, the ToRs are reviewed by the NEMC to ensure a certain level of quality.[22]

The SEKAB Bagamoyo project – analysis of the ESIA process The first stage of the ESIA process in the Bagamoyo project, the baseline study, was conducted from January to May 2008 with ORGUT as the lead consultant. The study produced by ORGUT consisted of 12 documents that were delivered to SEKAB on 8 May 2008, bearing the title 'Preliminary Environmental and Social Impact Analysis (ESIA)'.[23] The term 'preliminary' was used because SEKAB T had not provided a feasibility study for the investment project, and thus a final ESIA could not be produced. ORGUT had subcontracted ARU 'to carry out part of the assignment'.[24]

The second phase of the Bagamoyo ESIA process was conducted between May and July 2008. During July 2008, two versions of the Bagamoyo ESIA appeared. A short version of 64 pages was published by Swedish Radio. ORGUT does not recognize this product, although the signature of the ORGUT lead consultant appears on page two. ORGUT claims that this is a SEKAB T product. How this report found its way into the public sphere is unclear. The second version of the July 2008 report has 187 pages. There were amendments and additions to the July version as compared to the May one. ORGUT's lead consultant had commented on SEKAB's July version of the ESIA, and 'she signed the study team signature page for the study after SEKAB had explicitly accepted the changes she proposed' (ORGUT document, untitled, undated: 1). However, there were more changes and modifications in the SEKAB July version than ORGUT's lead consultant had been aware of. For instance, the following sentences were deleted in the July version: 'The [Bagamoyo district development] profile is clearly not geared towards new investment areas like biofuel or the size of investments planned by SEKAB' and 'The project may want to consider an alternative feedstock to produce ethanol that does not require irrigation.' This was not in agreement with the comments made by ORGUT's lead consultant. Either, then, ORGUT's lead consultant simply did not read carefully the version she signed (considering that the contract with SEKAB had already expired and payment had been finalized), or else changes were made to the ESIA after she had signed. However, it does not appear in the July version what changes were made to the May version and by whom. Changes may have been made by SEKAB T or by consultants from ARU, which had been hired directly by SEKAB T to assist in the preparation of the ESIA for presentation to the NEMC.[25] Yet, according to the lead consultant from ARU, the changes made by its staff before the document was submitted in July were just a matter of structure, not of content.[26]

The July version was passed to the NEMC for review, although ORGUT claims not to have been aware of such a transfer. However, according to our informant from ARU, the restructured report was sent back to ORGUT for its approval before it was submitted. In other words, ORGUT and ARU have quite different versions of what actually took place. On the question of the review, it is not unusual for the EIA department at NEMC to make a brief review of a document before it goes through a more thorough review, to see whether it will conform to the required standards.[27] ORGUT does not consider itself the owner of the July ESIA version over which it seemingly had not had influence.[28] The fact remains, however, that the signature of ORGUT's lead consultant did appear on the ESIA version for which it claims it could not take responsibility.

The NEMC's TAC is said to have assessed SEKAB T's ESIA for the Bagamoyo project, and to have carried out a field visit once the report had been officially submitted for review by the NEMC. Some of the informants we spoke to in the affected villages in Bagamoyo confirm that they received a visit from the NEMC. The reports made by the TAC based on the field visit and other reports by NEMC are supposed to be accessible to the public through the director of the NEMC. However, on our visits to the NEMC in October/November 2009 we could not gain access to the documents, nor could we get them from other sources. Hence, we have no direct insight into the conclusions and comments made by the TAC, or the comments from other relevant ministries, such as the Ministry of Water or the Ministry of Agriculture. Thus, we are unable to comment on the content of these reviews.

The final ESIA for the Bagamoyo project was handed over to the NEMC in December 2008. Information gained from interviews indicates that field studies in relation to the Bagamoyo ESIA had been conducted by SEKAB T and ARU consultants after July 2008. A message from Per Renman of SEKAB T to ORGUT of 20 March 2009 stated:

Box 6.1 Overview of major changes in the December 2008 ESIA for the Bagamoyo SEKAB T biofuel project, as compared to the May 2008 version

'Preliminary ESIA' has been changed to 'Final Report' in the title and throughout the document, and the explanation for why it was called a preliminary report has been deleted: 'It is unfortunate that neither the final plans for the sugarcane farm nor for the ethanol plant were available to the ESIA team for analysis, a fact which precludes many of the final and quantitative analyses which are normally part of an ESIA. The Environmental Information Statement is therefore a preliminary one and points to the most important information gaps which should be remedied before a final report can be produced.'

Text sections about the eight comprehensive baseline studies (vegetation, land use, wildlife, flora and fauna, water resources, socio-economic environment, stakeholders consulted, etc.) have been removed in the report, including the section on ToRs. These baseline studies were not handed in to the NEMC as part of the ESIA. (Deletions and additions: *italic* text shows what has been deleted and <u>underlined</u> text what has been added in the December 2008 ESIA, as compared to the May 2008 version.)

a   *There is a great confusion as to what the 'project area' actually entails.*

b   The socio-economic survey has documented a *relatively large* number of *pastoralist* activities in the area proposed for conversion to bioenergy crops.

c   In addition the people from adjoining villages (*Makarunge, Kdomole* <u>Makurunge</u> and Matipwili) use small bits of the former ranch area for permanent or temporary cultivation.

d   *Identification of Institutional Needs ... The Bagamoyo district developed an investment profile in 2007. Six areas are specifically mentioned: Fruit processing, tourism and hotel development, education, dairying, honey and small scale mining. The profile also highlights the district shortage of forest products and the dependence on firewood and charcoal for cooking. Further the abundance of arable land ... is stressed. Apart from listing jatropha as one of a number of tree species that may be planted in the area there is no mention of sugarcane or biofuel. The profile is clearly not geared towards new investment areas like biofuel or the size of investments planned by SEKAB.*

MITIGATION MEASURES – BIODIVERSITY

e   *... coastal mangrove areas, which may also be affected by the changes in water flow caused by increased intake of river water for project irrigation.*

SOCIAL ECONOMIC INDICATORS

f   *Indicator: Distance and time to collect forest products* g *Indicator: Number of compensation plans to address dislocations associated with the Project's activities*

IMPACTS OF WATER AVAILABILITY

h *Malaria is one of the major tropical diseases associated with irrigation schemes ... [which] lead inevitably to increased malaria in local communities.*

IMPACTS ON BIODIVERSITY

i Conversion of the present vegetation to sugarcane monoculture will have a *huge* significant impact on the local flora and fauna. Under this project most of the wildlife habitats will be destroyed during the process of clearing land for agricultural production.

j *Its [vinasse] acidic character, its high BOD content, and its enormous volume make its treatment the most decisive factor in the total environmental impact of an ethanol distillery.*

This is of concern due to the high COD and BOD levels of vinasse. If untreated vinasse is discharged into rivers and lakes oxygen level will decrease. This may result in death of fish and other aquatic life.

SUMMARY

- *The project may want to consider an alternative feedstock to produce ethanol that does not require irrigation.*
- The *sugarcane* irrigation water requirement is *high* significant. This suggests that, *at certain times of the year or certain years,* that sometimes – water supplies from the river may not *be available* sufficient – the *minimum available* water must be *maintained* left – in the river for geomorphologic and ecological functions.
- *There are serious issues of wildlife migration and loss of biodiversity ...*
- In particular, local governments and the local population should be well-informed about the *extent to which SEKAB BT views its corporate responsibility in terms of provision of social and physical infrastructure. The interviews have shown that there is a great deal of room or serious misunderstanding on these issues* practical implementation of sustainable biofuel production.
- Energy demand and consumption are among the main challenges currently facing the nation. Introduction of a Bioenergy project is a welcome opportunity. Such initiatives not only reduce the demand for fuel importation but also have an impact on poverty reduction through increased employment and income sources. [Does not exist at all in the May version.]

Source: Swedish EIA Centre (2009) Appendix 1 of 'A comparison of ESIA studies in the environmental assessment of SEKAB application to Sida for credit guarantee', prepared for Sida by the Swedish University of Agricultural Sciences.

As you will see in the document [the December 2008 version of the ESIA] we have together with Dr Mato [of ARU] spent considerable time on Quality Assurance of the document as the draft version was found to include many incorrect statements. You will also find from the document that we decided to perform/include a number of additional studies to a) raise the standard of the document to an acceptable level and b) meet the specific questions stated by the NEMC lead Technical Review Committee. For your information NEMC has now submitted the study to the Minister for Environment for final approval. We understand with a strong recommendation for approval. We therefore have nothing against that the study is circulated to Sida.

The lead consultant from ARU to some extent confirms the statement made by SEKAB T, as he claims that the review by the TAC and the relevant sectors raised a number of questions, to which answers had to be provided in the December ESIA report. However, according to the same source, it was not a matter of conducting new studies, but rather of including more information from the baseline studies in the final ESIA report. This was information that had not been considered important enough to include in the first version, but which the review by the TAC and the relevant ministries required.[29] Yet, according to a statement made by SEKAB T, additional 'soil, industrial, biomass and wildlife studies were conducted by a number of subject specific experts. The information was coordinated by EIA Experts from Ardhi University in line with ORGUT's expressed approval.'[30] ORGUT, however, distances itself from both the July version and the December version of the ESIA. A detailed investigation of the December version of the ESIA shows a number of changes to the content of the May preliminary ESIA version, made without the knowledge of ORGUT but still with the ORGUT team leader's signature. SEKAB T, however, through its leader, Anders Bergfors (interviewed on 30 October 2009), stated that SEKAB T had not altered any conclusions, but followed standard procedures as set out by the NEMC. This is in line with the statements on the process that SEKAB T has put up on its website as well.

As indicated above, SEKAB T, as well as ARU's lead consultant and NEMC informants, claims that the changes to the document were made in response to the NEMC's review of the ESIA and that they sought to enhance the quality of the work of ORGUT. The consultants from ARU claim to have been directly contracted by SEKAB T to do this job, but with permission from ORGUT.[31] In our interview with the ARU lead consultant, he particularly stressed that it was a stipulation of his for getting involved in the restructuring process before the formal review of the report took place that the content was not to be changed.[32]

The argument that changes were made in the July ESIA version after the May version to enhance its quality raises some questions. Apparently, the EIA department at the NEMC could have conducted an informal review of the report before it was formally submitted. The informality of the process at this stage is a weakness, as it gives grounds for speculation about what changes were required and why. Moreover, the difficulty of obtaining the written records of what the NEMC required in terms of changes/improvements to the ESIA once it was formally reviewed indicates a process that is not entirely transparent. And finally, contributing to the list of critical questions is the fact that all the important changes made in the December ESIA version (from the May version) have the effect of systematically downplaying issues and risks related to critical environmental aspects, and in particular related to water provision, wildlife and fuel wood (see Box 6.1). In addition, none of the original baseline studies for the ESIA conducted by ORGUT was submitted to the NEMC.

Assessment of the changes made in the various ESIA documents One major weakness of the Bagamoyo ESIA process was the lack of a project or investment feasibility study. It is evident that a sound and relevant ESIA could not be completed in such a context. ORGUT, however, resolved the problem by putting the word 'preliminary' in front of the collection of baseline studies and projects that it presented to SEKAB T (see note 23). In Tanzania, strict guidelines exist for the summary ESIA, which is a synthesis of the baseline studies and environmental and social mitigation approaches to address the impact of the project ESIA. As previously mentioned, for finalization of the ESIA to be submitted to the NEMC, SEKAB T contracted some of the same consultants from ARU that had earlier been subcontracted by ORGUT to prepare the baseline studies. It may not be unreasonable that SEKAB T employed researchers/consultants who had already gained knowledge of the site and area of the proposed project. However, the conflicting statements about the possible changes to the content raise certain questions about the independence and autonomy of the consultants at this stage.

It also appears that the NEMC had demanded further clarifications before it accepted the application for an investment permit. It is not clear what these demands were, since no written record of the NEMC's technical review could be obtained. It is clear, however, that SEKAB T again hired the same consultants from ARU to restructure the report according to NEMC requirements. SEKAB T claims that the final work on the report enhanced the quality of the preliminary ESIA, whereas a detailed review of the changes made between the May and the December versions of the ESIA shows a systematic change to the content to downplay the environmental and social aspects. This is highly questionable, not only because it reduces the reliability of the report, but also since a feasibility study for the project or investment never materialized. It is difficult to understand how the NEMC could accept an ESIA that lacked a feasibility study for the project and that did not come with the baseline studies attached. Considering the core importance of a feasibility study, it is difficult to accept or to understand that this could be explained by lack of capacity or competence solely in the NEMC and other relevant government quarters.

It is reasonable to expect that an ESIA might be improved following scrutiny (and demands) by the relevant government agency, in this case the NEMC. But what stands out in this case is the lack of transparency concerning the instructions about how improvement of the ESIA was to take place (in SEKAB T's case, the July 2008 version). The lack of transparency is particularly noteworthy in this part of the process, as it is prone to potential biases in execution, as is the work related to the original ESIA. We find that the discrepancies in the different versions of the ESIA challenge the accountability of SEKAB T in relation to the ESIA process and also in relation to general CSR guidelines. Limited transparency around the ESIA process in Tanzania makes it possible for SEKAB T to employ double standards: one set for the Swedish-based activities of the mother company, and another set for its subsidiary in Tanzania, SEKAB T. This, however, is not unique to SEKAB and SEKAB T.

ORGUT had a role both in preparing the ESIA and in legitimizing it. By not carefully verifying the full content of the July version of the ESIA, ORGUT came to give legitimacy to SEKAB's Bagamoyo project beyond the stage for which it took responsibility. Ownership of the process and the products associated with its various stages thus needs to be clarified in the ESIA process and be reflected in the contract between investment proponents and consultants. Making the ESIA process more open and transparent would also help various stakeholders to gain insights into the process, which might serve to enhance its quality and governance. Such openness around the processes of government budget allocations and the subsequent tracer studies has, in fact, proved effective, e.g. in the education sector in Uganda and Tanzania.

SEKAB's biofuel project in Rufiji district

Investments in Rufiji district A critical aspect of large-scale biofuel projects is access to land, either for acquisition or lease. The best option for access to land in Tanzania is through the long-term leasing of village land. In a note from February 2009, SEKAB T's land and agricultural manager outlines the process that the company was involved in to access village land for investment. Though a foreign company cannot own land in Tanzania, it can be given a user right or lease through the TIC. The TIC is given ownership of the land by the Commissioner of Land, and a foreign company is given a Derivative Right of Occupancy. This is based on a leasehold system, and the holder will only pay an annual administrative fee for the land. According to the SEKAB T manager, the difficult nature of the process had, by late 2008, led to 'very few foreign investors [having] so far been given such derivative rights'.

In order to access village land, the foreign investor and its local subsidiary – SEKAB T – were urged by the TIC to visit Rufiji district and village authorities, in order to identify and discuss the availability of suitable land. For a village to allow foreign investors to lease village land under derivative rights, the village assembly, which is constituted of all villagers over 18 years of age, must give its consent. Discussions at the village level, however, provide ample scope for misunderstanding, on account of language problems, cultural barriers and insufficient knowledge and information about local rights.[33]

Two major legal and regulatory processes governing village land demarcation and land use should, in principle, have been cleared before land was leased to foreign investors. The village should have received from the Ministry of Lands its 'village land certificate', which is based on cadastral surveys of village borders and a village land use plan (VLUP). As of 2009, fewer than 1,000 of the 11,000 registered Tanzanian villages had received their village land certificates. The VLUP is prepared by the National Land Use Commission and shows the zoning in different uses of village land. According to the commission, the preparation of land use plans 'is the only way to meet requirements for villagers scientifically and find extra land for the biofuels production'.[34] The process of preparing village land use plans is, however, also proceeding very slowly.

According to SEKAB T, the company set in motion the process of accessing village land in Rufiji by following the legal process step by step. By February 2009, SEKAB T was dealing with 13 of the approximately 90 villages in Rufiji district. However, since the VLUPs had not been finalized, SEKAB T 'decided to put the continued discussion with most of the villages on hold until the exercise was finalized'. In only four villages had SEKAB, by February 2009, managed to finalize discussions and demarcations with the villages and been given final approval by the village assemblies (Oscarsson 2009: 4). As well as detailing its handling of the complicated land access process, SEKAB T tries to provide information about its emphasis on sustainability and rights perspectives as guiding criteria for its operations, and about its willingness to enter into 'serious dialogue on how to best achieve social and environmental sustainability'.[35] This was done most recently in response to the draft World Wildlife Fund (WWF)-Sweden report of June 2009 (Roberntz et al. 2009).

Findings from WWF-Sweden's investigation of the SEKAB T biofuel development in Rufiji district The WWF-Sweden report on SEKAB T's plans for large-scale biofuel production in Rufiji district is based on a field trip in late March 2009, which included visits to and discussions with authorities and smallholders in villages where SEKAB T was involved.[36] By combining village maps (obtained in the villages), maps provided by SEKAB T (providing information about its plans), and maps of village land use plans (from the National Land Use Planning Commission), plus findings from interviews, WWF-Sweden emerged with rather a startling picture of SEKAB T's plans in terms of location and possible impacts. It reveals wide discrepancies with SEKAB T's stated objectives, which

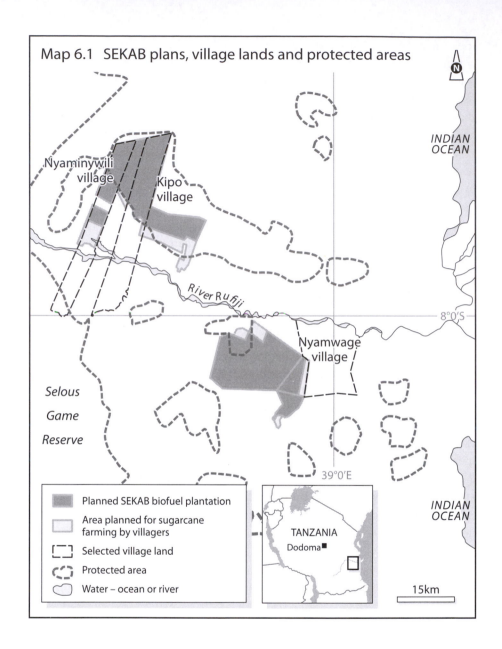

Map 6.1   SEKAB plans, village lands and protected areas

INDIAN OCEAN

Nyaminywili village

Kipo village

River Rufiji

8°0'S

Nyamwage village

Selous Game Reserve

39°0'E

Planned SEKAB biofuel plantation

Area planned for sugarcane farming by villagers

Selected village land

Protected area

Water – ocean or river

TANZANIA
Dodoma■

INDIAN OCEAN

15km

emphasize sustainability and local rights perspectives. The key information provided by WWF-Sweden (Roberntz et al. 2009, which is the basis for the two maps presented here) is as follows.

SEKAB T PLANNED INVESTMENT AREA WWF-Sweden was provided with maps by SEKAB T on two occasions. These indicated similar geographic locations of the project, but the second map showed a smaller area and was more specific in terms of outgrower areas and village boundaries. Whereas the original plan

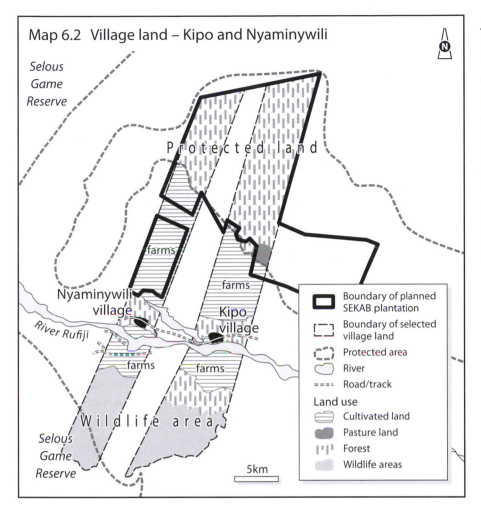

Map 6.2 Village land – Kipo and Nyaminywili

for SEKAB T's Rufiji project was to cover between 300,000 and 400,000 hectares with sugarcane cultivation, the first map received by WWF-Sweden indicated a total project area of only 175,000 hectares. In the second map received by WWF-Sweden, the project area had shrunk further and now totalled about 78,000 hectares (polygons in Map 6.1). About 15 per cent of this land (11,400 hectares) was earmarked for 'outgrower schemes'.

THE NATURE OF 'OUTGROWER SCHEMES' On the basis of interviews and maps that provide the basis for Map 6.1, WWF-Sweden discovered that the outgrower areas adjacent to the SEKAB T project were in fact to employ a sharecropping system, rather than outgrower schemes, which would have given smallholders some influence. The scheme was to be managed by SEKAB T, and any profits would be returned to the villages (after deduction of SEKAB's costs).

OVERLAP BETWEEN SEKAB INVESTMENTS AND CONSERVATION AREAS By combining SEKAB T's map for areas of planned investments with UNEP maps of protected areas in Rufiji district, the WWF-Sweden report shows that the location of the investments would intrude on two forest reserves, Katundu (about 6,000 hectares) located to the south of Rufiji River, and Ruahi River (about 80,000 hectares) to the north (see Map 6.1 and Map 6.2). According to UNEP, these forest reserves are not defined as key biodiversity areas, but as nationally protected areas.

According to the UNEP maps, the areas of SEKAB T's interest in Rufiji district have high (148–563 tonnes carbon/hectare) to medium (101–148 tonnes carbon/hectare) carbon content. According to WWF-Sweden, sugarcane plantations covering 200,000 hectares on such land would potentially transform land that currently stores between 20 million and 113 million tonnes of carbon. By way of comparison, the annual greenhouse gas emissions from road traffic in Sweden are about 20 million tonnes of carbon dioxide, equivalent to 5.5 million tonnes of carbon. Hence, according to WWF-Sweden, if all the carbon stored in the vegetation on 200,000 hectares were released as carbon dioxide, it would equal between four and twenty years' worth of greenhouse gas emissions from the current level of Swedish road traffic.

An initial risk assessment of SEKAB T's large-scale biofuel production in Rufiji district was published in June 2009 (SEI/IRA 2009). This report indicated that SEKAB T's planned production of biofuels would interfere little with carbon sequestration; yet at the same time it stated, somewhat contradictorily, that the risk had not been determined.

PLANNED INVESTMENT AREA, VEGETATION COVER AND CARBON When the WWF-Sweden team superimposed a vegetation map on the SEKAB T map showing the demarcation for sugarcane cultivation (including outgrower areas) on Nyamwage village land, it emerged that the planned sugarcane plantation would be located on wooded grassland. A field visit confirmed that the area was covered by Miombo forest, and it was estimated that the canopy cover exceeded 30 per cent. Old Miombo forests such as the one located in Nyamwage village attract high prices on the timber market, but they also store large quantities of carbon.

PLANNED INVESTMENT AREAS AND VILLAGE LAND USE PLANS Of the eight VLUPs that WWF-Sweden received from the office of the National Land Use Planning Commission, six coincided with SEKAB T's demarcated areas of interest of 78,000 hectares (Map 6.1). The following zonings of village land would, according to the WWF-Sweden analysis, be affected by sugarcane production (as examples, the village land use plans for Kipo and Nyaminywili villages are superimposed on Map 6.2):

VILLAGE	AFFECTED
Kipo (see Map 6.2)	Reserve land (forest), grazing land
Nyaminywili (see Map 6.2)	Reserve land (forest), farmland
Kipugira	Reserve land
Ndundunyikanza	Forest reserve
Ngorongo West	Village forest, investment land, rice fields
Ngorongo East	Investment land, village forest, settlement area

WWF-Sweden's detailed findings at the village level show that SEKAB T's sugarcane plantations will affect village land to different degrees, but in the range of 15 per cent to 77 per cent. The planned sugarcane plantations would, furthermore, reduce farmland available in some villages. Nyaminywili village would transfer 60 per cent of its farmland to sugarcane production, and Ngorongo West 49 per cent (Roberntz et al. 2009: 19). SEI/IRA (2009) assumes that a low risk exists in terms of sugar plantations interfering with food production. However, it fails to provide any documentation of relevant VLUPs. This assumption is in contrast to the findings of WWF-Sweden.

CONSULTATIONS AND COMPENSATION According to interviews conducted by WWF-Sweden in Rufiji villages, SEKAB T's strategy, when consulting with villages and reaching agreements, seems to have been to address one village at a time.[37] WWF-Sweden argues that this approach is likely to undermine the possibility of villages benefiting from fair negotiations, and tensions between villages may emerge as well if there are large discrepancies in the agreements. Interviews conducted in villages indicated that promises had been made by SEKAB T on social development, e.g. the building of schools. No information, however, is provided on the follow-up to such promises. WWF-Sweden is of the opinion, after its brief fact-finding trip, that lack of knowledge among villagers implies a special responsibility on the part of investors to ensure that local livelihood compensation and social development are adequately addressed (Roberntz et al. 2009: 21).

Some assessments The field findings provided by WWF-Sweden regarding SEKAB T's approaches and plans for large-scale biofuel production in Rufiji district show only limited consideration for environmental sustainability. The large-scale sugarcane plantations will partly be located on reserved forestland and will result in land use changes, with negative implications for climate change. Accordingly, it is highly questionable whether the production of biofuel by SEKAB T in Rufiji will adhere to EU sustainability criteria. In addition, the local food security situation is negatively affected by the planned encroachment of large-scale plantations on to village farming areas. The organization of the outgrower schemes seems more like a sharecropping arrangement than a scheme where smallholders can influence production and marketing conditions.

The SEI/IRA initial risk assessment of SEKAB T's investment plans for biofuel production in Rufiji district raised far fewer questions regarding investment risks, climate impact, intrusion on to farming land and natural reserves. However, the analysis and findings of that report were supported by limited cartographic documentation – far less than the findings of the WWF-Sweden report, for which much of the cartographic documentation was obtained from official Tanzanian agencies. The SEI/IRA study is also weak in its analysis of the environmental implications of the planned large-scale irrigated biofuel plantations and, in particular, their impact on environmental flows and fragile downstream ecological systems, although the report does recommend that the issue should be investigated further (Widengård 2009b).

The change in ownership of the Rufiji biofuel project from SEKAB T to EcoDevelopment in Europe does not imply that the challenges related to large-scale biofuel production in Rufiji district are no more. The people responsible for SEKAB T's initiation and for the first phase of implementation of the project are those people who run and own EcoDevelopment in Europe. The rapid expansion and changes connected with large-scale acquisitions and lease of land for biofuel and food lend urgency to the need for legal regulations that can be applied everywhere.

SEKAB T's application for a Credit Enhancement Guarantee

The application The application for a Credit Enhancement Guarantee was submitted to Sida on 28 July 2009. In the application, SEKAB T claims to be a company 'engaged in developing state of the art AgroEnergy projects in Tanzania'. If it received credit, that would enable SEKAB T 'to take the first of our projects to Financial Closure early in 2010 and continue development of the second project [i.e. Rufiji] to activate the first AgroEnergy cluster development in Africa' (SEKAB Bioenergy Tanzania 2009). The application further disclosed that SEKAB, Sweden, was ready to sell SEKAB T and all its East African operations to the minority owners, EcoDevelopment in Europe AB, and furthermore that ethanol purchase and sales agreements were in place between SEKAB T and SEKAB, Sweden, and were ready to be activated. Such agreements, according to the application, 'are essential for continuity and will come into force subject to sufficient funding being secured for the continuing operations in Tanzania'.

The motivation for the sale of SEKAB T to the minority owners is 'an attempt to both separate the African ventures from the municipalities in northern Sweden as well as to maintain the Swedish connection and assure the continuity of the process'. Furthermore, the application makes clear that the Government of Tanzania had been invited to become a 10 per cent shareholder in SEKAB T, and a memorandum of understanding was about to be signed with the Tanzanian Petroleum Development Corporation to work towards its becoming a shareholder of SEKAB T, thus creating the first public–private partnership in the agroenergy sector in Tanzania. The application states that ethanol produced from sugarcane and also electricity co-generation are emerging as major products that can reduce carbon emissions and also provide significant volumes of renewable fuels and electricity to the domestic and international markets. Moreover, the whole undertaking could become an engine for sustainable development in rural areas.

Two districts, Bagamoyo and Rufiji, had been identified for the Tanzania projects. Bagamoyo was at a more advanced stage: 'Land has been identified and demarcated, environmental and social surveys undertaken, and a sugar cane seed farm is established.' The application further argued: 'Equity participation is in place and an agreement with a strategic partner for building the factory and running the agricultural and factory operations is also in place. The project is ready to be taken to the financial market and financial closure is possible early in 2010 when a separate company will be created for the continued operation of the project.'

SEKAB T stated that in Rufiji areas had been identified and secured, soil tests had been carried out and studies conducted to support the planning of potential projects within these areas and to develop a pipeline of future projects for commercialization. It was claimed that 'close and trusted working relationships have been established with the Central Government, local authorities and communities'.[38] In addition, the application stated that detailed risk analysis had been undertaken, in particular in relation to water availability and socio-economic and environmental issues. SEKAB T was advised by local banks in Tanzania that they were unable to lend SEKAB T funds unless a Credit Enhancement Guarantee was in place. The application was signed by the managing director of SEKAB T, Anders Bergfors.

Sida's assessment, preparation and decision on the Credit Enhancement Guarantee Sida's AKTSAM was responsible for the assessment and preparation of the decision on SEKAB T's application for a Credit Enhancement Guarantee. The application and review process was followed with great interest both inside and outside Sida and in government circles in both Sweden and Tanzania. The lobby groups in favour of renewable fuels and rapid agricultural modernization in Africa worked on many levels to support a positive outcome for the application. On the other hand, NGOs, journalists, researchers and activists in Tanzania, Sweden and elsewhere, who had followed the SEKAB case for some years, argued against Swedish government support for SEKAB T's developments in Tanzania.

Sida professionals were also divided in their views and beliefs on the virtue of large-scale biofuel production in Africa and Tanzania, and the organization therefore opted for a thorough assessment of the application. Part of this assessment was conducted by the Sida Help Desk for Environmental Assessment[39] (henceforth the Sida Helpdesk) at the Swedish EIA Centre (SLU). Some of the general comments of the assessment were that:

1 The application documents provided by SEKAB T to Sida made it 'impossible to assess the economic, social as well as the environmental sustainability of the proposed intervention' (the application contained a brief application document, a comfort letter from the Tanzanian Ministry of Energy, and a memorandum of understanding between SEKAB T and the Tanzanian Petroleum Development Corporation).

2 Information was lacking about the funding needs that SEKAB T had vis-à-vis Tanzanian banks and what exactly funding was to be used for. SEKAB T, however, indicated that one project/unit of 20,000 hectares in Rufiji would require an investment of US$450 million. SEKAB T's vision of developing between 200,000 and 400,000 hectares of biofuel production in Rufiji would thus amount to 10–20 units, implying an investment cost of US$4.5–9 billion.

3 The question was raised as to whether the Tanzanian Biofuel Task Force, representing various ministries, had been informed of SEKAB T's application, and if so, what its views were.

The Sida Helpdesk assessment also discussed, at length, the fact that various ESIAs for the project has taken place and that disagreement about the authenticity of the July and the December versions had emerged between the lead consultant company, ORGUT, and SEKAB T. The changes that were made between the 8 May and the December 2008 versions are identified in detail, of which the most important are shown in Box 6.1 above. The assessment also argued that SEKAB T's claim of aiming for full compliance with the EU Renewable Energy Directive (RED) criteria was brought into doubt by the finding of WWF-Sweden that there were considerable overlaps of plantation sites with communal land in use and forest reserves with high carbon stock and species protected by the Convention on International Trade in Endangered Species.[40]

It is also pointed out that, according to the Environmental Management Act, Cap. 191 and the Environmental Impact Assessment and Audit Regulations of 2005, SEKAB T's projects in both Bagamoyo and Rufiji districts were subject to an independent participatory ESIA. In addition, the Rufiji project, due to its size and various potential impacts, could benefit from a SEA, or preferably a SEA at national level could guide investments at the national level.

The Sida Helpdesk assessment went on to make brief conclusions about opportunities and risks associated with the projects, based on a number of studies.[41] The areas assessed include (i) water, (ii) socio-economic, (iii) land use/smallholders, (iv) biodiversity, (v) climate change, (vi) Tanzanian regulation and policy framework, (vii) national economy, (viii) sustainability of large-scale biofuel investments. The assessment concluded that:

It is important to look at alternative development pathways for Rufiji and Bagamoyo mentioned in the reports on which this assessment is based, referring to current livelihoods and natural resource use, needs and traditions locally, and compare it with risks and opportunities provided by investments suggested by SEKAB.

The major concerns expressed include SEKAB T's adjustments of the ESIA study, the lack of clarity regarding exactly where and for what the borrowed money would be used, the risks for environment and social well-being expressed in studies reviewed, and the fact that the Tanzanian regulation was not yet prepared to handle biofuel investments of this scale. Moreover, due to the overlap in Rufiji with forest reserves, the investment did not, in its current form, fulfil EU sustainability criteria (Sida Helpdesk for Environmental Assessment 2009).

Sida's decision on the Credit Enhancement Guarantee was dated 29 October 2009, and the main reasons for rejecting the application were as follows:[42]

1 The request for a guarantee does not fulfil the requirements of the new ordinance – Development Loans and Guarantees (e.g. one of the criteria is that procurement of products or services shall be made with international competition).
2 Guarantees are intended to support specific projects, not the financing of development costs.
3 The social and the 'green' environmental risk are deemed to be high (impact on sensitive and already threatened environments) in relation to the potential advantages of the project.
4 Uncertainty whether the EU's sustainability criteria will be met.
5 Tanzania's legal framework is too fragile to manage biofuel investments of the type and magnitude proposed by SEKAB.

Main conclusions regarding SEKAB's biofuel plans in Tanzania and their implications

There are three main issues that call for concluding comments based on the above findings. One concerns the Tanzanian capacity to deal with large-scale, cross-cutting projects like biofuel investments, and particularly the capacity of the NEMC to handle these. The second issue concerns the consultants and how they relate to the proponent, as well as to government agencies involved in the ESIA process. And thirdly, there is the issue relating to the ethical conduct of the investors, in this particular case SEKAB and SEKAB T.

It seems that the NEMC has an elaborate structure that can ensure the promotion of high-quality ESIAs. Yet there is lack of clarity and transparency on the follow-up process once an ESIA has been submitted to it. That the

NEMC provides unofficial reviews of the quality of ESIAs before the formal transfer of an ESIA document leaves room to question not only the transparency of the process, but also the relationship between the project proponent and the NEMC. With reference to the Bagamoyo ESIA report, the informal review conducted by the NEMC before the July 2008 ESIA submission gives grounds for questioning the reliability of the report. Moreover, due to certain restrictions on access to review material from the TAC and relevant sectors, the ESIA process – particularly in the period July–December – was not transparent and lacked clarity on responsibilities. The NEMC needs to be clear as to its formal procedures, and must follow these closely in all cases, in order to avoid any doubts emerging about the legitimacy and accountability of the ESIA process, and hence the content of an ESIA report. Easing access to written documentation on ESIA reviews would improve the transparency of the process, as would some clarification on the responsibility of an independent executor of an ESIA study and on what 'independent' means in relation to the proponent of the project. As the experience in the Bagamoyo case has shown, unless this is clarified, environmental and socio-economic issues risk being inadequately addressed in the ESIA process.

It also emerges that the NEMC needs to increase its capacity to assess ESIAs for major projects of a cross-cutting nature, and to be able to carry out control of mitigating measures once projects are approved. A particular weakness in the Bagamoyo biofuel project is the lack of a feasibility study as an input for the project ESIA. The decision by the NEMC to grant an investment licence to a project without baseline studies being submitted and without foundation in a proper feasibility study indicates that the problems go beyond lack of competence and capacity.

With reference to the role of the consultant, it is clear that the lead consultant, ORGUT, and its sub-consultants from ARU should not have compromised on the need for a proper feasibility study. Adding 'preliminary' to the title of the May version of the ESIA does not absolve ORGUT of its responsibility to promote sound procedures. However, the company is probably not the first to have made such compromises. This reflects a challenge that the consultancy industry faces generally, both as individuals and as companies, in the struggle to generate income. SEKAB, Sweden, can also be held responsible, as the majority owner of SEKAB T, for not ensuring that formal procedures were followed properly for the production of the ESIA for the Bagamoyo project.

SEKAB, Sweden, is an experienced and municipally owned Swedish energy company with a vision of contributing to sustainability. However, the role played by SEKAB T in the ESIA process in Bagamoyo and in its project plan for biofuel development in Rufiji district shows that the companies have failed in important areas to deliver on the recommendations of research institutions and UN agencies.[43] How can a company that is held in high esteem internationally for its technological developments in Sweden plan its activities in Tanzania with the shortcomings and faults presented above? The weaknesses of the ESIA and the planning processes in both Bagamoyo and Rufiji give not only reason to question some of the Tanzanian bureaucratic processes, but also SEKAB's ethical standards for its Tanzanian operations, as well as the responsibilities and rights of the consultant in the follow-up process. It emerges, too, that voluntary standards or guidelines for biofuel production will most likely not be adhered to. Internationally accepted codes of conduct for large-scale land acquisitions and leases are needed to address the situation – codes that have 'teeth', i.e. that can be enforced. So far these are still lacking.

It should be acknowledged, however, that SEKAB T has taken an active and constructive role in creating a space for the discussion and promotion of regulations and guidelines for the bioenergy sector in Tanzania, in cooperation with donors such as Sida and Norad, and in dialogue with relevant Tanzanian ministries and agencies. On the basis of meetings, interviews and field visits to Tanzania, we found that SEKAB T had acquired the relevant competence, both Tanzanian and foreign, to initiate the process of acquiring land for biofuel production. Operation managers and SEKAB T officials on the ground had sufficient experience to understand the complexities of accessing land for biofuel production. But the leadership of SEKAB, both in Sweden and Tanzania, took shortcuts in the ESIA process, and this compromised its quality.

With regard to the role played by donors and NGOs, the Swedish embassy in Tanzania took a positive view of biofuel developments in the country – in particular the plans of SEKAB T. The Swedish and the Norwegian aid agencies both supported Tanzania in developing much-needed guidelines and a regulatory framework for the biofuel sector, and subsequently also biofuel policies. NGOs have played a critical role by exposing the content and implications of SEKAB T's plans in Bagamoyo and Rufiji through reports from the field and advocacy work. Important information that was not properly identified or assessed in the various consultancy reports supporting the EIA and planning processes has been made available, and this has thrown new light on SEKAB T's projects. The NGOs have thus shown their capacity to provide insights into the complexities of biofuel promotion in Tanzania and Africa generally. However, the rapid appraisals and studies – although at times employing considerable ingenuity, e.g. the WWF-Sweden report of Roberntz et al. (2009) – also reveal a lack of knowledge of context and the absence of a critical faculty when assessing the information retrieved from interviewees.

7 | Agro-investments in Zimbabwe at a time of redistributive land reforms

Prosper B. Matondi[1]

Introduction

The acquisition by big investors of large areas of land for the production of agricultural commodities, for forestry, mining and the provision of environmental amenities has recently attracted considerable interest. The phenomenon has been described as 'land grabbing' when large-scale acquisitions of land in Africa, Latin America, Central Asia and South East Asia are undertaken – by international and domestic investors alike – as an investment in land-related developments (Cotula et al. 2009; FAO, IFAD, UNCTAD and the World Bank Group 2010). Various terms have been bandied about in the media on the subject of land grabbing in Africa, 'land grabbing' being defined as the search for and accessing of land outside the borders of one's own country for the purposes of investment. Alongside 'land grabbing', we hear such terms as 'commercialization', 'colonization', 'climate colonialism', 'new imperialism', 'agro-investments', 'new land invasions' ... Large-scale land acquisition can be broadly defined as the acquisition (by purchase, lease, etc.) of land areas of over 1,000 hectares (Cotula et al. 2009). Land acquisition includes not only the purchase of ownership rights, but also the acquisition of use rights, for instance through leases or concessions, and may be short or long term. Cotula et al. (2009) then characterized the land deals in their basic form as deals that involve at least two parties, arguing that:

> On the one hand, there is an acquirer. In the African context, this is generally a private or joint equity company, but it can also be a foreign government acquiring land directly. On the other side of the deal is a land provider, either a government or, much more rarely, a private land-owner.

In the case of Zimbabwe, all aspects of land acquisition are handled by government, with local communities retaining the rights to use and manage land. In this case, government can compulsorily acquire customary land, because the land is government owned, held in trust by the president.

The terms 'grabbing' or 'invasion' have been used to draw attention to the impact on local communities and to the potential for dispossession (Hall 2010; Cotula et al. 2009). Yet, in the Zimbabwean context, it would seem that the type of land grab is different, as will be explained in this chapter. Zimbabwe experienced land occupations (also termed land invasions) of white-owned farms from 2000, which led to the fast-track land reform programme. The occupations were done by local Zimbabweans and grabbed international headlines (which have remained a constant feature over the last ten years). However, the domestic land occupations (or land grabs) are distinct from the current wave of land grabs, which have an international dimension and are driven by interests other than poverty reduction. The land grabs in Zimbabwe also differ because domestic private elite interests in the economy are partnering foreigners who are leasing state land for agro-investments. This is different from what Colombant (2010) described as

> the trend of buying up farmland by private investors from food-insecure, but land-rich nations in third world countries, especially in Africa, which is displacing people ... but more important, it is called 'land grab' because it is the grabbing of resources, which are absolutely essential for ensuring food security in these countries.

However, the agro-investments in Zimbabwe by domestic investors do still pose serious threats to the land rights of local people. The current agro-investments are not informed by local needs and interests, which creates a situation whereby a few elites, in partnership with foreign investors, seem to (or will potentially) benefit from the agro-investment deals. The private sector (national and international) has partnered with the state to benefit economically from land that ideally would have been intended for public resettlement. It would seem that some former landowners who lost their land are coming back with a new model of partnering the state to get back into agriculture. In this chapter, I draw attention to Zimbabwe's new forms of land investments, which have been highly contested at the local level (*Sunday Mail* 2010).

Three public and private agro-investment projects are analysed as a basis for understanding Zimbabwe's position with respect to domestic corporate investors who partner foreign investors in accessing land. It should be said that the three projects emerged and were funded by a public parastatal, domestic and international private interests. The first project is a jatropha project, implemented by the government throughout the country with the intention of producing fuel internally, at a time when the country faced serious fuel shortages due to the economic crisis. Government was unable to pay for fuel supplies due to the economic crisis it faced then. The second project, in Chisumbanje, Manicaland province, is a private–public partnership between the government – through the parastatal Agriculture and Rural Development Authority (ARDA) – and domestic and local investors in a private company called Zimbabwe Bio-Energy Ltd. The project utilizes ARDA estates to grow sugarcane for biodiesel. The third project involves a private trust (Development

Trust of Zimbabwe) that belongs to the former Zimbabwe African People's Union Patriotic Front (ZAPU-PF) (which was led by the late Joshua Nkomo, one of the leaders of the national liberation struggle). This trust has teamed up with local investors in Zimbabwe Bio-Energy Ltd, in a project to utilize Nuanetsi in Mwenezi, Masvingo province. The two latter projects thus have in common a single private investor driving the agro-investments.

Zimbabwe's dilemma of foreign investment in land

Zimbabwe embarked upon a land reform programme in 2000, whereby land has been transferred through compulsory acquisition from large owners to small and medium-sized farmers. The land reform and resettlement programme affected ownership of the large-scale commercial agricultural sector. Some 160,000 new owners (on close to 7 million hectares) displaced 4,500 mainly white, large-scale farmers, who occupied roughly the same area of land across the country. It is estimated that, of the 12.4 million hectares of commercial land, government has acquired 10.4 million. The remainder is still owned by large commercial farmers, and some of it is still contested, by being occupied, without legal authority, by new land 'owners'. In less than ten years, the large-scale commercial sector has been transformed and is largely in the hands of small-scale producers. As the transfers have taken place, a large part of the land in the possession of smallholders has been taken out of production on account of a variety of factors (Matondi et al. forthcoming).

A key result of this massive land transfer, which has occurred over a short period of time and without adequate resources, has been land underutilization, and this has affected a range of agricultural commodities. In response, the government decided to allow the revival of large-scale commercial farming on uncontested land. Such land may have been deliberately omitted from acquisition because it was being productively used for agricultural purposes. However, it is also the case that some land owned by the government, or by trusts in which the government has shares, seems to have been spared from the resettlement exercise. At the same time, the Zimbabwean government has been encouraging the targeting of land owned by its parastatals for agricultural revival, so that they might contribute to food security. In the case of the ARDA-owned land in Chisumbanje, domestic and foreign investors identified an opportunity to make a contribution to agricultural revival by partnering government in agro-investments.

Given this context, the accessing of land by foreigners in Zimbabwe does not, strictly speaking, follow the same trends as on the rest of the continent and beyond. Given Zimbabwe's experience of forced land takeovers, it hardly makes sense for foreign investors to want land in Zimbabwe. Yet, it would seem that outside interest in Zimbabwe's land remains very high. In a comparison of land grabbing in Africa, Sam Moyo (a Zimbabwean land expert), speaking at a conference in Cape Town in March 2010, described Zimbabwe's experience of international investment in its land as 'dissident with conformity'. Thus Zimbabwe's agro-investments need to be understood differently from the global rush for land by foreigners, as is seen in other parts of Africa and in Latin America. It is also different in the sense that it comes at a time when Zimbabwe is implementing a land reform programme that has largely targeted foreign-owned land.

Context of large-scale foreign land ownership in Zimbabwe

Foreign land investment in Zimbabwe is not new. Though the area under former white landowners has been reduced, foreigners still retain a large amount of land under bilateral promotion and protection agreements (BIPPAs). Such BIPPA farms have all shades of foreign ownership – British, German, Malaysian, South African, Malawian, Dutch, Chinese, etc. Yet, some of the land is still owned under non-BIPPA arrangements by foreign-owned multinational companies that are not domiciled in Zimbabwe. However, some individual landowners are said to have claimed BIPPA protection when such agreements did not exist, in order to avoid the land being compulsorily acquired for resettlement by the government (MLRR 2009). This forced the government to review all BIPPAs, especially in relation to land and agriculture. The outcomes of this review have not been made public. Since the start of the land reform programme, and in view of Zimbabwe's international isolation, government began to establish relations with countries such as China, Libya and Iran that have different political ideological relations with Africa compared to Western nations, under what was dubbed the 'Look East Policy' (Horta 2008).[2]

The media reported that Libyans had tried a 'land for fuel' deal at the height of the fuel crisis in 2002, but that it failed to work.[3] In addition, internet reports indicated that the Chinese were buying massive tracts of land for agriculture and agro-industries – one source indicated that, in 2008, they acquired 101,171 hectares for agricultural purposes (Horta 2008). The Malaysians were said to have invested in agriculture in the eastern parts of the country through a company called Matansuka Investments, but under BIPPA arrangements. However, it is the presence of Brazilian technicians, who are assisting in the establishment of an ethanol plant in the south-eastern part of the country, that raises questions about the role of emerging countries in biofuel investments.

The Zimbabwean government has a specific aversion to land ownership by foreigners, which has been apparent in its land reform programme. The racial dimension of the ownership of land and the associated discrepancies – large land holdings by whites (an average of 2,000 hectares) in generally the most fertile parts of the country versus less than one hectare held by most blacks, in mainly poor or degraded communal areas – were sore points that were translated into political action. In addition, the presence of multinationals with strong international linkages, and the affluence of those with land at a time when the majority of Zimbabweans were poor provided a motive for the political protests, which resulted in the land reform programme. While some commercial farms under BIPPA performed exceptionally well in terms of production, overall the majority of companies tended to underutilize their land. Zimbabweans were also unhappy about the nationality and citizenship of large landowners, and felt that BIPPAs were unfair, because no Zimbabwean could easily gain access to land in the countries with which BIPPAs existed, and yet this was a key condition of the agreements (MLRR 2009).

Government officials acknowledge that, because of the speed with which the land reform programme was undertaken, there was no proper prior consideration of how foreign-owned land that the government had agreed upon would be handled. At the outset of the land reform programme in 2000, the principle was that farms covered by country-to-country bilateral investment agreements were exempt from the redistribution efforts. However, in the period between 2000 and 2003, the government came to review this policy (Utete Report 2003). Dakarai (2009) noted that there were 14 countries (out of 51 BIPPAs) that owned 277 farms, with a total of 1,015,288.286 hectares. Of these 277 farms, 214 had been resettled in the A1 or A2 model,[4] with about 6,011 beneficiaries. It was established that some of these agreements had still to be ratified by parliament. Government then established a cabinet committee to investigate the question of BIPPA farms, paying particular attention to possible criteria for listing or delisting some of the farms, based on whether the farms had met the investment thresholds after the signing of the agreements. In addition, the committee was tasked with examining whether the properties concerned were covered by export regulations, and whether there was any possibility of swapping such properties, depending on their suitability for resettlement.

On the BIPPA-owned farms, government took steps to evict some land occupiers for failing to comply with the BIPPAs. However, in some cases it also had parallel programmes for negotiating land sharing through a process called 'coexistence', whereby, in problematic cases, where the removal of settlers appeared difficult, the BIPPA owner was left with part of a farm and the settlers had some land. Government also promised compensation, although it had no resources to pay it. The issue of foreign ownership of land needs to be viewed in the context of the international politics of Zimbabwe's land reform programme. The government may have had the feeling that, because it was isolated by Western nations, whose citizens were also the beneficiaries of BIPPAs, it had no obligation to honour those BIPPAs. The benefits of the BIPPAs in agriculture were questioned, in light of the pressure for access to land and the fact that some of the properties were above the maximum farm size thresholds set by government. Therefore, in seeking to explain foreign investment in land at a time when Zimbabwe's land reform programme has not been resolved completely, we encounter a lot of questions. What is it that gives foreign and domestic investors confidence in what seems to be a risky market?

History of agrofuels in Zimbabwe and the context of sugarcane production

Agriculture for fuel production is not a new phenomenon in Zimbabwe, since the production of ethanol extracted from sugarcane was initiated and concentrated in Zimbabwe's (Rhodesia's) Lowveld region in the early 1960s. The Anglo American Corporation (AAC) built an ethanol plant at the height of international sanctions against the white minority government of Ian Smith, the last prime minister of Rhodesia before Zimbabwe's independence in 1980. The objective was to hedge against international sanctions imposed on the Smith administration. The plant produced ethanol from sugarcane grown on vast estates owned by AAC and other firms, in the country's hot south-eastern region (Dove 2007).

The project was abandoned at the height of the Economic and Structural Adjustment Programme in 1991, due to the high costs (relative to fuel imports) and because the ethanol produced accounted for only a small proportion of the country's fuel requirements. The drought of 1991–92 also affected operations in the Lowveld areas, reducing sugarcane production. The fuel component was therefore de-emphasized. Because of its harmful effects, the use of benzene was banned in the extraction of ethanol from sugarcane, and this also contributed to the closure.

The sugar-growing sector in Zimbabwe has always been dominated by private multinational companies. The country has two large sugarcane milling companies: Hippo Valley Estates (a local public company, with just over 50 per cent of shares owned by Triangle Sugar Corporation) and Triangle Limited (owned by Tongaat-Hullet, a large South African conglomerate). The two factories receive 30 per cent of their sugar from private independent commercial growers and the remainder from their own estates called Mkwasine. Thanks to the excellent growing conditions, they can produce 600,000 tonnes of sugar at low cost (by world standards). In 1999, sugar was being produced on about 43,000 hectares (with an output of 463,000 tonnes); by 2007, this had dropped to 36,000 hectares (and an output of about 300,000 tonnes). These figures prompted the government and stakeholders to search for ways of arresting the decline.

Under a sugarcane production adaptation strategy supported by the European Union, government sources indicate that they intend to increase the area under sugarcane to more than 140,000 hectares and to reduce fuel imports by 15 per cent. Most of the sugar produced is sold on the domestic market, though some is also exported to the EU and the USA (a quota of 12,800 tonnes). The push for agro-investments in the production area in the south-eastern parts of the country is within this context of agricultural revival. Yet the biofuels discourse and the international interests it has generated seem to have suited Zimbabwe's history of ethanol production. In fact, policy-makers have identified a new stream of opportunities that could benefit the country by attracting foreign and domestic investors into the agricultural sector.

The push for large-scale commercial land investments

In 2005, the government approached several local and international companies, including Anglo American Zimbabwe, with a proposal to revive the defunct Triangle ethanol-processing plant, located in Lowveld in Masvingo province. In return, the government was offering to restore some of the land it had seized from Anglo American as part of its land redistribution programme. By 2010, the Triangle processing plant was producing alcohol and other chemical substances, though in relatively small quantities. But the installation of new dehydration technology as part of the revival of the Triangle plant was expected to result in the production of enough ethanol to help the government meet its target of reducing its fuel import bill by 15 per cent by 2010. At the end of 2010 it was clear that this target – for private companies (including the Triangle and Chisumbanje plants) and the jatropha ethanol plant in Harare managed by NOCZIM – would not be met. While the NOCZIM plant in Harare was operational, it suffered from lack of enough jatropha to produce diesel. On the other hand, the Triangle and Chisumbanje plants were slow to build up their infrastructure, and hence the actual production of ethanol had to be deferred several times.

In 2004, Triangle Ltd engaged Praj Industries (a leading ethanol distiller and production company listed on the Bombay Stock Exchange and the National Stock Exchange of India) as a technical partner and consultant to design and install the ethanol plant. This was after negotiation with the National Oil Company of Zimbabwe (NOCZIM) a government parastatal that was to be a key partner. NOCZIM was supposed to be the key customer for the ethanol produced from Triangle sugarcane, which NOCZIM would process and sell as fuel and other byproducts to the public. This project was, however, overtaken by new domestic investors, who entered into a land leasing arrangement with the Development Trust of Zimbabwe (DTZ) at Nuanetsi ranch to create Zimbabwe Bio-Energy Ltd (ZBE), which will be discussed below.

In view of the economic crisis, and specifically the energy crisis that Zimbabwe faced, the government expressed an interest in this and started to work towards resurrecting ethanol production. Over the years, investment in energy has expanded to include general agricultural commercial production, spearheaded by ARDA. At the preparatory stage, politicians lauded the project

---

Box 7.1 Testimony of a former parastatal chief executive officer

Back in early 1994, having come out of the devastating drought of 1991/92, as chief executive of the Grain Marketing Board (GMB), I was approached by Clive Nicolle, representing the Lions Den Syndicate. This was a group of commercial farmers stretching from Banket through Chinhoyi to Lions Den. He had a biofuel project, whose raw material was going to be maize and soya beans.

These farmers wanted my and GMB's support for this project, which was going to provide fuel and save this country large amounts of foreign currency. Large swathes of land were going to be put under maize and soya production for biofuels. After a careful study of the effects of the project; considering that Mashonaland West was the main producer of food; considering further that there was no offer or plans for expansion in order to maintain the land taken for growing crops for biofuels, I told the farmers that we could not support their project. Failure to get our support as GMB then killed the project.

Source: Gasela (2009).

---

as one of the largest agro-investments by 'local Zimbabweans' in Manicaland and Masvingo provinces. The ZBE entered the Zimbabwean agriculture sector with aggressive media campaigns. Advertisements featuring land use layout plans were splashed in the newspapers.

Speaking on a television programme called *Business Talk with Supa Mandiwanzira*, the chairman of ARDA's board was upbeat about the prospects of 'heavy' investment in agriculture to unlock value 'unparalleled' since independence. At the same time, the white managers, many of them former commercial farmers whose land had been taken during the land reform programme, have been at the forefront in presenting the project to the Zimbabwean public as the greatest investment ever in the country's agriculture. The project is depicted as a high-technology and complex agrarian investment in Zimbabwe. With the high-tech machines now a regular feature in the south-eastern part of the country, this suggests optimism in a country that has been starved of investment. The high technology has been a key feature in selling the project to the broader public, and complex 'green' architectural designs and plans have appeared in the print media.

Yet behind this aggressive media campaign there are real fissures about the implications of the agro-investments. For a start, local people and local politicians have voiced strong objections to the projects in both Chisumbanje and Mwenezi districts. In the case of the DTZ and the Nuanetsi ranch, there were moves to remove people who had moved on to the farm by force at the height of the domestic land grabs in 2000. When DTZ and ZBE decided to invest in the new project, the people who had forcibly occupied the land were deemed illegal occupants. Government defended the investors by noting that the Nuanetsi ranch was not part of the land to be compulsorily acquired, because it was indigenously owned by a private trust that was owned by blacks (and controlled the land, which had belonged to ZAPU-PF before it united with ZANU-PF in 1987). However, this did not amuse politicians in Masvingo province, who started to question the rationality of the promised investments vis-à-vis the objectives of the land reform programme. Some local politicians in Masvingo province argued in a literal sense that: 'it does not make sense to remove some whites and to bring whites on the same land we are taking from them'. Kahiya (2009) wrote:

> Zanu PF leaders in Masvingo registered their intent to take away the estate from DTZ two years ago when [the] then provincial governor ... wrote to [the] Land Reform minister ... demanding that the government acquire Nuanetsi ranch to resettle thousands of villagers in the area on the pretext that the land was lying idle. 'It would be unfair to leave such land idle when thousands of Zimbabweans need land,' he reportedly said. The attempt to settle people on the estate was blocked ... But parts of Nuanetsi have been occupied by villagers at the behest of politicians. Attempts to move them have failed ... There are now accusations that DTZ is driving out black farmers to bring dispossessed white farmers onto the land.

Yet, despite local political pressure and protests, the investors and technical managers have continued with their project. It seems that access to higher political authorities provides leverage in dealing with the political landmine that is the Zimbabwe land issue. The investors have continued their agricultural revival work, knowing full well that, for the time being, the government seems desperate for an injection of external cash and technical expertise to get commercial agriculture moving again.

Government-led investments in agrofuels

Arguments for going green through jatropha Zimbabwe faced a serious fuel crisis between 2001 and 2008, to the extent that it needed to rethink its energy strategies, given its inability to pay for external fuel. The jatropha-growing project sought to mitigate the negative impacts of the steady rise in international fuel prices. The aim was largely to improve the security of fuel supply and to ensure self-sufficiency in the face of dwindling foreign exchange reserves. At the same time, Zimbabwe used environmental reasons, such as the contribution to reducing carbon emissions and the rehabilitation of degraded land, as key arguments for promoting the growing of jatropha. Yet jatropha production was not entirely new, as commercial producers had attempted it in the 1990s.

In 1992, a group of large-scale commercial farmers formed the Plant Oil Producers' Association (POPA) with the objective of producing jatropha on a large scale (Dove 2007). The activities of POPA slowed down when the farmers discovered that jatropha fuel profit margins were lower than expected, especially because there was no possibility of mechanically harvesting the seeds. The NGO sector also attempted the commercialization of jatropha by initially introducing two plant oil projects in Zimbabwe. In 1996, the Binga Trees Trust and the Biomass Users' Network (in Binga and Mutoko districts, respectively) were targeted for production, following the discovery that the plant was abundant in these areas (Tigere et al. 2006; Dove 2007; Wyeth 2002). A key objective was to promote the commercial exploitation of jatropha, as a living fence, to produce oil for use as fuel, especially for the benefit of smallholder farmers.

Jatropha production strategies In Zimbabwe, jatropha was reintroduced as a 'fuel wonder crop' in the 2005/06 farming season. Government set up a National Biodiesel Feedstock Production Programme, targeting communal farmers, new farmers, schools, private companies and national institutions. The feedstock was to be grown as hedges, scattered plantings, on contour bunds, along highways, on degraded lands and gullies, as dedicated fields and as large-scale plantations (SIRDC 1998). The government of Zimbabwe set up a taskforce to promote a programme for community-owned jatropha nurseries in various districts. According to the government, there were approximately 2.5 million seedlings in individual nurseries. As of 2010, an estimated 6,000 hectares of land were under jatropha. This was achieved through the efforts of institutions, individual farmers, youth and women's groups and commercial estates. The outgrower scheme was poised for expansion over the rest of the country, especially in the semi-arid areas.

In Zimbabwe, areas that have been found to have a higher concentration of jatropha include Hwange, Victoria Falls, Binga, Shamva, Mutoko, Masvingo and parts of Manicaland. The government aimed to purchase 60,000 tonnes of jatropha seed for planting to meet the national target. The planned full-scale jatropha production was to contribute to a strategic local liquid fuel content of at least 10 per cent of Zimbabwe's annual fossil diesel consumption (110 million litres of biodiesel) by 2010. However, this implied that at least 122,000 hectares of jatropha would be required to meet the national target (Tigere et al. 2006; AREX 2006).

Trend analysis of the production patterns of jatropha is difficult because much of the information is not in the public domain. Based on media reports and a NOCZIM press statement, we found that, in the 2006 production season, the targeted area for production was 40,000 hectares, and that this target

Box 7.2 Outcomes of investment in jatropha for biodiesel in Zimbabwe

Little oil trickles out of bio-diesel plant

The country's first commercial bio-diesel plant, commissioned amid pomp and fanfare last year, is operating at less than five percent capacity, investigations revealed last week. Workers at the gigantic plant in Harare – once touted as the panacea to the country's perennial [*sic*] – said they were producing 'a few hundreds of liters' of diesel and cooking oil a month. They attributed the false start to an acute shortage of Jatropha, cotton seed, sunflower, soya beans and maize to produce diesel and cooking oil.

When standardbusiness visited the plant just before midday on Thursday, the plant with a capacity to produce between 90–100 million liters of diesel annually was silent. 'For the past year, we have been using cotton seed for the production of diesel and cooking oil but it has run out,' said a worker speaking on condition that he was not named. 'We can't use maize or soya beans because there is hunger. People need them for food.'

At least 500 tonnes [*sic* – 500,000 tonnes] of seed oil is required annually to produce the targeted 100 million liters of bio-diesel. 'We have to wait for the Jatropha seedlings to mature otherwise we are wasting our time,' said another worker. It takes between two and three years for a Jatropha seedling to mature. The worker said when the fuel is available at the plant anyone can buy using foreign currency. He said initially they were selling the diesel for US$1.35 a liter, but the price was being reviewed following the drop in fuel prices globally. Only one of the tanks was said to be full of diesel, which was being sold in foreign currency.

... During the plant's commissioning last year, government officials said it would meet 10% of Zimbabwe's annual diesel requirements, which translates to foreign currency savings of US$80 million annually. RBZ Governor Gideon Gono said the central bank has set aside funds to support a Jatropha feed stock growing programme. 'Under the programme beneficiaries of Zimbabwe's land reform programme will receive support to grow Jatropha on marginal land as the country works towards its target of achieving fuel self-sufficiency by 2010,' said Gono. He also announced government would set up one bio-diesel plant for each of the provinces by 2010. However, the project seems to have stalled ...

Experts however say there is need to guard against diverting productive land and food crops to the production of biofuels at the expense of regional food security. The World Food Programme (WFP) says over five million people will need food aid at the beginning of next year.

Source: *Zimbabwe Standard* (2008).

area decreased to 35,000 hectares in the 2007/08 farming season. Yet in 2008, only 10,000 hectares were put under jatropha. In the 2007/08 season, about 30 million seedlings were made available by NOCZIM to generate 50,000 litres of biodiesel. In the 2008/09 farming season, the targeted area increased to 65,000 hectares of jatropha. Whereas large farmers had initially viewed the crop with great anticipation, many gradually ended up not regarding it as a crop of choice. This led the government oil company NOCZIM to turn its attention to the smallholder outgrower scheme.

In anticipation of higher jatropha output, in 2004 the Reserve Bank of Zimbabwe (RBZ) invested in a test vehicle and bio-reactor at Harare Polytechnic College. In 2007, construction was completed of an agrofuel processing plant, built by the South Koreans with funding from RBZ. The plant was described as the only one of its kind in Africa and only the fifth in the world. The high-tech processing plant had the capacity to produce more than 100 million tonnes of fuel annually. The cost of the plant was stated to be more than US$80 million. At the national level, successful experiments on conversion to biodiesel were conducted at the Harare Polytechnic. Before 2008, the RBZ was involved in quasi-fiscal activities, including funding of this project, but this was stopped when the government was restructured following the formation of the Inclusive Government. The project seems to have been de-prioritized as the role of the RBZ shifted to monetary policy management. There is not much information on the jatropha project, but small community jatropha production and processing promoted by NGOs continues in such areas as Binga and Mutoko. One of the questions to reflect on is whether it was a good strategy on the part of the government to invest in jatropha on such a large scale.

The contested economics behind jatropha production The issue of biofuel production in Africa raises pertinent emotional and moral questions. The fact that biofuels are about satisfying international – and particularly Western – demand for energy fuels such tensions. Zimbabwe requires 5 million litres of diesel and 3 million litres of petrol daily. If the country were to put 500,000 hectares of land under jatropha – and assuming a high yield of 4 tonnes per hectare – about 2,000,000 tonnes of jatropha would be harvested. A tonne of jatropha produces 300 litres of diesel. This means that 666,000 litres of diesel could be generated. What would be the effect of putting 500,000 hectares under this crop, as against food crops? These are good questions in view of the very optimistic estimates, which biofuel production has so far been unable to meet.

Jatropha as a crop for the poor Jatropha oil is an important product in terms of the cooking and lighting needs of the rural population. Replacing firewood with plant oil for household cooking in rural areas will not only alleviate the problems of deforestation, but will also improve the health of rural women,

TABLE 7.1 Key production characteristics in Chisumbanje and Mwenezi project agro-investments

Province	Enterprise	Area/Quantity	Expected production output
Manicaland (Chisumbanje and Middle Sabi)	Sugarcane	40,000 hectares of land are under sugarcane production (2010)	525,000 litres of ethanol and 18.5 MW of power daily (to light 24/7 a city like Mutare, with a population of close to 1 million)
	Wheat	1,000 hectares planted in winter of 2009 (against projections of 3,000 to 4,000 hectares)	?
Masvingo (Mwenezi)	Sugarcane	100,000 hectares of land out of the entire estate of 350,000 (1 per cent of Zimbabwe's land area)	?
	Crocodile farming	100,000 (the target is 300,000)	For export
	Cattle	5,000 herds of cattle (target is 50,000)	Local and export beef markets
	Tourism	Game farming and tourism (chalets)	Local and international markets

Source: various media sources.

who are subjected to indoor smoke pollution from cooking with inefficient fuel and stoves in poorly ventilated space. Jatropha oil performs very satisfactorily when burned using an easily adapted paraffin wick, and can largely be used for lighting the homes of rural people (Mapako 1998). If fully tapped, jatropha could save rural women time for other productive purposes (instead of spending much of their time fetching firewood for household use).

About one-third of the energy in the fruit of jatropha can be extracted as an oil that has a similar energy value to that of diesel fuel. Jatropha oil can be used directly in diesel engines, added to diesel fuel as an extender, or 'transesterized' to a biodiesel fuel (SIRDC 1998). In theory, a diesel substitute can be produced from locally grown jatropha plants, thus providing rural communities with the possibility of becoming self-sufficient in fuel for vehicles. The key issue, then, is how best jatropha can be used as a basis for rural industrialization in the short and medium term. The production of domestic oil to replace imports, especially in marginal rural areas, is the most attractive feature of jatropha oil, as noted elsewhere.

Private-sector-led initiatives in agro-investments

Private sector in public partnership with government The Zimbabwe Bio Energy Company, in partnership with the government and DTZ, was in full production by 2010. In Chisumbanje, the project was jointly managed with ARDA, Macdom (Private) Ltd and Ratings Investments on a build–operate–transfer basis. The government set the operating procedures and guidelines, and was involved in the land negotiations with local authorities and the Ministry of Land and Rural Resettlement. Other key interested ministries were Energy and Power Development; Indigenization; Agriculture; and Industry and Trade. The Zimbabwe Investment Authority was also involved.[5] The smallholder farmers are largely beneficiaries, in the sense that they gain from employment opportunities. In the Mwenezi project, for example, over 2,000 people were said to have been employed by the company by early 2010, in various departments.

Biofuels within integrated agricultural investments The investing companies in Zimbabwe have adopted a model along the lines of integrated systems. The integrated agricultural investments have some of the following features: technological transfer, skills development, the adoption of high-yielding crop varieties, hybrid livestock varieties, agro-tourism, integrated markets and supply chains. The investments in technology are also seen to be particularly beneficial, both in terms of water supply and distribution to smallholder farmers, who, it is envisaged, will be outgrowers for the main estates. At the same time, the new hybrid varieties, when adopted by smallholders, are seen as a technical improvement in their farming systems. In the sugar-growing sector, integrated approaches are being adopted in response to the popularity of biofuels. But there is also a sense in which the country needs to increase sugar exports, to get foreign currency. However, sugar production in Zimbabwe has declined considerably, to the extent that the country is relying on imports, especially from South Africa.

Analysis of trends and patterns

Maximization of land use through agro-investment options Land ownership and use in Africa and elsewhere is a highly emotive subject. Land is a contested resource, because assumptions of abundance of land may not be correct, yet in a country such as Zimbabwe land is central to 'identity, livelihoods and food security'. The driving force for the 'land grab' is usually economic, with an eye to deriving maximum rates of return on land that is perceived or considered to be underutilized in the present period. At this stage in Zimbabwe's economic development, there are economists and politicians who believe that in the wake of the land reform programme there is a need for pragmatic solutions to the challenges that agriculture faces, and also that it makes economic sense to tap into foreign investments, given that the country is under sanctions. In addition, the economy is not performing well, to the extent that it is difficult to capitalize agriculture using domestic resources alone.

The above arguments have been advanced by Zimbabwe Bio-Energy, fronted by the chairman of ARDA and the vice chairman of DTZ. The agro-investments in Chisumbanje and Mwenezi make sound sense from an economic perspective. Some of the positive features noted include the availability of uncontested land, the existence of private companies that have invested in technology (tried and tested), water resources, prime climatic conditions and the availability of employees (locals targeted for low-level jobs) to work in various areas of the commodity chain. In addition, the investors have begun to address challenges and anomalies in the production supply chain. The challenges to be addressed were the lack of finance, obsolete equipment, technology, inadequate water storage facilities, and deteriorating public infrastructure (roads, railways). The parastatal ARDA itself acknowledged that it had failed to fully utilize the land, and therefore could not derive value due to its inability to mobilize financial resources. As far as DTZ was concerned, it had huge swathes of land that were not being fully utilized – to the extent that parts of the Nuanetsi ranch were occupied by illegal settlers during the land reform programme.

DTZ and ARDA argued that their land was indigenously owned and therefore excluded from the land reform programme. Yet, when one undertakes a careful examination of the plans for the project in Chisumbanje, there is a clear mismatch between available land and the plans of ARDA. This means that, at some stage in the lifespan of the project, additional land will be required to meet the project's needs. In the Chisumbanje project a total of 40,000 hectares were said to be available for the project. Yet, the project will require an additional

20,000 hectares to meet its plans (Sibanda 2010). Based on the geography of the area, these extra 20,000 hectares can only come from adjacent land owned by communal smallholder farmers. This has the potential to prejudice smallholder farmers, and to create conflict over land – still a burning issue in Zimbabwe. In Mwenezi, about 100,000 hectares (out of a total of 350,000 hectares of DTZ-owned land) were said to be available for the project for sugarcane production. The land appeared to be free of conflicts, yet in reality smallholder farmers were arguing that it was too large and were demanding that part of the land be given to them. However, the involvement of the state in the ownership of the trust means that the investment project may well succeed.

Contradiction in Zimbabwe's land reform Zimbabwe's land reform programme was premised on correcting historical wrongs of land dispossession. In doing so, it targeted the land of white owners, who were generally regarded as 'foreign', since they hailed from generations of settlers who had forced black people from their ancestral lands a century or more ago. Although, four or five generations on, many of those affected are indeed indigenous Zimbabweans, there is a view that they have tended to isolate themselves from the broader Zimbabwean indigenous social formations, have lived an affluent life, oblivious to the poverty around, and have practised poor social relations. Even though the land reform programme was premised on social and economic equity, it seemed to target mainly white owners, because they formed the majority of landowners. Here, then, lies a contradiction with the desire for foreign agro-investments.

Another area of concern is the impact of agro-investments on local people, especially with regard to land and resource rights. In both the Mwenezi and Chisumbanje project areas, communal people have weak claims to land vis-à-vis the state, which is involved in the agro-investments. There is no guarantee that they can assert their land rights, given that the government retains stronger rights to liquidate land rights on the grounds of public good. In the case of Nuanetsi in Mwenezi, some settlers moved into the property at the height of the land reform programme. This was because the property was seen to be oversized and parts of it were underutilized, thus making the property suitable for occupation. This was despite the fact that the property was owned by black indigenous owners, who are excluded by the government from the criteria for compulsory acquisition. However, the land occupiers are to be displaced because they are what is termed 'illegal settlers'. The number of illegal land occupiers is said to be between 232 and 5,000. However, because they are illegal, it is difficult to establish the numbers affected. Those to be displaced are from the Chisase, Lundi and Mutirikwi areas.

The government has a policy that no illegal settler shall be removed from state land, for any reason, without the provision of an alternative source of land. In the case of the DTZ in Mwenezi, the investors are impatient, and so too is government this time around, as it wants the illegal settlers to go. The vice chair of DTZ advanced the argument in the media that it had set aside 60,000 of the 350,000 hectares for the resettlement programme, to satisfy the land needs of the illegal settlers on the property.

In Chisumbanje, an interesting case has emerged with regard to the bene- fits and costs of the agro-investments. Reports from the *Sunday Mail* and the *Herald* show how one chief in Chisumbanje area was negotiating with the proponents of the project. In the Chisumbanje project, there have been accusations that the investors working with ARDA have also been trying to get access to land in the communal areas. This meant that the company wanted to expand the land area for its project, which could potentially have affected large populations of communal dwellers. The *Sunday Mail* (2010) reported this story and what the chief had to say:

> When the company came in at first, we were told that we would not be moved but instead be offered employment on the plantation. This development has left us pondering our future. We want development that benefits rather than exploits our people. I am chief in this area but if we are moved, I will lose my chieftainship because I will be residing in a new area with its own chief …

The chief further noted in the article that the company was clearly encroach- ing on villagers' fields, because boundaries in communal areas, though not registered, are 'known' through customary systems. He went on to note that villagers in Machona, Machikwa, Munepasi, Nyamukura, Matikwa, Nepasi and Chinyamukura were set to lose their fields, and that some had already been affected by the projects. The chief then complained bitterly:

> Where do we go from here? This is our land of birth and we have lived here from time immemorial. Our ancestors were here before this animal called ARDA. Why would ARDA allow the company to displace us when we were the first to arrive here?

Within a month, the same chief had performed a U-turn and was praising the project, after food (30 tonnes of sorghum, plus the promise of 30 tonnes of wheat) had been donated, and there had been promises of schools and doctors for the area. With all this excitement, the chief urged the people of his area to be beneficiaries of the project:

> Chief Garawa urged Government and its partners to ensure workers were well looked after. He hoped the 40,000-hectare Greater Chisumbanje project would not displace people. 'We do not expect our people to be moved from the area. They should be the beneficiaries of this development,' he said. (Mandebvu 2010)

One of the key challenges is that there are no specific guidelines in the public domain on how communities can respond to investments that may take their land. In Zimbabwe, land in rural areas is a key resource that anchors the livelihoods of the local people through a range of benefits. Therefore development must not be seen to be displacing people; rather they should be ring-fenced by clear policies on land matters, implemented openly by relevant institutions. For instance, government has a legal instrument governing maximum farm sizes, and it would seem that the farms in both Chisumbanje and Mwenezi are over the prescribed size. This runs counter to government policy, and would seem to imply that, where the government is a direct participant in an agricultural project, the rules can easily be waived. It would seem that there is one set of rules for new beneficiaries and the remaining white farmers, who are subject to maximum farm sizes, and another set for preferred 'investors' (who seem to include the parastatal ARDA, which has gone into massive agro-investment deals).

Agro-investment for national food security There are other persuasive arguments for the investments, in a country that has struggled with its agriculture and economy. In Mwenezi, the planned targets for wheat and beef could contribute to food security, if the products generated are not exported. Zimbabwe has had to import most of its food, and this could present an opportunity to get food from local supplies that are known and can be planned. For production to go ahead, the foreign investors and local partners will need to replace the obsolete equipment owned by ARDA. Some of the benefits of investment include the building of roads, the construction of dams for water storage, access to electricity and some CSR measures. The complementary investments in tourism provide an opportunity to raise foreign currency for Zimbabwe. In addition, there is the possibility of high levels of employment creation for local people in the adjacent areas.

Development can be elusive, and there is no guarantee that foreign investment will benefit local people in the long term. This is especially true of marginal areas, where poor people with limited skills, low rates of literacy and a desperate desire to move out of poverty may be taken advantage of by outsiders through agro-investment projects. Often the local women may end up mere onlookers at the projects, since most of the jobs created are manual, and require mostly men. Conversely, large-scale agro-investments also imply the use of high technology, which may not require high levels of labour. Therefore, development becomes synonymous with huge tractors, caterpillar trucks and combine harvesters, and these may have negative environmental impacts. In the case of Tanzania (see chapter 6), there was evidence that the planned agro-investments would lead to deforestation and environmental hazards, and the investing companies were not prepared to take responsibility for these in terms of rehabilitation and mitigation initiatives.

In terms of food security, targeted cash-crop production for biofuel could create food insecurity problems, especially in view of volatile food markets. The idea of taking arable land to produce agricultural feedstocks, on the assumption that the net gains from employment incomes outweigh the people's own production, may be misplaced. As the Ethiopian cases show, smallholder lands are used for the production of food for foreign countries rather than local markets. In the process, precious water is diverted from food crops to irrigate the biofuel plantations (Meinzen-Dick 2010).[6] Many of the estates in Zimbabwe collapsed following the land reform programme, and some were divided up and allocated to smallholder farmers. The remaining estates were unable to attract agro-investments because the country became too risky for investment.

However, following the formation of an Inclusive Government, it seems that estates are gaining popularity in government, and there is a fear that, over time, such estates have the potential to reduce smallholder agriculture, as they may target land owned by indigenous people, as appears to be the case in Chisumbanje. Smallholders will not be able to compete for access to water with the larger estates, and nor will they be able to compete in the marketplace if the agro-estates enter the domestic market. The agro-estates have a penchant for using the 'latest farming technologies', with chemicals, pesticides, herbicides, fertilizers, intensive water use, and large-scale transport, storage and distribution turning landscapes into enormous monocultural estates. While this may sound desirable, the question is whether Zimbabwe is ready for such monoculture when over 70 per cent of its people depend on farming for their livelihoods – most of them women (Oxfam Australia and Ruzivo Trust 2011, forthcoming).

Employment creation arguments and labour implications The question is how to balance agro-investments in light of what it means for the livelihoods of local people. Rarely are social impact analyses carried out to establish the benefits and costs of agro-investments, because of the pressure for FDIs, which Zimbabwe is greatly in need of. Therefore, the inclination to suspend social impact analysis is much greater among bureaucrats who are bent on getting foreign currency and on reaping the benefits that come with it. However, the benefits of employment have to be weighed against the cost to long-term livelihoods, because in the long run not all the people in Chipinge or Mwenezi districts will be employed by the ZBE. The greatest promise is of employment; yet in countries where agro-investments have been implemented there is a sense of broken promises over wages and job opportunities.

The job-creation potential of the biofuel provides contrasting opportunities. On the one hand, the establishment of the plant at Chisumbanje has, in the short term, created employment opportunities for 100 skilled people during construction of the plant. The employment potential in this particular project has grown from a projected 7,000 jobs to 10,000.[7] However, the sectors in which these jobs will be created in the ethanol production project are not specified. If the jobs are to be realized, and if they target local communities, then this will be significant. However, there are a lot of 'ifs', and the project will need further assessment once it is fully operational in terms of production of ethanol.

On the other hand, given that the companies are investing in future out-grower schemes, the majority of the smallholder communal farmers are likely to switch to biofuel feedstock production, which may affect their food security. This means that, though they may not necessarily be directly employed, they will be operating at the behest of the ethanol company by virtue of mono-production. This may create insecurity, as they will be subject to domestic and international market trends in terms of the performance of ethanol.

Employment and income benefits are also assumed through increased feedstock production: this means more cultivated land, which implies more people needed to clear and use the land for sugarcane production. If labour-intensive (i.e. less mechanized) forms of agriculture constitute the approach of the ethanol company, it may indeed generate the promised jobs. However, the company is promising 'highly mechanized operations', and this is where there are problems in establishing precisely where the promised 10,000 jobs would come from and what they would do. The employment-creation potential of the processing side depends on its labour intensity, as well as on a constant supply of feedstock from the production side. In general, ethanol production requires more capital and tends to be more technology-intensive than biodiesel production. So the jobs promised through biofuels may be elusive.

Chisumbanje and Mwenezi have experienced a massive surge in infrastructure developments on the two sites. In a *Herald* newspaper article, ARDA officials engaged the traditional leaders on the project. The outcome of the meeting went as follows:

> Chief Garawa said the community had already started benefiting from joint venture between Government and MacDom and Rating Investments. Over 80 village heads under the chiefdom were in attendance. 'We had some of the poorest roads in Zimbabwe and as you can see the company has already graded them. The project has provided employment for our children,' Chief Garawa said. 'We also expect hospitals and clinics in the area will be refurbished and with more workers coming in, more schools will be built,' he added. (Mandebvu 2010)

However, foreign investors have a penchant for bringing external experts in to manage operations, while the mass of the people are promised or given shop-floor jobs, in many cases on a temporary basis. Experience in Ethiopia demonstrates the contradictions in employment claims by foreign investors in agriculture:

Box 7.3 Template for changed agrarian relations due to foreign investments

Transforming small farmers to small workers who have to fulfil the rules and requirements of the company means switching to new agro-labour relations, where one literally has to live and act in the interests of the company. It also means changing agrarian relations, where the small-holder farmer is transformed into an employee. Being an employee means being forced (default) to be dependent on a 'foreign' company with its own conditions of service, some of which include:

- Contracts designed to safeguard the interests of the company
- Employees subject to conditions of service, mostly favourable to the needs of the company
- Poor performance leading to loss of income and job
- Termination of contracts without prior notice
- Contested packages in the event of death/injury
- Duration of contracts normally short term (renewed on performance)
- Retirement benefits for local poor (bicycle, barrow or small amount of cash)
- Accidents at workplace not adequately compensated
- Personal victimization

All the above new conditions apply to people who may have lost their land rights on the promises of agro-investments:

- Loss of land upon which they may have been dependent for generations, where their ancestors are buried
- Loss of cropped land and grazing that directly affect their food security and economic well-being
- Loss of access to natural resources – water, ecosystems products (fruits, medicinal plants, access to wildlife for meat, etc.)
- Loss of trees that can be used for multi-purposes in their homes
- Loss of personal worth, viable self-fulfilling family life, destitution and sense of belonging

The farm manager shows us millions of tomatoes, peppers and other vegetables being grown in 500m rows in computer controlled conditions. Spanish engineers are building the steel structure, Dutch technology minimises water use from two boreholes and 1 000 women pick and pack 50 tonnes of food a day. Within 24 hours, it has been driven 320 km to Addis Ababa and flown 1 600km to the shops and restaurants of Dubai, Jeddah and elsewhere in the Middle East. (Vidal 2010)

While this quote provides an international dimension of land grab, where African people do not feature much, the subject of the global 'race' for farmland is complex. African governments perceive the economic benefits of external investment in their countries as offering the opportunity for their people to escape from poverty. The realities of new developments are such that small farmers are either displaced or incorporated in projects of this nature. The experience of large-scale investments in Africa, which may not be entirely different from the future of Zimbabwe's own investments, shows a marked impact of foreign agro-investments. Certainly at the outset of the investments, there are prospects for poor people to gain from the investments, but there are incipient challenges and issues that need to be addressed.

One of the key mitigating measures is to involve locals beyond mere shop-floor employment. The minister of agriculture, irrigation and mechanization development urged ARDA to enter into partnerships reflective of the country's indigenization policies. He was quoted as saying:

I am very concerned about ARDA going into joint venture operations that do not reflect the 51:49 government-stipulated shareholding structure. ARDA has land and machinery in Middle Sabi, Chisumbanje, Balu and Sanyati and is free to enter into joint operations as long as they reflect the 51:49 ownership structure or even better than that. (Kawadza 2010)

This is an important observation in a country where externally driven land use arrangements through agro-investments may create new and worse inequalities than before the land reform programme.

Lessons from agro-investments

What specific lessons should we draw from the new agro-investments in Zimbabwe at a time of land reform? The subject is complex, given that Zimbabwe is emerging from a decade of economic crisis caused by internal policy failures, external interventions resulting from the policy and practical contradictions of the land reform programme, and recurring negative weather patterns. Today, Zimbabwe requires assistance and a complete regeneration of its agriculture. Since 2002, a combination of negative weather conditions (droughts and floods), contested land reform programme, lack of international agricultural support (seeds, fertilizers, tillage, etc.) has meant that the country failed to feed its citizens. In addition, the industrial sector has collapsed because it could not get products from agriculture. Hence, like a cascade, production across the economic sectors declined, with industry at one time during the economic crisis operating at less than 10 per cent of capacity. For this reason, there are strong reasons why agro-investments are the preferred option to kick-start the agricultural sector: they tend to be capital intensive; and they can attract foreign cash injections, while generating foreign currency by unlocking value and through economies of scale. However, the challenge is how to balance such agro-investments against national and local food security and the long-term livelihoods of the local populations.

Can the Zimbabwean land investments be characterized as land grabbing in the same way as elsewhere in Africa and in other parts of the world? The answer to this question veers towards a strong 'yes', even though it is contextual. It is land grabbing when publicly owned companies make deals with foreigners that exclude the people in the deal, and where the locals may not benefit. One of the key enigmas that is difficult for local people to understand is the whole motif of the land reform programme. It would seem that the Zimbabwean government has redrawn the benchmarks for acceptable and unacceptable white landowners or land users. The Chisumbanje and Mwenezi projects have seen the reintroduction of whites to large-scale farming. Yet the dominant tendency has been the removal of some white farmers on the basis of correcting wrongs that, historically, had created land ownership imbalances along racial lines.

At the same time, there are lingering threats of the removal of people currently classified as 'illegal' land occupiers, in order to make way for white-led agro-investments. In the case of Zimbabwe, apart from the instance in Chisumbanje and the threats to remove illegal occupiers in Nuanetsi, there is no strong evidence that private companies are targeting land owned by indigenous people. In fact, the government parastatal has partnered on state-owned land, which makes it difficult to conclude that land has been grabbed. However, when a poor villager is contracted into a large-scale project that changes his livelihood on the promise of a better future, however uncertain, that is indeed land grabbing. This is all the more so when the large-scale projects are implemented without regard to flora and fauna that are of benefit to locals and the environment.

Can government-led promotion of agrofuel crops (jatropha) be classified as land grabbing? In a way, these are not land grabs, as smallholder farmers retain their land rights and have the freedom to choose what crop to produce. It also seems that smallholders in Zimbabwe did not embrace jatropha as the government had expected, thus causing the government's plans for jatropha expansion to fail.

At another level, it is interesting to look more closely at the new rules and regulations governing foreign investments in large-scale commercial farms. Besides the BIPPAs that the government has reviewed, there is limited enforcement by it of the rules and regulations governing agro-investments, because it needs investors more than ever before. So, more and more frequently, the rules are waived for the convenience of external investors, though they are still applied to some domestic investors. Thus the government is employing double standards.

Clearly there is a need to monitor and enforce the regulations on agro-investments better, in order to minimize the negative impacts. There should be:

- Monitoring of specific cases of how long-term livelihoods are compromised and/or threatened; and
- A clear land administration system, with open and transparent channels of decision-making, as well as openness about the factors influencing decisions and about how such decisions are communicated. This is required because the country is emerging from a political crisis in which land featured prominently and which caused the land administration system to become inconsistent and to develop unclear operational procedures.

In terms of rules and regulations for the implementation of agro-investment, there should be moral guidance to signal to stakeholders the costs and benefits for the local population of the various public policy choices made. Human rules, however laudable in their construction, are violated from time to time. Through policy measures, there is a need for institutions to continuously monitor progress on biofuel investments.

Conclusion

Zimbabwe is emerging from a decade-long, deep-seated economic and political crisis and has arrived at the stage where resources are required to drive its economy. Agro-investments provide an opportunity to kick-start the agricultural sector and make it more dynamic, offering as they do potential advantages for food production and the 'promise' of employment generation. In this chapter, we have demonstrated that Zimbabwe is at the stage where agro-investments are starting to be negotiated. This process is necessarily political, given the sensitivities and historical issues associated with the land issue. Domestic investors have taken the risk of partnering with government in various agro-investments, because they need state protection to initiate and sustain their projects. Yet, in doing so, they need to negotiate carefully with communities, which today may be happy to embrace 'development' but in time may grow wary and realize that their livelihoods have been negatively affected by elusive promises.

Agro-investments that include local people and communities in all structures of the operations (shareholding, technical management, shop-floor labour) have better prospects for sustainable development that benefits the rural population than do models that rely on external or foreign technical people and investors who have a limited understanding of complex rural contexts. The absence of domestic professionals and skilled workers necessitates the creation of a capacity-building programme for locals. Over time, foreigners can move away and trade relations can be established. This is not to say that investors should finance projects without any expectation of reaping any rewards; instead, as they generate profits, a primary objective for them should be the prudent transfer of responsibilities, based on clear and long-term development for local people, communities and institutions. This will also require a developmentally oriented state. In the case of the two projects highlighted, it would seem that the build–operate–transfer model has been embraced, but this needs to be backed up by political will and robust programmes for local skills development and ownership.

The overall challenge is thus to find constructive methods of weighing the costs and the benefits of agro-investments. Clearly, for Zimbabwe in its present state, the government should be seen also as a protector of the poor. In the longer term, the livelihoods of the poor should be safeguarded in any large-scale development programme, which should apply to agro-investments that have the potential to push poor rural people off their land. The poor require protection because they have a limited ability to organize and lobby to gain benefits from agro-investments. The dispossession of land also leads to a loss of national identity and an invitation to political conflict, which may hinder the potential success of agro-investments. The government needs to rethink agro-investment strategies in view of the possibility that any future land conflict could further damage agriculture, which seems to be on the road to recovery following the contested land reform programme.

8 | Competition between biofuel and food? Evidence from a jatropha biodiesel project in Northern Ghana

Festus Boamah

Introduction

Ghana is gradually becoming one of the havens for biofuel investments in Africa. At the moment, there are biofuel investments in almost all ten regions of the country, undertaken by both foreign and Ghanaian investors. As a consequence, large areas of land have been outsourced by traditional landowners for biofuel production. However, in the twenty-first century, biofuel production has coincided with food security emergencies worldwide. In 2008 the realities and fear of starvation caused the food insecure to embark on street demonstrations and picketing in such countries as Côte d'Ivoire, Ethiopia, Cameroon, Guinea, Morocco, Senegal, Mexico, Thailand and Pakistan. The demonstrators demanded from their governments sound policies to stabilize the soaring price of food. The increases in global food prices were attributed to the high oil prices and to a consequent increase in the cost of producing and transporting agricultural commodities (Flammini 2008: 8). The food supply emergency was predicted to worsen with a surge in biofuel production (ibid.: 9). It is estimated that global food prices increased by about 140 per cent between 2002 and 2007 due to a number of factors, including increased demand for biofuel feedstocks. Agricultural prices are expected to increase by a further 30 per cent by 2020 because of biofuel targets (Fischer et al. 2009: 22). Similar concerns regarding long-term dire consequences of biofuels are expressed by some international research agencies (IFPRI 2007b; ActionAid International 2008; Oxfam 2008). The large land areas required for biofuel production, coupled with scanty empirical research into biofuels, has generated controversies among interest groups in Ghana in the form of reports and media debates that address the implications of biofuels (Boamah 2010). These controversies motivated my interest to enquire into the food security implications of the BioFuel Africa jatropha biodiesel project being implemented in some villages in Northern Ghana.

Socio-economic background of the project villages in Northern Ghana

The three study villages of Kpachaa, Jimle and Jaashie are in the Yendi Municipal Assembly (formerly Yendi District Assembly). The district has a population density of 26.6 persons per square kilometre. Mean annual rainfall for the district is (January to December) 1,125 mm. Mean wet season rainfall for the district is (April to October) 1,150 mm, while the mean dry season rainfall (November to March) is 75 mm (ibid.). Rainfall is thus seasonal and unreliable, and this limits food crop production to the short rainy season. The three villages share the same rainfall characteristics as the district. People live in the project villages only temporarily, mainly because of the limited economic opportunities. Since farming – the predominant livelihood in the project villages – is determined largely by rainfall, most of the residents have a permanent residence in Tamale or the other nearby towns (Biljini and Sang), and only stay in the villages to farm during the rainy season. Most of the people, then, alternate between the villages and their permanent place of residence for the farming season and the off-season (dry season) (Boamah 2010).

As peasant village communities, the basic source of food in the household is farm produce. Farming is a predominantly male occupation, and the major crops cultivated include yam, maize, groundnut and rice. Other sources of livelihood include the charcoal and firewood business, the shea nut business, and some petty trading activities, which are predominantly undertaken by the women. The contribution to household food provisioning is highly gendered, due to the gender division of labour in the three study villages. Gendered differentiation of livelihoods becomes more pronounced during the dry seasons. Most males become idle during the seven-month-long dry season (November to March/April), when the villages endure a severe drought that limits farming activities. Nonetheless, women are less vulnerable financially than are men, because their predominant livelihood activities (firewood and charcoal businesses, petty trading and shea nuts) are not limited to a particular season of the year. Because of the strategic location of the three villages along the Tamale–Yendi major road, there is a ready market among road users for shea nuts, firewood and charcoal.

The income from these businesses is used for the upkeep of the households. Women thus become breadwinners in their households during the dry season. However, in the years when tradable products (shea nuts, firewood and charcoal) decline either in volume or in terms of price, the living conditions of the households decline correspondingly. Households thus either resort to borrowing or else the men engage in temporary labour migration to Tamale and other neighbouring towns, and return during the next farming season. In short, the livelihoods in the villages are not lucrative enough to reduce economic vulnerability, especially in the dry season.

BioFuel Africa jatropha biodiesel project in Northern Ghana

The environmental benefits of biofuel are well-recognized and acknowledged throughout the world: carbon emission reductions, increased fuel economy, reduction of dependence on fossil fuels. But the creations of a biofuel industry in developing economies, like Africa, go far beyond environmental concerns. Jobs are being created, economies are being impacted, infrastructure is being built, services provided and lives profoundly changed ... We believe in partnering with communities, tribes and governments to create lasting economic infrastructures and change lives. (BioFuel Africa 2008)

The above quote is the rationale for the BioFuel Africa jatropha project. Inspired by BioFuel Africa's argument, the Environmental Protection Agency in Ghana gave it the go-ahead in February 2008 for a jatropha biodiesel project on land totalling 23,762 hectares in the Central Gonja and Yendi districts of Northern Ghana (ibid.). BioFuel Africa Ltd was formerly owned by BioFuel AS. However, the two founders of BioFuel AS, Arne Helvig[1] and Steinar Kolnes,[2] acquired 100 per cent of the shares in BioFuel Africa Ltd on 13 March 2009, when the mother company was forced to file for bankruptcy after corruption allegations (reported on the BioFuel Africa Ltd website in 2009). The two men bought all the shares in BioFuel Africa Ltd, assuming all its debts as well as acquiring all its assets. This paved the way for BioFuel Africa Ltd to continue its operations in Ghana. A new company, Solar Harvest AS, was formed in Norway and is now the sole owner of BioFuel Africa Ltd. The company aims to undertake an environmentally friendly jatropha project to produce biodiesel for use in Ghana and also for export. The company believes that producing biodiesel from jatropha oil will have fewer negative environmental consequences and will boost food security in the project villages, because the plant thrives on less-productive land.

BioFuel Africa Ltd first embarked on a jatropha project in Alipe, a village in the Central Gonja district of Northern Ghana, in November 2007, but encountered local opposition in Ghana from ActionAid-Ghana, Regional Advisory and Information Network Systems (RAINS) and some environmental activist groups, on the grounds of perceived dire implications for local livelihoods and food security (Boamah 2010). The project was abandoned in Alipe after a month of operation. After abandoning its operations in Alipe, BioFuel Africa Ltd moved to a new project site in the Yendi district of Northern Ghana and established a jatropha plantation in March 2008. The jatropha plantation is located along the Tamale–Yendi road. The location of the plantation is about 55 kilometres from Tamale, the regional capital of Northern Ghana. The project was established on land belonging to the surrounding villages, but Boamah (2010) focused on three of the villages: Kpachaa, Jimle and Jaashie. These villages are within an approximately 5km radius of the plantation site; Kpachaa is the closest village.

Recruitment of workers and subsequent lay-offs At the peak of the project, in October 2008, about 400 people (both skilled and unskilled) were employed on the plantation. The skilled workers, who included mechanics, building field supervisors and machine operators, earned monthly wages of between Ghana new cedi (GHS) 200 and GHS 1,000 (US$138–690). The unskilled workers – fieldworkers (people weeding, pruning and harvesting in the plantation), security personnel, fire volunteers and cleaners – earned monthly wages of between GHS 77 and GHS 150. In addition to the monthly wages, insurance payments and other statutory tax obligations are paid by the company. The range of the monthly wages offered by BioFuel Africa Ltd far exceeds the current national minimum monthly wage of Ghana, which is GHS 61.

By November 2008, BioFuel Africa Ltd faced financial crisis, due to funding problems caused partly by the global financial crisis, but also by the local opposition to the project, which continued in Yendi, even after the project had been abandoned in Alipe. Funders and potential investors in the company withdrew their financial support. As a consequence, BioFuel Africa Ltd had to lay off about 300 of the 400 workers in the first half of 2009. At the time of the study's fieldwork (June–August 2009), the number of workers had declined to below 100.

Because the three villages depend largely on land acquired to cultivate food crops and to collect shea nuts, the study sought to examine the effect of the jatropha project on food security among those households whose livelihoods depended on the acquired land. The subsequent sections will show the controversies surrounding the BioFuel Africa jatropha project and the empirical evidence for its food security implications on the affected villages.

Discourses underpinning biofuel debates

Discourse refers to a specific delimitation of the shared meaning of a phenomenon (Svarstad 2002: 67). 'Each discourse rests on assumptions, judgments and contentions that provide the basic terms for analysis, debates, arguments and disagreements' (Dryzek 1997: 8). The adherents of a discourse contribute to it in varying degrees regarding its production, reproduction and transformation through written and oral statements (Adger et al. 2001: 683). 'These statements possess certain regularities not only as to content (or message) but also by the use of some shared expressive means in terms of, for instance, certain meta-narratives and rhetorical devices such as metaphors' (Svarstad 2002: 68).

Meta-narrative is used to conceptualize an abstract structure or pattern to which specific narratives within a discourse may belong (ibid. 2002: 77). However, the study concentrates on narrative production. The expressive means here refer to the ways in which the message of a discourse is communicated (Adger et al. 2001: 685). Narratives are important expressive means of discourse. Narratives are pragmatic, in the sense that they compel the audience to act or believe in something through the telling of a story that creates a scenario in which something will inevitably happen, given a certain set of conditions. The incontrovertible logic in narratives authenticates development action (Fairhead and Leach 1995: 1024). The worth of a narrative as an expressive means of discourse is evident in its usefulness in simplifying the uncertainties and ambiguities that bureaucrats and policy- or decision-makers face in development issues (Roe 1991: 288). Explaining the tendency to meet complexity with narratives, Roe (1999: 2) asserts that:

> one of the abiding ironies of rural development practice – and not just in Africa – is that narrative and complexity are deeply reciprocal. The more complex things are and the more things there are to be complex, the more widespread complexity becomes at the macro-level and the greater the demand for standardized approaches with wide application to deal with complexity.

Adger et al. (2001) look at the ideas of the global environmental managerial discourses and populist discourses to address climate change, and also their associated narrative structures (the cast of 'victims', 'heroes' and 'villains' that emerges in the narratives). Although both discourses claim the existence of climate change as an environmental problem, they offer alternative explanations as to the causes and the appropriate mitigation measures. Debates about the food security implications of biofuels are underpinned by the two discourses, and their implied messages are expressed through the use of narratives.

Proponents of the managerial discourse Global environmental managerial discourse (or 'managerial discourse' for short) expresses optimism in development projects that involve the transfer of technology and financial payments to address climate change problems (Adger et al. 2001). The discourse holds that financial payments should be encouraged to conserve forests and biodiversity, and to support the adoption of 'clean technologies' (ibid.). Financial support, it is argued, will revive local economies by improving livelihoods and ensuring environmental resource sustainability to mitigate the effects of climate change. Proponents of the managerial discourse thus see environmental problems as symptoms of poverty, underdevelopment and population pressure (Hermann and Hutchinson 2005). Within the managerial discourse, local farmers, peasants and the landless poor become 'victims' and 'villains' of climate change, while scientists, aid bureaucrats and civil servants become 'heroes' by calling for urgent intervention (Adger et al. 2001).

In the biofuel debates, managerial discourse sees biofuel investments as a way of mitigating the impact of climate change through a reduction in the emission of global greenhouse gases into the atmosphere, at the same time as livelihoods are improved through job creation. The renewed interest in biofuels is thus inspired by managerial discourse.

In Ghana, the proponents of the jatropha project include BioFuel Africa Ltd, chiefs and the majority of residents in the project villages, and Rural

Consult Ltd, an NGO that claims biofuels could create a win-win situation for all parties involved and thus should be encouraged. BioFuel Africa Ltd claims that biofuel investment contributes to environmental sustainability at the same time as it improves food security and livelihoods in the project villages (BioFuel Africa 2008). Inspired by the managerial discourse, the policy of BioFuel Africa Ltd was to undertake an environmentally friendly jatropha biodiesel project for the global oil market and also to create sustainable livelihoods for affected communities:

> Our policy is further to increase food production in terms of volume and land area to ensure food security on a local level ... BioFuel Africa is helping to transform economies and the environment to create a more sustainable future for us all. (BioFuel Africa 2008)

Moreover, the chiefs of Tijo (Tijo-Naa) and Kusawgu (Kusawgu-Wura) who leased out the land areas to BioFuel Africa Ltd also expressed optimism in the jatropha project, in light of the vulnerability of livelihoods in the project villages. Because the villages have large areas of unused land, the chiefs hoped the project would improve livelihoods. Explaining the perceived spin-off effects of the jatropha project on local livelihoods, Kusawgu-Wura remarked:

> I decided to lease a land size of 300 hectares initially for the start of the project and if I find out any sign of positive development, then part of the vast idle land will be given to them to continue their operations ... We need them because we believe that their operations will generate employment for our people and create development for us.[3]

In addition, Rural Consult Ltd conducted research in the three Yendi project villages to investigate the consequences of the project for livelihoods. An article published by the NGO in Ghana's leading newspaper, *Daily Graphic*, opined that, despite the land use changes and some losses in the project villages, the positive impacts on livelihoods far outstrip the negative impacts (Rural Consult 2009a). It concluded that it is imperative to weigh both the positive and the negative impacts before drawing conclusions as to the implications of the biofuel project (ibid.). The NGO emphasized the win-win effects of the jatropha project for both the company and the project villages. Furthermore, the local people in the project areas shared the project optimism expressed in the managerial discourse by expressing hopes for job creation during the project.

Proponents of the populist discourse Populist discourse, however, focuses on the perilous local environmental effects of so-called development projects that claim to solve climate change problems and deal with biodiversity loss. This discourse sees biodiversity loss and climate change as a consequence of the interests and the institutions of capitalism (Adger et al. 2001). Within the populist discourse, those international NGOs and local community organizations working to mitigate environmental degradation become 'heroes', while global capitalism, TNCs and colonial power become 'villains', and local people become 'victims' (ibid.). The formation of community-based approaches to conservation and forest management are thus promoted by this discourse, to protect the rights of local people and to empower them (ibid.). In other words, the discourse implies a deepening of environmental problems at the local level, as a result of the external interventions; local communities would be better off left to their own devices (Hermann and Hutchinson 2005).

In the biofuel debates, the populist discourse sees biofuel investment as a potential threat to climate change, and as a catalyst for the destruction of local livelihoods through 'land grabbing'. Opponents of biofuels adhere to the populist discourse. In Ghana, the opponents of the jatropha biodiesel project included ActionAid-Ghana, RAINS, the Directorate of Crop Services and some local farmers. Inspired by the populist discourse, the first opposition to the jatropha project surfaced in the form of an article by a resident of Kusawgu (near Alipe) who worked with RAINS. Entitled 'Biofuel Land Grabbing in Northern Ghana', it begins with a crisis scenario:

> This is the story of how a Norwegian biofuel company took advantage of Africa's traditional system of communal land ownership and current climate and economic pressure to claim and deforest large tracts of land in Kusawgu, Northern Ghana with the intention of creating 'the largest jatropha plantation in the world' ... When given all the information the community successfully fought to send the investors packing but not before 2,600 hectares of land had been deforested. Many have now lost their incomes from the forest and face a bleak future. (Nyari 2008: 1)

The article predicted dire consequences of the jatropha project for livelihoods because of the destruction of shea nuts. It influenced the global biofuel debate, because it had a large readership throughout the world on the internet. One NGO, ActionAid-Ghana (AAG) was incited by the article and also joined the campaign against the jatropha project. AAG is a Ghanaian affiliate of ActionAid International. The NGO published an article claiming that, without giving the local people prior warning, BioFuel Africa Ltd had caused the massive destruction of shea nut trees during the jatropha project. The article, entitled 'The Biofuel Debate', predicted dire consequences of the jatropha project:

> AAG works with poor and excluded people to eradicate poverty. Consequently, right to food is one of our four thematic areas. It is in furtherance of that, when we noticed that large tracts of land were being taken for biofuel production, we [AAG] initiated the research to determine its implications for food security in

particular and development in general. The results indicate that the plantations pose a potential threat to food security of the people ... Because the destruction of the economic trees has become an issue, the company has the intention to replant them. What happens to the poor women and their families who hitherto earned their livelihoods from these economic trees after the good number of them have been destroyed? They now have no choice but wait and go hungry for the 20 years during which the replanted trees grow. (ActionAid-Ghana 2009)

The publications by RAINS and AAG sparked concerns about the implications of biofuels in Ghana. In Ghana, investments that influence food production are steered by the Directorate of Crop Services. At the time of the study, there was only a draft policy on biofuels, spearheaded by the Centre for Renewable Energy under the Ghana Energy Commission. Because there was no codified policy on biofuels in Ghana, the directorate relied on reports by AAG and on other biofuel reports. The director of crop services admitted the country's need for alternative energy like biofuels, but asserted that Ghana would not promote biofuels at the expense of food. Interviewed in 2009, the director remarked:

I am told the jatropha plant thrives on marginal soils. If an investment is made on marginal soils, it yields marginal output ... therefore jatropha plant must be undertaken on arable land to reap maximum yields. Cultivating the plant, however, on such arable land poses a threat to food security through competition with edible food crops for land. With this ... I think the jatropha investment should not be encouraged.

Moreover, before the project, some farmers with very large households and a heavy dependency burden perceived the jatropha project to be a threat to food security (Boamah 2010). The limited income-generating activities in the study areas led these farmers to view 'land grabbing' as a threat to food security and the shea nut business. One resident of Alipe lamented the perceived massive shea nut destruction by BioFuel Africa Ltd, remarking that 'shea nut is the cocoa in this community'.[4] This metaphor expresses the worth of shea nuts as a major livelihood strategy for the rural economy of Alipe, comparing the value of shea nuts for the region to the value of cocoa as a cash crop for Ghana. In other words, in Ghana, the opposing opinions about the jatropha project were found not only among the various interest groups, but also among the local people.

Narratives associated with the discourses underpinning the biofuel debates

As explained above, narratives are used as the expressive means of the two discourses underpinning debates about the jatropha project. In the debates about the jatropha project, the food security implications are expressed in story form, as described by Roe (1991: 288). The messages in the biofuel narratives convey presumed consequences of the jatropha project for food security, and thus the need for appropriate policy responses towards biofuel projects. The narratives identified in the debates about the jatropha project include the narrative of 'land grabbing leads to food insecurity' (associated with the populist discourse) and the narrative of 'development projects lead to improved livelihoods' (associated with the managerial discourse).

Narrative of 'land grabbing leads to food insecurity' As explained above, AAG, RAINS, the Directorate of Crop Services and some local people from the study areas adhered to the populist discourse, telling a story to explain the daunting implications of the jatropha project in the project villages in Northern Ghana:

- The story begins by setting the premise (or assuming) that before the jatropha project, there was harmony between the local livelihoods and land resources. The local people depend on the land for farming and economic trees to make a living. The jatropha project implementation causes land use change through 'land grabbing'.
- In the middle of the story, the consequences of the jatropha project are expressed thus: 'Land use change interferes with local livelihoods through the encroachment on farmland and destruction of economic trees such as shea nuts.'
- The 'dead end' comes when the local people's command over food is at stake, leading to food insecurity.

The local people, and especially farmers, are represented as 'victims', since they are perceived to suffer the consequences of the jatropha project; BioFuel Africa Ltd becomes the 'villain', due to the perceived livelihood destruction through the encroachment on farmland and the destruction of shea nut trees; while NGOs like AAG and RAINS, the Directorate of Crop Services and local environmental activist groups calling for the abandonment of the jatropha project become 'heroes'. The role of these 'heroes' in the case of the jatropha project in Northern Ghana was to protect land resources from being diverted into jatropha (biofuel) production by BioFuel Africa Ltd and thus to safeguard the local people from economic marginalization.

Narrative of 'development projects lead to improved livelihoods' BioFuel Africa Ltd, Rural Consult Ltd, the chiefs and some residents of the project villages adhered to the managerial discourse to explain the economic spin-offs of the jatropha project on livelihoods. These proponents expressed optimism in the project:

- Their story begins by claiming that livelihoods in the affected communities are vulnerable. The establishment of the jatropha plantation creates spin-off effects in the affected communities.

- In the middle of the story, it is claimed that 'the spin-off effects lead to livelihood diversification through employment creation, in addition to a boost in the traditional local livelihoods'.
- The story ends by concluding that 'diversified livelihoods lead to improved livelihoods'.

In the narrative of the managerial discourse, local people are represented as 'beneficiaries' of the project instead of 'victims'; AAG and RAINS, which oppose the jatropha project, are seen as 'villains'; and BioFuel Africa Ltd emerges as the 'hero' thanks to its environmentally friendly biodiesel project, which boosts local livelihoods. It is implicit in the managerial discourse that biofuel investments should be encouraged because of the presumed positive spin-off effects.

Our study focused on the discourses that underpinned the jatropha biodiesel project debate, and analysed the messages and narrative structures associated with the mainstream discourses, based on the evidence from the study areas.

Narratives and 'de-narrativization'

Roe (1999) recommends engaging in the production of counter-narratives. In the production of counter-narratives, the conditions in narratives are subject to rigorous investigation of their true complexities (through what Roe calls 'de-narrativization'), in order to highlight the flaws or oversimplifications in the narratives – such as those that adopt an activist stance or that simply foster externally driven solutions to Africa's problems. This study thus sought to examine the narratives in the jatropha project debates, based on empirical findings from the study villages (Boamah 2010). The discussion below shows the complexities surrounding the two narratives.

De-narrativization of 'land grabbing leads to food insecurity' As already indicated, the adherents to the populist discourse perceived 'food insecurity' to be an inevitable consequence of the jatropha project, with farmland encroachment and the destruction of shea nut trees. Shea nut trees were supposed to have been destroyed during the land preparation stage of the project (Nyari 2008; ActionAid-Ghana 2009). Because livelihoods in the project villages depend on land resources, 'land grabbing' has dire food security implications. The word 'grabbing' means 'to grasp or seize suddenly and eagerly' (Oxford English Dictionary). Land grabbing thus refers to a sudden seizure of land areas. However, the study found that, of the 1,100 hectares of land cleared by BioFuel Africa Ltd, 400 hectares were initially planted with jatropha. Before the jatropha project, there were only 25 farmers on the 400 hectares used for the jatropha plantation. The land preparation period of the project ran from March 2008, which is when farmers prepare their land for farming. After consultation and negotiations with the affected farmers and the chiefs, the 25 affected farmers were asked either to relocate to new farmland areas in the cleared land or to continue farming on the jatropha plantation. Five of the 25 farmers continued farming on the plantation, while 20 accepted relocation. The company ploughed about 0.8 hectares for each of the farmers in the new land areas, and encouraged them to expand on their own.

Four of the 20 relocated farmers feared a reduction in yield in the 2009 farming season because it was their first time farming in the relocated farm fields, and because of the reduced farm sizes. However, the remaining relocated farmers (16) and other farmers from the study areas remarked that relocation to new farmland was compatible with the usual bush fallowing system practised. This is because that farming system is characterized by a move to new land areas when the fertility of the soil begins to decline. Under the bush fallowing system, farmers move to new land and allow the previous land areas to remain fallow for some years, so that it can regain its lost fertility. Residents remarked on the declining fertility of the 400 hectares of land used for the jatropha plantations, and added that, apart from the difficulties involved in removing stumps and big trees using crude implements like axes and cutlasses, relocation to new farmland usually increases crop yields, because of the relatively high soil fertility levels. In short, the project saw the relocation of farmers from less fertile and almost abandoned farmland areas to relatively more fertile farmland areas without any distortion of the farming system. Therefore, the establishment of the jatropha plantations did not lead to the 'seizure of farmland' in the project villages (Boamah 2010).

The storyline of the narrative continues that food insecurity is a consequence of the project because of the encroachment on farmland areas. However, because of jatropha's tolerance of other plants – even on marginal soil – the jatropha rows were used for maize production. Moreover, part of the 1,100 hectares of cleared land was set aside for the production of maize: 16 hectares for villagers living in the project area and a further 10 hectares for the benefit of workers on the plantation. BioFuel Africa Ltd promoted the crop production in accordance with its 'food first policy'. Moreover, farmland areas under cultivation within the cleared land (1,100 hectares) increased during the project, relative to the period before. These increased farmland areas led to a marked rise in crop production.

In addition, despite the increases in farmland during the project, a large part of the cleared land remained 'unused' on account of the low population density in the Yendi district – 26.6 persons per square kilometre, which is far lower than a peasant community such as Asante Akim North district (with a population density of 109 per square kilometre, according to the Asante Akim North district profile for 2006), or indeed Ghana's national population density of 98.4 per square kilometre (Europa Regional Surveys of the World 2009).

Even in Alipe, where the project was abandoned on the grounds of perceived farmland encroachment, brief interviews and personal observations reveal the opposite: BioFuel Africa Ltd began its land preparations in November, and the farmers confirmed that they had finished harvesting their crops by then. Therefore it is valid to question whether the local people became 'victims' of food insecurity through farmland encroachment during the project (Boamah 2010).

Another dimension of the story was that shea nut destruction by the project led to food insecurity. However, many factors have contributed to the destruction of shea nut trees in the study areas. The study found that destruction had begun some years before the jatropha project. Although some shea nut trees were indeed destroyed during the land preparation stage of the project, the local farmers confirmed that they, too, had contributed to the destruction of shea nut trees during their preparation of the land for farming. Because the vegetation in the three villages is dominated by many species of shea nut trees, even a small area cleared for farming involves the destruction of many trees. Village residents mentioned farmers as the main cause of the shea nut tree loss and the consequent decline in access to shea nuts. Moreover, residents explained that the 400 hectares of land used for the jatropha plantation had once been farmland, and so the farmers had already cleared most of the economic trees, including shea nut trees, before the project. Some residents also mentioned that trees were felled by the local people to make charcoal to sell.

Farmers in Alipe similarly admitted their part in the destruction of trees. The empirical findings from the project villages do not necessarily disprove the loss of some economic trees or the land use change caused by the jatropha project, as reported in ActionAid-Ghana (2009) and Nyari (2008). Nonetheless, it is not so straightforward to relate tree loss during the jatropha project to livelihood destruction, or food insecurity in the project villages to farmland encroachment. Even with the reduction in the number of shea nut trees in the three Yendi villages and Alipe, I observed women still trading in shea nuts. In addition, despite the land use changes, food production increased during the project from its previous level. Thus, the central idea of the storyline – that 'land grabbing' by BioFuel Africa Ltd caused food insecurity – needs to be qualified.

De-narrativization of 'development project leads to improved livelihoods' The study found that an important consequence of the project was employment creation, both direct and indirect. About 60 per cent of the workers on the jatropha plantation were recruited from the three villages and their environs and earned between GHS 77 and GHS 150. As rural peasant villages with almost nonexistent alternative livelihoods, monthly wages for plantation workers were an important source of income. Income sources also increased indirectly during the project, through a boost in petty trading activities due to the increased demand for food and groceries. Women started petty trading activities, such as food sales, while village residents who secured employment on the plantation bought shea nuts in the villages and resold them at higher prices in neighbouring towns. Other residents also invested in farming. First, farmers could hire the company's tractors for ploughing at a lower cost than before. Second, part of their wages went towards buying seeds for cultivation. Third, wage earners were able to hire extra labour on their farms.

It would seem that livelihoods did improve during the period of the project (this will require long-term monitoring and assessment). However, as was mentioned above, within just two years of the plantation being established, the funding problems faced by BioFuel Africa Ltd led to lay-offs that affected 300 of the 400 workers. The lay-offs reduced the gains from the project, since the petty trading activities contracted and the plantation workers lost their wages. Most of the village residents lamented the sudden loss of the gains from the project and the consequent effects on household welfare occasioned by the lay-offs.

After the lay-offs, the residents did not become worse off than before, because they went back to their previous livelihoods. However, the inability of the project to continue to create sustainable livelihoods in the project villages raises questions about the sustainability of so-called development projects and about the spin-off effects that are claimed by proponents of the managerial discourse. Thus, the narrative that a 'development project leads to improved livelihoods' needs better qualification.

Both narratives associated with the discourses underpinning the debates about the jatropha project are thus in need of some qualification, as the evidence from the study reveals many complexities.

Constructing a 'better narrative'

As explained above, the study identified the narratives surrounding the jatropha project and food security. Roe (1991; 1999) further suggests that we should construct a better narrative to represent a 'truer' and 'more productive' knowledge. However, Roe also cautions that the better knowledge should not necessarily lead to displacement of earlier narratives, but should provide an equally straightforward narrative that tells a better story (Roe 1991: 290). To Roe, this takes the form of 'reversing the old pattern of thinking' (Roe 1999). This section thus seeks to improve on the biofuel narratives based on the evidence from the BioFuel Africa jatropha biodiesel project, by positing four conditions under which biofuels influence food security.

Biological characteristics of the biofuel feedstock The biological characteristics of the feedstock used for biofuel production have some effect on both food consumption and production (Boamah 2010). The poisonous nature of the plant makes jatropha inedible. The plant is not even browsed by livestock and cannot be compared to biofuel feedstock like sugarcane, soya beans, millet or maize, which are important global food sources. Moreover, the drought-resistant perennial characteristic of jatropha and its ability to thrive in most ecological zones (Cocks 2009: 139) make its cultivation suited to drought-prone Northern Ghana. This implies that, despite its long gestation period (of about 50 years), jatropha is less likely to monopolize arable land needed for the production of staple food crops like millet, groundnut, yam and maize, which are usually produced by farmers in Northern Ghana. Thus the biological differences between the above-mentioned biofuel feedstocks mean that producing biodiesel from jatropha does not directly deny people food, which is not the case when edible crops like maize, sugarcane and cassava are converted into ethanol.

Population density and availability of unused land The availability of 'unused' land is another important factor when considering the impact of biofuels on food security. The effect of encroachment on land areas used by densely populated communities for food crop production is totally different from the effect on sparsely populated farming communities. The study found that, even after the implementation of the project, a large part of the acquired land remained 'unused'. Thus, the establishment of the jatropha project did not create competition with food crop production or other land-based livelihoods. This is different from the case of Rajasthan state in India, where a government-led jatropha project that sought to revive the livelihood of the rural people is in fact creating competition with agriculture and other livelihoods, on account of the state's high population density (about 165 persons per square kilometre) (Tompsett 2010).

Social responsibility of biofuel investors The social responsibility of biofuel investors also has an effect on food security. The strategy of the investors determines to what extent the biofuel project will be compatible with previous livelihoods, local food production and respect for the labour rights of the local people who will be employed (Boamah 2010). To show its social responsibility, BioFuel Africa Ltd adopted a participatory approach with the project villages, in order to ensure that the effects of the jatropha project were win-win. Farmers who ceded their farmland areas during the project were duly compensated through farmland relocation and employment on the plantation. Food crop production was promoted, especially maize (a total of about 26 hectares) and rice. Local people (including some female workers on the plantations) were also encouraged to cultivate crops in the jatropha rows, as well as on the edges of the plantation. The humane social responsibility of BioFuel Africa

Ltd thus rendered the land use change brought about by the jatropha project compatible with the economic land use pattern in the three villages.

In addition, BioFuel Africa Ltd provided a hammer mill to grind food crops like dried maize and dried cassava. The mill helped to ease food processing by community members. Two people are employed working at the mill, and they earn between GHS 80 and GHS 120. In other words, the socially responsible policy of BioFuel Africa Ltd had spin-off effects on food production, food purchases and food processing in the three villages, without compromising local livelihoods.

Contribution to livelihood diversification The importance of livelihood diversification to achieving food security has been noted by many researchers (Swift and Hamilton 2001; Maxwell and Smith 1992). Livelihood diversification involves a spread of economic activities away from reliance on the primary enterprise, whether livestock or cropping activities, and typically seeks a wider range of on- and off-farm sources of income (Swift and Hamilton 2001: 86). Inevitably food must be purchased to supplement a household's consumption, over and above the farm's own produce. Because the livelihoods in the three Yendi villages yield meagre and irregular incomes, additional sources of income are required in the villages to make ends meet.

During the project, there were new opportunities for the residents, either through direct employment on the plantation or through a boost in petty trading activities and farming (Boamah 2010). The diversified livelihoods that accompanied the project created diversified income sources. The residents of Kpachaa, Jimle and Jaashie spend a large proportion of their incomes on food. The existence of 'food sharing' in the households meant that the diversified income sources improved household food security. To the extent that they contributed to livelihood diversification, the biofuel investments thus had an effect on food security.

Why are there crisis narratives in most biofuel reports? The influence of 'interests'

The study has thus contributed to the literature on biofuels, by showing how the mainstream biofuel narratives fail to illuminate the complexities surrounding the relationship between biofuels and food security. I therefore support Roe at this stage that 'there is no story to tell until the facts are in' (Roe 1999: 10). The study found that there is interest in reports about the implications of biofuels (Boamah 2010; 2011). There is the perception that NGOs investigate the problems of, and prospects for, investment projects at the grass-roots level by identifying themselves with the poor. As a consequence, reports published by NGOs are widely circulated and are well received, with high confidence in the reliability of their information – especially when they create crisis scenarios on undeveloped Africa (Boamah 2010). AAG claims to be concerned for the plight of the poor, and so publishes reports on projects that appear to affect the livelihoods of the poor. When such reports predict doom, the NGO solicits funds from donors to arrest the situation. In the quest for funding, crisis narratives are used as a tool for lobbying. They appeal to the emotions of donors and urge the need to act to restore a certain ideal situation or to avoid some impending agony. A thought-provoking question is: will there be any basis on which to solicit funding when there is no crisis?

The study found that regular visits were not made to the project villages to establish the consequences of the project. Rather, AAG visited the plantation and took snapshots of farmland areas, which, it claimed, were encroached upon by the project. It used these to try to explain the daunting implications of the project on local livelihoods. During interviews with people from the Food Span and Food Rights units of ActionAid-Ghana, it seemed to me that they magnified the potential problems of the jatropha project, while ignoring the benefits and not even attempting to find out about what was going on in the plantation and the project villages.

In addition, the article by RAINS highlighted a doom-laden scenario in order to gain the support of environmental activists and other interest groups in opposing large-scale biofuel investments in Ghana. This is evident from a quote:

> We need a more aggressive campaign to halt land grabbing. We need to engage with traditional rulers, District Assemblies and Politicians about this ominous phenomenon. We need visibility through print and electronic media to put our message across effectively to a wider audience ... we cannot afford to be caught unawares in this war with the biofuel companies. The ancestors are on our side and we shall win the war! (Nyari 2008: 6)

To make the messages more compelling, elegant and authoritative, certain phrases or statements with some negative connotations were woven together into a kind of story to predict impending doom from the consequences of biofuels, if governments and policy-makers remained aloof (Boamah 2010). There were other reports, too, by environmental activist groups, which claimed that the project would have dire consequences because of material interests. There were even cases where individuals joined the campaign against the jatropha project after some selfish demands were rejected by BioFuel Africa Ltd.

Undeniably, there are instances where some of the reports about the jatropha project contained valid evidence. Nonetheless, interest groups that opposed the jatropha project built up crisis scenarios, using fear of the devastating effects that biofuels and other capitalist investments have had on local livelihoods and food security elsewhere. Yet, in spite of the numerous negative reports about the project that were circulating in the Ghanaian media, most village residents hailed the spin-off benefits of the project on local livelihoods and household food security. Because 'interests' determine what is investigated, what is published and what is suppressed (Herring 2008), the information presented in reports about biofuels should be treated with some caution.

Conclusion

The discussion here elicits the fact that, thanks to the demographic and ecological conditions in the Yendi district, coupled with the goodwill of Bio-Fuel Africa Ltd, the BioFuel Africa jatropha project improved household food security in the three villages whose livelihoods depended on the land areas acquired. However, loss of funding for BioFuel Africa Ltd in the midst of the global economic crunch and negative reports about the project contributed to its failure. The chapter concludes that analyses of the food security implications of biofuels should be located within specific contexts, and consideration should be given to local variations in land use patterns, land availability, farming seasons, household composition, the resilience of livelihoods, the strategy of biofuel investors and the biological characteristics of the biofuel feedstock. This is because these factors determine the amount of resources diverted from food production to biofuel production. And that determines the extent of competition between biofuels and food. Because the relationship between biofuels and food security is very complex, it is vital to rethink biofuel narratives so that they contribute a more nuanced knowledge of the biofuel and food security debates.

Conclusion: land grabbing, smallholder farmers and the meaning of agro-investor-driven agrarian change in Africa

Prosper B. Matondi, Kjell Havnevik and
Atakilte Beyene

Introduction

The subject of land grabbing in Africa and related issues of food security and the search for alternative energy have moved the centre of relevant academic discourse to issues of continuity in global economic and power relations on the one hand and poverty, injustice and the 'squeeze' of smallholders on the other hand.[1] Issues of climate change and economic recession have also featured prominently in the global discourse, in what seems to be continuity in the historical relationships between Africa and the rest of the world. The enigma is that there seems to be a pretence by most actors, including international institutions, of having been ill prepared for the rapid interest in and growth of agro-investments. The search for energy and food security has resulted in processes that converge in land grabbing of unexpected intensity, with a number of implications that threaten to undermine broader development objectives related to poverty, land rights and environmental issues. This has intensified the furious search by international institutions for 'guidelines', 'best practices', 'responsible' or 'win-win' solutions for agro-investments where large tracts of land have to be acquired. Current studies have often concentrated more on the global aspects of land acquisition and less on the impact on African smallholders. By way of African case studies, this book presents findings on land grabbing by examining investments in agrofuels (jatropha, sugarcane, soya beans, etc.) and export food production in several countries. We examine biofuels, food security and energy from a number of perspectives, including environmental and ecology issues, rural development and agrarian change, political science and institutions.

Land grabbing in Africa today seems to be a reincarnation of the colonial land expropriations of the late 1800s, which were driven by capitalist expansion and were connected to the specific competition among European countries to access land, labour, natural resources and markets. This wrought economic, social, cultural and political havoc in Africa and endogenous processes of change and state formation were undermined (Ki-Zerbo 1995). The politics of land grabbing in Africa is driven by commerce (money) rather than by force (weapons). The process is viewed as strategic by wealthy foreign nations, anxious to enhance their food and energy security, and at the same time to create wealth for their own citizens through the investment and state-related companies. This time the competition for African land and resources has widened to include transition countries in Asia with large populations, Arab nations with abundant petro-dollars but limited capacity for food production, and Brazil, which boasts the longest experience and the highest technological level of biofuel processing and use. Although global processes, such as peak oil, climate change and food security, are the essential driving forces in current agrofuel development, we stress that these have implications for local people in Africa and cannot be discussed in a vacuum. At the end of the day, many African states are key stakeholders who will be impacted by these processes. The desire to attract, or even to compete for, FDI in order to 'modernize' their agriculture and reduce their dependency on imported oil is driving African states to hastily promote guidelines and policies for biofuel production. This is leading to a situation where the access of international companies and external states to African rural land and resources, including labour, is gradually increasing and being protected. The problem here is that this is occurring at a time when the governance of African land and natural resources has not yet been settled. Not only is this unresolved issue a major (current and potential) source of conflict surrounding land access across Africa, but it has also allowed African states to apportion land at the expense of their own people.

Biofuels, land grabbing and the narratives in global relationships

Biofuel investments and land-related activities have generated fresh debates about North–South and South–South relations. A political view emerging in Africa is that the North is primarily interested in controlling resources because of growing competition over the past decade from such transition economies as China, India, Brazil and the Arab countries. This might also explain why Northern countries are shying away from implementing the Paris Declaration of 2005, which seeks to give aid-recipient countries more influence over their own development strategies (cf. the meagre outcome of the subsequent Accra agreement of 2008).

The biofuel narratives are, in important ways, shaped by the emerging transition economies, and therefore inspire many African leaders to search for other alliances and new future development paths. A case in point is Brazil – the world's largest producer of bioethanol. The bioethanol expansion in Brazil is also founded on such problematic premises as the invasion of tropical forests, labour problems, monoculture, land degradation, increased concentration of land and landlessness (Hollander 2010).

Economic and social progress in the transition countries, with their growing urban populations, has increased the demand for food and energy. Yet such growth has also created global price volatility and a growing distrust in the international trade system. The response has been a search for alternative sources of energy and food in the context of bilateral investment treaties and agreements (see Chapter 1). The grabbing of land in Africa and elsewhere is also based on fears that the world prices of energy and food will continue to rise, making land, water and associated resources critical and increasingly scarce factors. This has made these resources increasingly strategic in the North–South relationship. Yet there is also some land speculation by global risk capital through quick acquisition in anticipation of large capital gains.

Nonetheless, the discourse of land grabs in the context of continuity in global relationships raises questions about the role Africa plays in the global policy discourse. When carefully examined, land grabbing is part of globalization processes, in which African land has two main functions: (i) it has become part of the internationalization of capital, investment and trade, and (ii) it has come to constitute an integral part of enhancing food and energy security in developed and transition countries. The process by which nations that are rich in cash, but vulnerable in terms of their own future energy and food provisions, secure African land retains similarities with historical paradigms linked to mercantile trade, colonialism and neo-colonialism. In the new 'scramble' for Africa, governments of developed and transition countries encourage private investors, state companies, large investment and sovereign funds to acquire, lease or buy land in Africa.

However, behind this process lie deeper 'security narratives'. These shape the search for land for biofuels and food, reflecting the fact that powerful nations cannot leave security provisioning to economic liberalization, markets and trade. Thus, the narrative of land grabbing for biofuels and food is often introduced and communicated as 'development' of a poor continent. This may be supported by sub-narratives related to 'conservation' and 'environmental concerns', in order to convince the general public and sceptical taxpayers that, for example, biofuel expansion is also addressing climate change. However, many Northern taxpaying consumers, whose resources subsidize the search for cleaner energy, tend to take a dim view of corporate and municipal companies pushing an agenda for profits, especially beyond their own borders.

The North–South differences also played out at the 2009 Copenhagen Conference on Climate Change. The developing nations demanded a stake through monetary compensation, which the developed nations were prepared to concede only to a limited extent. The narratives were shaped not just by policy-makers, but also by researchers and scientists. The problems ranged from scepticism over climate change data and evidence to uncertainty over the proposal to curb greenhouse gas emissions (in which biofuels feature as an alternative option). In this context, the discussion on climate change is transmuted to the 'virtues' of biofuels and the need to put 'idle' land in the South to use. It is in this context that countries with land targeted respond by insisting on general monetary compensation. Nonetheless, such compensation for land in Africa does indicate that there is a market for transactions around land. However, more than 90 per cent of African lands are owned under various tenurial regimes (customary, leasehold, freehold title, permit), which differ from Western types of ownership. This implies that there is no standard global measure for compensation.

Biofuels as a limit of 'development' from the North

In the last decades, there has been a declining interest in Africa's agricultural and rural development, in spite of the fact that the majority of the African people reside in rural areas. Despite technological advances and global economic progress (albeit with increasing differentiation between nations), people in Africa continue to be mired in poverty. In the 1980s and 1990s, a range of scholarship emerged, asking questions about the 'positive' prospects for the neoliberal agenda of promoting economic liberalization in Africa. Havnevik and others wrote *Tanzania: The limits to development from above* (1993) and *African Agriculture and the World Bank* (2007), detailing how the neoliberal agenda was failing and had failed to generate agricultural and broad-based development in Tanzania and sub-Saharan Africa. Today, we might characterize land grabbing in the same vein, as the 'limits to development from the North'. Many African states are weak, following implementation of externally led economic reform programmes (Havnevik et al. 2007). However, the specific Northern worldview, supported by that of transition countries, has shaped the biofuel narratives over the last decade or so. Why this interest?

There is a contested view as to why and when exactly biofuels started to feature in the global debates, because biofuels, in the form of ethanol, have a long history both in the North and in the South. Those lobbying for biofuels point out that sufficient progress has been made with ethanol on a small scale, and, in view of climate change, the need for biofuels has become imperative. The pro-biofuels lobby views those who are anti-biofuel as having insufficient understanding of the role of biofuels in technological and economic progress. The pro-biofuel people acknowledge that the world food crisis around 2007/08 convoluted the progressive development of biofuel development. The anti-biofuel movement uses the food crisis as a foundation on which to attack the development of biofuels by connecting it to food insecurity. Sengers et al. (2010: 18) found that:

> The practitioners also mention that the image of biofuels in the eye of the
> public has changed considerably for the worse over the last few years. One of

the interviewed mentions that 'Before [the food crisis] biofuels were THE green alternative'. Or, as another one of the practitioners puts it: 'When we started in 2004/2005 people saw biofuels as "a solution for everything"; good for climate, good for trade, good for farmers; pretty much good for everything. The undertone was much more positive then ... Only when the food crisis came along, was there attention for the negative side effects. What I read in the papers was a sort of mantra; when a piece on biofuels appeared in the media there was always the notion "but it has problems; forests and food". I'm talking about 2007/2008, when this is always mentioned.'

The 'agriculture for biofuels' narrative is predominantly within the confines of the 'agro-exporter' model, based on the neoliberal logic of market-based development, privatization and the transformation of natural resources – i.e. land, water, forests and fauna. This model is assumed to lead to maximization of investors' profits, an increase in land-based export production and the modernization of agriculture. This model does not arise out of national political processes, aimed at community welfare and the provision of clean sources of rural energy. The logic of the neoliberal model has resulted in an increased concentration and control of land, resources and production in the hands of African elites and external interests. Influence over the value chain of food and natural resources has increasingly been placed in the hands of a few multinational or transnational companies (Gibbon and Ponte 2005).

This development has made Africa assume a new importance for cash-rich nations. De Schutter (2009: 5) indicates that 'resource-poor but cash-rich countries have turned to large-scale acquisitions or rent of land in order to achieve food security'. Developed and emerging countries have led the race for land grabbing for the production of biofuels and food based on strategic political interests. African countries have largely been (or are intended as) recipients of foreign investments. Africans are expected to embrace foreign investments and external innovations because the continent is regarded as poor and backward. Therefore, when private companies enter the continent, they do not expect Africans to question the development that the investments are supposed to bring. Biofuel production has so far been pushed in a 'Big Brother' attitude that resembles the historical relationships of colonization. Africa and Africans are viewed as 'inferior and backward', needing development from outside. Since development assistance has failed to deliver in the African context over the last four decades, interest has turned to FDIs in the quest for dynamism and economic growth. This worldview is embedded in Western and transition states and global corporate institutions, and 'legitimizes' the global push for biofuels.

Corporate institutions in Western and transition countries that have taken the lead in biofuel investments have done so also on the basis of a strong claim that the world needs clean and cheap energy (Chapter 3). There is, however, limited evidence of constructive technology transfers, of genuine involvement of smallholders, or even of anything approaching equal partnership in relations between external and domestic investors. Domestic investors are given the opportunity to share a fraction of the equity (e.g. in the Tanzanian case, 1.5 per cent), while they are given the responsibility for paving the way for access to the major sources of the investment – land and labour (Chapter 6).

The agricultural systems of Africa have been heavily disinvested over the last three decades – to the extent that the World Bank's *World Development Report* on agriculture (2007) called for greater attention to be paid to agriculture by the international donor community and African states. In this context, it is argued that renewable energy, led by bioenergy, represents an opportunity to reverse this trend and turn African agriculture into a dynamic and dominant sector for broad-based development.

In 2010, the World Bank, in cooperation with other international organizations such as IFAD and the IMF, elected to provide voluntary principles for land acquisition in foreign lands (World Bank 2010). In fact, it argued for a land governance that is open, especially for public purchase and leasing. The World Bank defined governance in terms of how public officials and institutions acquire and exercise their authority. In terms of land governance, it noted that the conduct of public officials in relation to property rights to land and to the exchange of such rights (as well as their transformation) is critical. The public authorities have weighty responsibility for oversight of land use, management and taxation. The public should have sufficient confidence in how land is administered, and clear knowledge of what is state owned and of how land is acquired or disposed of. In fact, the nature and quality of land ownership information available to the public, and the ease with which it can be accessed or modified, are likewise important elements in accountability and transparency. The development of these guidelines emerges from the reality that the bulk of the poor African population resides in rural areas. Therefore, while the modernization of African agriculture could help reduce poverty, at the same time these people remain exposed to greater negatives if such land acquisitions are hidden (Partners for Africa 2005). While the arguments advanced by the bank sound rational, there are questions of procedure in how they develop. The development of governance principles has largely come from the North (including from leading financial institutions and donors), which questions the 'political' motives, given that there has not been adequate consultation.

Challenging the neoliberal paradigm in land grabs

A significant number of the people in sub-Saharan Africa live in rural areas and pursue agriculture as a main livelihood, although diversification of rural economic activities and rural–urban migration have increased since the onset of the African crises in the late 1970s. The land issue continues to be crucial in many respects: land rights, identification, status and recognition of customary rights (formalization and certification processes), tenure and rights of 'communal', national and protected lands.

Our assessment is that there is a need to go beyond the rhetoric of the benefits of a weak state – a notion that was driven by the neoliberal framework in Africa in the 1980s. This notion was pursued with less intensity in the late 1980s and early 1990s, when it was acknowledged that it could not deliver (World Bank 1989). This abdicationist stance on the part of the state left communities exposed to local elites, ready to share the spoils of the promised investments in biofuels and food security. There is a need for the state to take a more central role in land deals and to ensure that the rights and interests of rural people are protected against investors. This calls for a strengthening of laws and policies on the management and administration of land, related to tenure reform, land redistribution and land restitution, which many African countries have struggled to develop over the past two decades. The lobbying of external investors, banks and financial institutions has made it extremely difficult for many African governments to arrive at land policies with a clearly defined role for foreign companies and investors, given the sensitivities that arise from property rights internationally. For instance, a ten-year domestic land policy and law process initiated in the early 1990s in Tanzania was confused when external donors (in this case the Norwegian aid agency), in alliance with the country's president, made the country one of two African pilots (the other being Egypt). The government of Tanzania gave Hernando de Soto, author of *The Mystery of Capital*, the task to find ways to speed up village and urban land titling processes. In so doing, but without proper consultation of current land legislation, new confusion was inserted into the village land certification process.

As global and national demand for agricultural products (energy and food) puts greater pressure on the land, so the widespread allocation of large areas to investors for food and biofuels can be problematic. De Schutter (2010: 39) writes:

> global population increases by some 75 million individuals each year, diets evolve, demanding greater amounts of animal protein. But these facts matter only to the extent that, combined with the unsustainable levels of consumption in rich countries – the demand for meat and the thirst for agroenergy, in particular –, they lead to increased pressures on natural resources, encouraging in turn speculation over land and large-scale dispossessions of the poorest and the most vulnerable, particularly smallholders and indigenous communities that lack adequate protection and political support. It is not by producing more that we will effectively combat hunger: it is by protecting those who are hungry today, hungry because they are disempowered and marginalized.

The process of acquiring land for food and energy needs to be seen in relation to the broader land tenure policies of African states and rural conditions. We have shown that land targeted for biofuels includes both customary-owned land and land under freehold tenure. The governments of some countries have also ceded some of the land they own as statutory lands, by providing leases to biofuel companies. Issues related to customary land ownership of so-called 'unused' lands have created a huge controversy in Africa, because rural people hardly conceive any land to be unused. Some of the land that is assumed to be unoccupied is used for pastoralism and some for accessing natural resources important to people's livelihoods. In addition, many rural people see themselves as the stewards of land for future generations. Unused land will always be used.

The pitfalls of reverting to plantation agriculture

In many contexts, the large-scale acquisition of land also highlights a renewed interest in plantation-based agriculture. This is fuelled by an increasing scepticism regarding the effectiveness of market mechanisms and international trade in guaranteeing access to basic food and energy supplies. Loewenson (1992: 3) reminds us that 'violent land expropriation, the destruction of peasant farming and the often forced recruitment of slave, tenant or wage labour marked the earliest development of plantation agriculture'. History has shown that small family farms are much more efficient than large-scale farms (World Bank 2007). Plantation agriculture displaces local producers, who often have the knowledge to produce sustainably and who would be in a position to do so, with even higher yields, if they were provided with an enabling agricultural policy environment and with proper learning platforms and communication networks.

The implication is that large African land areas are appropriated for forms of economy and organization that are intended to promote efficient and voluminous food and energy feedstock production, and that may not accommodate small farms. Yet large-scale farming in Africa has historically faced specific difficulties. Large farms have only prospered in Africa when they have been able to capture some form of public subsidy. Many large-scale commercial Zimbabwean farmers who have emigrated elsewhere within the continent have found life hard without state subsidies.

However, the economics of biofuel production remains speculative, because the investments are largely subsidized, meaning they are not economically competitive. The economic sustainability of investments in biofuel is not actually clear (Chapter 3). Currently the biofuel product is, to a great extent, financed by subsidies. If the 'real price' were charged, without tax reductions and other benefits, bioethanol would probably be considerably more expensive than petrol is today. (That said, fossil fuels are also, in a way, subsidized, since the costs of their negative impact on the environment and on health – the result of their production and consumption – are not included in the price.)

The World Bank's *World Development Report* (2007) stressed the difficulties that African smallholders face in trying to compete on the global market. Poverty levels in rural areas remain high and have been spreading to urban areas along with migration. The opportunities for generating incomes in rural areas have diminished. In this context, biofuels are seen as strategic in generating employment and income for rural areas, and they may help stem rural-to-urban migration. However, in large part, food insecurity is increasing. This is indicated by African countries' rising levels of food imports and famine relief. African governments and Western donors have called for renewed investment in agriculture, while drawing attention to the importance of global value chains, private capital, contract farming and different scales of farming units.

Smallholders, it is suggested, should scale up their input procurement and technology usage through producer organizations. Focusing on biofuels and food production, the issue of the scale of agricultural production and marketing is being reintroduced as a key one, especially in less-favoured areas. Yet smallholders face multiple threats. One of these – competition from cheap imports – often undermines indigenous farming units and forces people to migrate to urban areas, or else to move in and out of wage labour cyclically.

Pushing people into wage labour or migration forces them increasingly to purchase imported foods or food produced by large-scale farms. The linking of sectors to export markets frequently creates increased pressure on the rural poor to give up farming for employment. In most chapters of this book, we provide background and insights showing that much hinges on how biofuel production 'pans out' with respect to large or small agricultural production units. On the one hand, the current trends in agribusiness agitate for 'efficient', large-scale, capitalized biofuel production, as opposed to the efforts of scattered, small-scale farmers. On the other hand, the equity and livelihood of large segments of the rural population could suffer if such efficiency considerations were prioritized to the exclusion of welfare aspects.

Biofuel assault on the food security and sovereign rights of the poor

Rural areas in Africa are experiencing processes of globalization, commoditization and monetization. In the various chapters of this book, we have tried to make sense of how a number of global processes and relations with respect to biofuels and food security affect Africa. The rich nations' search for land for biofuels and food security no longer takes the form of veiled plundering of resources, based on the 'civilizing' motives of the pre-colonial period. Instead, new forms of accessing Africa's land and resources come through the economic interests of rich nations seeking to sustain their economies, which are marked by affluence and high resource consumption. One key issue emerging in many countries is the fact that there is limited land to satisfy the food needs of their own populations. This has triggered a rush for African lands in a world consumed by a human-led economic crisis. Eide (2008: 12) concluded that:

Any diversion of land from food or feed production to production of energy biomass will influence food prices from the start, as both compete for the same inputs. Putting it starkly, the 'food versus fuel' game could make it possible for a car owner in a developed country to fill his or her tank (50 litres) with biofuel produced from 200 kilograms of maize, which would have been enough to feed one person for one year. The purchasing power of the owner of the car is of course vastly higher than that of a food insecure person in a developing country; in an unregulated world market there is no doubt who would win.

Many African countries have large unemployed populations in both rural and urban areas. Though HIV and AIDS seem to have slowed population growth somewhat, especially in southern Africa, in general a high rate is still being maintained. As was pointed out in the Introduction and in Chapter 1, land and natural resources offer opportunities for labour-intensive food production. Many Africans in rural areas are tied to the monetary economies only to a limited extent, and exchanges happen informally on the basis of trust and relationships. Hence, although they may not be living sophisticated lives, they are secure in terms of food. Therefore, when foreign companies acquire land, as in Ethiopia (Chapter 5), the human right to food and life is compromised.

We have also noted that many foreign land acquisitions are oriented towards excessive profits and are largely for export. This implies that countries receiving such investments may see an industrial agricultural mode of production being developed. In the case of Zimbabwe and Ghana, massive mechanization is followed by massive land clearance for arable crop production. The process is ecologically destructive and will have far-reaching consequences for micro-climates. Land, water and forests form ecosystems that offer a wide range of 'services', ranging from cleaning of the natural environment, to water (aquatic resources), to fruits, etc., which can be damaged by land clearance or by the damming of rivers for large-scale irrigation. If contingent conservation measures are not put in place, there will be massive loss of nutrient-rich soils, destruction of biodiversity and large amounts of CO_2 released.

Agro-investments are premised on their supposed ability to increase agricultural production. However, as past efforts to promote the 'Green Revolution' show, the modernization of agriculture, which may well result in more food production, does not imply enhanced food security for local communities. In fact, the expansion of cash-crop monocultures has a severe impact on local availability of food, as it diverts food-producing resources and labour to cash-crop production. As a result, communities are forced to depend on the market, putting them at the mercy of volatile food prices. The lack of local food availability and the high level of dependence on food from elsewhere also reduce the quality and variety of the diet of communities and alter their food customs.

Natural heritage and environmental narratives

At another level, all the chapters in this book discuss how the politics of energy and food production impact on the livelihood of local people. This is with specific regard to the access and use of natural resources. Although it may seem that the land targeted for biofuels and food security is small, it will increase in proportion over time, due to peak oil and climate change. Climate change seems to be deepening and to have the potential to reduce the areas favourable to agricultural production. This means that large-scale, capital-intensive and energy-dependent agricultural production systems will compete with smallholder farmers on the most productive land. This is likely to exacerbate land conflicts. At the same time, as agriculture encroaches on wetter and ecologically productive areas, the ecosystem habitats (flora and fauna) are most likely to be casualties of resource competition.

The degradation of 'the commons' has also been used to justify the allocation of land to large-scale users, on the pretext that small farms are unable to mobilize financial resources. The argument is also that smallholders misuse natural resources because of pressure per unit of land caused by both livestock and human activities. In the context of local livelihoods, the transfer of skills and knowledge is embedded in the livelihood processes of local communities. This has been characterized as indigenous knowledge systems that are more likely to be lost with the creation of monocultural estates. Investors in large-scale farm units are rarely as concerned with flora and fauna as indigenous people are.

Smallholders are likely to have an adaptive advantage relative to large-scale producers for a number of reasons: (1) their in-depth environmental knowledge of their home areas; (2) their farms, which represent dispersed production units affording diverse, decentralized experimentation; and (3) their combination of subsistence and commercial cash cropping, which has accustomed them to growing an array of crops and livestock-sustaining products, and which comprises a diverse foundation for experimentation that can reduce risks to livelihood. Large-scale production, on the other hand, often does not have indigenous knowledge at its disposal and has a tendency towards monoculture. Costly investment in agriculture on the basis of economies of scale, could, in the face of climate uncertainty, prove to be ill judged and unsustainable.

Economic and social justice questions

In Africa, smallholder farmers account for the majority of the rural population, and constitute the economic, social and cultural bulwark of the African countryside. African governments face a kaleidoscope of pressures with respect to their smallholder farming populations. On top of productivity and welfare concerns, the opportunities and threats posed by the emergence of biofuels are increasingly coming to the fore. Balancing land and labour allocation, energy dependency and food supply in Africa is difficult for policy-makers, who often end up taking part in projects such as biofuels without adequate feasibility analysis (see Chapter 6). People in Africa more often lack basic services and economic opportunities. The opportunities for Africans to invest in biofuels for the benefit of Africa are limited because of the market constraints and the context in which the majority of the people struggle to access food. Local people are primarily concerned with improving their living conditions, while taking responsibility for their own areas. Income and non-income inequalities are high in Africa, with the level of inequality being lower in rural areas. Countries with high initial income inequality find economic growth to be less efficient in reducing poverty. The pace of poverty reduction would have been substantial had it not been for the dampening effects of a rise in inequality in the wake of economic growth.

Many African countries see agricultural commercialization as an opportunity to achieve economic development and thereby stimulate their trade relations across regions. However, there are also concerns as to how such processes can contribute to a reduction in rural poverty. One major risk for many African countries is their over-dependence on land as an incentive for attracting foreign investors. In fact, as Chapter 5 of this book shows, some countries even go so far as to provide large pieces of land for lease or acquisition, low land rents and long lease terms to attract companies with an interest in biofuels. The private investment perspective has increasingly become the dominant discourse, after the failure of development assistance in Africa. This helps promote the assumptions, perceptions and interests of those shaping investment policy. However, this investment discourse, including that of biofuels, focuses too narrowly on technical and economic change, to the exclusion of structural, social and behavioural issues, which influence local people's perceptions of technological innovation. In general, current investment policies hardly try to embed biofuels within rural livelihoods, such as through the provision of clean and affordable household energy, by improving rural health, or by enhancing the gender and environmental impacts of rural energy. The policies fail to envisage a role for agrofuels in the rural transformation, through the localized consumption of biofuels, or through the technological, entrepreneurship and organizational requirements of the rural agrarian contexts.

Despite the paradox and conceptualization of a 'failed continent', rural Africans demonstrate a capacity to produce their own food, to supply food and labour to urban areas, to sustain indigenous and formal education systems, to endure deprivation and to reconstruct economic and social systems. They may not be doing this at the pace and in forms that policy-makers at the national or global level may wish. However, smallholders are living their own lives, which the proponents of biofuels and land grabbing have placed at stake.

The introduction of biofuels also has a specific impact on gender, labour and generational divides, all of which ultimately impinge on household welfare. The biofuel investment comes with a specific focus on commercial production, on a continent where agriculture is dominated by female smallholders. It is most likely that men will willingly give up their land for shop-floor labour on the estates, resulting (among other things) in gender-differentiated labour migration (particularly male outmigration). At the same time, when contract farming and outgrower schemes are introduced, it is the landholder – usually the man – who will gain (though often only in the short term). There is a real possibility of a decline in the irregular (but critical) income that women earn from agriculture and contribute to the welfare and food security of their families. At the broader community level, Africans live in structured villages, following specific cultural norms and rules. Many of these are likely to be broken or weakened by new economic systems centred on agro-investment farms, without leading to the creation of new and sustainable rules and norms that can provide rural people with meaningful livelihoods and social orientation.

Individualism is likely to replace community collective effort and rules, thus undermining the orderly, however discriminatory, resource governance systems inherited from the past. Without the complexities of paperwork, these governance systems, based on oral tradition, were effective in determining land ownership, looking after natural resources and allocating land. Instead, with large-scale agricultural modernization, more competition and conflicts over land will emerge within families and communities, as they defy tradition by engaging in opportunistic behaviour, competition for profit and contract relationships that assume importance at the expense of family and community. Thus, in the long term, Africa is more likely to see the loss of community responsibilities, including access to and transmission of knowledge, the defence and negotiation of rights, and the regulation of relations between winners and losers. This development is likely to occur because there are limited options for the majority of rural African people to escape poverty. The loss of land, when capacity for industrialization is weak, creates grounds for conflicts, which may negatively affect the biofuel companies.

Complexities shaping policy-making on biofuels in Africa

On the question of narratives and ideologies that shape policy-making in developing countries, Scott (1985: 318) writes the following:

> If there was a dominant, hegemonic ideology ... [it] would require that the beliefs and values of the agrarian elite penetrate and dominate the worldview of the poor so as to elicit their consent and approval of an agrarian order, which materially, does not serve their objective interests. Its function would be to conceal or misrepresent the real conflicts of class interests ... and to make of the poor, in effect, co-conspirators in their own victimisation.

In Africa, there is still a policy vacuum, which the proponents of large-scale biofuel development are exploiting quietly and often with a lasting impact on smallholders. On the continent, competition for FDIs (Chapter 4) has seen policy-makers override even their own policies, as they try to attract investors. The policy-making process is not linear or orderly, because behind the scenes of the schemes various deal-makers are active in the land acquisitions. The chapters of this book confirm that the policy-making process is non-linear, complex and incremental, influenced by practices, interest groups, actors and policy networks in which agro-investors and political leadership in the host country play a significant role.

External investors see African lands providing scope for them to make easy money on a continent without strong regulations (see World Bank 2010). In addition, cheap land is a motivating factor for companies and host governments. Weak land and environmental laws mean that mechanisms for protecting local rights, interests and welfare tend to be disregarded. African policy-makers are increasingly responding to external pressures for biofuel investments in ways that dislocate them from people within their own countries. National interests and agendas are at stake, especially when they are tested with the lure of money directed towards an agriculture that underpins the livelihoods of the majority. The attraction of technological investments through estate agriculture in neglected areas is seen as a signature of economic progress that African governments find hard to resist. The emerging alliance between external investors and elite domestic investors in Africa has been highly secretive within the context of agro-investments.

While a number of African countries have tried to craft policies that can attract foreign investments, there remain policy inconsistencies with respect to land that touch on national interests. The asymmetric power relations caused by domestic class interests make it difficult to see the (otherwise obvious) need for legislative protection of land held by smallholders. In any case, foreign investors have identified the loopholes in local systems of land management and administration. The weaknesses that are reflected through lack of policy on land and indicators that need to be considered when public lands are targeted create conditions ripe for underhand deals. In most cases, public officials have capitulated to the money dangled by the corporate investor negotiators. At times the corporate negotiators go straight to the villagers and their traditional leaders, who seem to lack the protection that can only come from strong policies and an alert public bureaucracy (which is hard to find in most African countries).

There is no doubt that Africa does require economic development and external investment capital to unlock the greater economic value of its land and resources for its own peoples. However, the current trajectory has been dominated by investment in large-scale plantation agriculture, which most often replaces and undermines the livelihoods of African peoples. Mechanization makes wage labour opportunities on plantations scarce, and only a limited proportion (if any) of the income generated from this form of agriculture is ploughed back into smallholder agriculture or into improving the welfare of rural people in other ways. A pertinent question needs to be raised: at what price should Africa give up its land?

Therefore, the political and governance contexts – in both the investor and the host countries – shape the discourses and narratives related to land grabbing (Roe 1991). In land grabbing, investors are manoeuvring complex political processes in varied contexts, because they compete for limited land and resources. Often external investors or companies find willing hosts, alliances and partners, both commercial and political, to make it possible for them to access land. At times, the local 'hosts' also act as a buffer between them and the people affected by the grabbing.

Emerging civic and community resistance to biofuel production

A range of civil society organizations inside and outside Africa have realigned their activism agenda to oppose large-scale African land grabbing – on behalf of the smallholder farmers. Africa has seen its fair share of such organizations, including RAINS and others that collaborate with international networks. At the international level, the FoodFirst Information and Action Network, the World Wildlife Fund, the Ecumenical Advocacy Alliance, GRAIN, etc. have all played a critical role in disseminating messages and knowledge on biofuels, food security and land grabbing. Multilateral institutions, led by the World Bank and the FAO, have been at the forefront of developing voluntary guidelines for win-win solutions in agro-investments.

In the preceding chapters, through the various authors, we have given space to voices 'from the field', talking about how communities and local policy-makers are responding to land grabs. In general, the media and academics have picked up the biofuel and land-grabbing discourses and have strongly opposed the apparent trajectory – the massive land grabs, the increased food insecurity and the greater poverty – and have projected this into the future. The poor are not involved in public debates on land issues and foreign investors, yet the investments are billed as beneficial to them. Instead, the engagement is happening at the international level, based on limited knowledge of what biofuels have already done in local communities in Africa.

In Africa, NGOs involved in advocacy have noted an increase in the voices that oppose land grabbing by multinational companies. The opposition from people affected by land grabs does not follow any rational course, but is rather based on the practical realities they face as their ecosystems and resources disappear as the land is cleared. While Boamah (Chapter 8) argues that, in Ghana, there is evidence that civil society has built anti-biofuel narratives on very shaky ground, the voices of village women suggest otherwise:

'Look at all the sheanut trees you have cut down already and considering the fact that the nuts that I collect in a year give me cloth for the year and also a little capital. I can invest my petty income in the form of a ram and sometimes in a good year, I can buy a cow. Now you have destroyed the trees and you are promising me something you do not want to commit yourself to. Where then do you want me to go? What do you want me to do?' (Nyari 2008: 6)

The Tanzania case, however, reveals (Chapter 6) that there is an epistemic community promoting biofuels, ranging from environmentalists fighting for clean fuel energy to large-scale investors and sectoral associations. They actively raise issues and frame debates, outline possibilities and lobby governments, agencies and institutions. Unfortunately, since they are given their information by advocates for biofuels, governments have largely been weak in responding and non-committal as to whether they are willing to stop land grabbing that prejudices the poor. However, activists and researchers following the grabbing issues are carefully presenting their views and insights and sharing these with the media, in order to shape the public's views in the North on biofuels and their impact on African people.

In addition, issues of human rights, food and nutrition rights, and ecological concerns have been placed higher in the public domain, forcing multilateral institutions to think again about agro-investments by crafting what they call 'codes of conduct'. However, the issue is: what does this mean when these frameworks are to be applied in the villages and at the local level? In Africa, a combination of poverty, illiteracy, lack of democratic liberties and economic deficiencies will make it difficult to implement the codes of conduct. Moreover, the codes are voluntary and are not underpinned by institutions or resources to monitor and enforce compliance. Our fear is that such voluntary guidelines, oriented towards 'how things should be done', will divert attention from what is happening on the ground (see Chapter 1).

Setting the agenda for protecting the rights of smallholder farmers

Many studies have shown that investment to increase productivity in owner-operated smallholder agriculture has a great impact on growth and poverty reduction. Investments to bring about such productivity increases in Africa have historically amounted to only a fraction of what was spent in Asia at the height of the 'Green Revolution'. This is often seen as one of the reasons for Africa's dismal record in terms of agricultural growth and rural development. Investment in rural areas, based on African agrarian development vision, can close this gap. The challenge is to ensure that such investments respect the rights of existing land users and increase productivity and welfare in line with existing strategies for economic development and poverty reduction, but without further widening income gaps.

Private investment in the agricultural sector offers significant potential to complement public resources, and many countries with reasonably functioning markets have derived significant benefits from this. At the same time, there is evidence that, if rights are not well defined, if governance is weak, and if those affected lack voice, then such investments carry with them considerable risk. The investments may lead to the displacement of local populations; to the undermining or negating of existing rights; to corruption, food insecurity, local and global environmental damage; to loss of livelihoods or opportunity for land access by the vulnerable; to nutritional deprivation, social polarization and political instability. In the past, many large farming ventures have been unsuccessful. Mistaken beliefs in economies of scale in agricultural production, rather than value addition, have historically saddled several countries with subsidy-dependent large-farm sectors that provide few economic or social benefits.

Rural entrepreneurship and organizational issues provide another critical dimension. Rural producers do not respond as individual and independent actors to the political and economic imperatives. The entrepreneurial and organizational aspects of rural people are crucial in the dissemination of technical and management know-how, access to rural finance and connections to potential markets. The right to form economic associations that can be recognized by formal/state systems (as firms and economic actors) is a critical step towards securing access to different resources.

Developing African capacities

It is evident that the current land grabbing in Africa is happening in a policy environment that has not been sufficiently developed or that does not exist at all. As such, many national governments are 'muddling through' with little guidance on how best to respond, given the complexities of investment (technical) language, with which local bureaucratic institutions may be unfamiliar. The lack of clarity on land negotiations calls for action and research to build a knowledge base of the many dimensions of land grabbing and agro-investments. There is growing consensus within Africa on the need for alternative development frameworks, as well as on the need to develop poverty-reduction and food security-enhancing strategies. This is underpinned by renewed and increased interest in addressing Africa's land tenure and agrarian reform questions. This is coupled with an increasing recognition, both outside and inside Africa, of the importance of agriculture to rural livelihoods and broad-based national and global economic development. However, this recognition has yet to be turned into firm policy programmes to guide land deals in Africa. In fact, agriculture, as a sub-sector, remains underfinanced, while land tenure reform programmes are not yet coherently formulated or are framed with major problems in their implementation.

In the chapters of this book, we have demonstrated that land deals have been negotiated with governments. However, there has only been muted response from African-based institutions and intellectuals. The media globally only picked up on the issue when the food and energy crisis went global in 2007/08. In Africa, where the land deals are being made, it was only in 2009 that the African Union started to talk of a code of conduct for land deals. The capacity for engaging in these matters in Africa is weak and is further compromised by the lack of platforms and opportunities on which to engage on issues. Furthermore, it has become the norm that inventions and technological solutions, such as those related to biofuels, are made in the developed countries, with little regard for the circumstances and rights of the Africans.

In terms of capacity, the economic decline that characterizes present-day Africa has translated into limited research opportunities, thereby impacting negatively on the development of an African body of knowledge. It is important that such a body of knowledge should command a technological grasp of African socio-cultural contexts; it should also understand the conditions and the potential of biofuel production. The problems have been compounded by the 'brain drain' from the South to the North, which has left African public institutions lacking capacity and unable to contribute to national policy development. Ironically, the environment shaping livelihoods has undergone considerable strain and has changed significantly, so this requires deeper knowledge. New theoretical constructs have been developed, which could enhance understanding of the processes of rural change. However, theoretical and methodological approaches, though they have become more comprehensive, are still largely disconnected and fragmented. Using the case of African land grabbing, we have demonstrated the complex connections of livelihoods, natural resource tenure, governance and environmental sustainability.

There is clearly a need for further enquiry into land grabbing, because awareness of the full impact is only in its infancy. There need to be technical inquiries; research projects need to be commissioned; and policy-making and implementation need to be monitored as agro-investments go ahead. At the same time, there is a need to develop a questioning voice from within Africa, so that the deals secure sustainable benefits for the broader African societies. The issue is about identifying what works and then scaling it up in such a way that it works better for the people of Africa. This requires knowledge about the impact of land grabbing to be pooled and shared as packages of options for Africa's smallholder development. Africa will need to identify actions to spread the benefits as wide as possible, particularly among the poor and marginalized. Supporting positive change, therefore, requires more targeted approaches to research, focusing on learning from successful experiments and experiences on the ground, particularly in relation to critical success factors, including institutional innovations.

Take-away message

The major concern of our book has been to provide the background and the stories and the narratives on how foreign investments connected with land grabbing affect smallholder farmers, now and potentially in the future, and to explain why such processes require a precautionary approach. Most of the chapters have addressed the positive and negative impacts of biofuels on the livelihoods of smallholder farmers, and they have also reflected on policy implications for the production of biofuels at the global, the national and the local levels. The authors have re-examined critical issues that affect smallholder farmers across Africa, as the continent moves towards being a 'bio-economy' characterized by the use of nature to prop up global economies and lifestyles. These issues have been analysed in light of economic, social and political justice, where biofuel seems to have compromised the food security of present and future African generations. Suggestions are made for improvements, and solutions incline towards the establishment of a more level playing field in relationships between developing and developed nations, and also within countries. We hope the suggestions will contribute to the setting of a new agenda for Africa that contains genuine win-win situations and that avoids a zero sum game at the world, the national and the local levels.

The combination of higher and more volatile commodity and oil prices, population growth and urbanization, globalization and climate change is likely to imply that biofuel demand and investments will be of even greater importance in the future. The issues of land grabbing for biofuels, for food and for other strategic reasons in Africa raise political and economic questions about global relations. Clearly, the conditions (economic, political, social and ecological) in Africa differ. Precise local knowledge needs to be developed on the meaning and impact of this 'new' phenomenon. This is because land grabbing affects local people's livelihoods, their food and their assets. It would seem that foreign private international companies, backed by their governments, are coming into Africa to make land deals with host governments that render it easier for them to venture into large-scale commercial production of agro-crops. Apparently, in many countries (such as Zimbabwe, Ethiopia or Tanzania) the shortage of agricultural land will, in the coming decades, prove an obstacle to the launching of ambitious programmes of land grabbing in Africa. However, for strategic and security reasons, developed nations and transition economies such as China, India and Brazil will push strongly to gain control of natural resources and land in the South.

In seeking a more level playing field, much will depend on the pace and direction of technological progress in the agricultural production of food, biofuels and industrial crops. Even more will depend on the ability to design integrated food-production systems that imitate natural ecosystems, instead of imposing monocultures. The main difficulties are likely to arise in the realms of land tenure, of access to land for small farmers, and of devising production functions and organizations that are knowledge- and labour-intensive (and at the same time eliminate hard manual work) and that are also capable of economizing on capital and resources. These are the issues that researchers and activists will need to address as land grabbing escalates across the African continent and elsewhere.

Notes

Introduction

1 For example, African sugarcane export production, which has been hard hit by the European Union's 2006 sugar reforms, now has domestic and export biofuel market potential.

2 Jatropha, for example, is generally grown in large monocultured block plantations, although there are arguments that it can be intercropped with other food crops. To address this constraint, the International Crops Research Institute for the Semi-Arid Tropics (ICRISAT) has been running trials on sweet sorghum, which yields bioethanol but does not preclude the grain from being eaten; it can also be intercropped with other plants.

3 For example, sudden flooding in Mozambique in 2000 resulted in the dislocation of 2 million people, as well as the loss of 350,000 jobs, which affected the livelihood of up to 1.5 million people (Nkomo et al. 2006).

4 There is a provision in the declarations on agriculture and food security of both the African Union and the Southern African Development Community for the allocation of 10 per cent of national budget to agricultural development. The African Union declaration was signed in Maputo, Mozambique, in July 2003, while the Southern African Development Community declaration was signed in Dar es Salaam, Tanzania, in May 2004.

1 Grabbing of African lands for energy and food

1 This is part of a larger paper that was first presented at the 4th Initiative for Policy Dialogue's Africa Task Force meeting in Pretoria, South Africa, on 9–10 July 2009. I am grateful to the organizers, Joseph Stiglitz and Akbar Noman of Columbia University, for the invitation and the inspiration that comments and discussions at the meeting gave me for my further work on these issues.

2 A comprehensive listing of overseas land investments is available on IFPRI's website at www.ifpri.org/pubs/bp/bp013.asp

3 In September 2010, the World Bank published a major report on the topic, *Rising Global Interest in Farmland: can it yield sustainable and equitable benefits?* (World Bank 2010). This report presented seven principles for responsible agro-investment that were merely a repetition of the five 'consensus' principles mentioned above. The only significant addition was what was termed principle 5: Responsible agro-investing. It states: 'Investors ensure that projects respect the rule of law, reflect industry best practices, are economically viable and result in durable shared value' (ibid.: x, box 1). This report was done in cooperation with the African Union, the FAO, IFAD, UNCTAD, IIED, the International Land Coalition, the Working Group on Land of the European Union and the Global Donor Platform for Rural Development, (ibid.: viii). However, already in April 2010 a statement by La Via Campesina, FoodFirst Information and Action Network, the Land Action Research Network and GRAIN, responding to a draft of the World Bank report, claimed that, 'The WB's principles attempt to create the illusion that land grabbing can proceed without disastrous consequences to peoples, communities, eco-systems and the climate. This illusion is false and misleading.' Instead four actions are seen as essential: keep land in the hands of local communities, heavily

support agro-ecological and smallholder farming, promote food sovereignty; and support community-oriented food and farming systems (GRAIN 2010: 2). A quite complete overview of the content of the many recommendations and principles related to land grabbing can be found in Anh-Nga Tran-Nguyen, 'Global land grabbing: issues and solutions', Paper presented for Pain pour le Prochain, September 2010.

4 Directive of the European Parliament and of the Council on the promotion of the use of energy from renewable sources, 2008/0016 (COD). Art. 15, 'Sustainability criteria for biofuels and other bioliquids'.

5 World Bank (2010: xvi, table 2) states that potential availability of uncultivated land in different regions amounts to about 446 million hectares, of which 202 million hectares are located in sub-Saharan Africa and 123 million hectares in Latin America and the Caribbean. In total, this amounts to about 75 per cent of the potential available uncultivated land globally. The World Bank, in presenting these figures, refers to a report by G. Fischer and M. Shah (2010) and prepared for the World Bank, 'Farmland investments and food security, statistical annex', Laxenburg, Austria.

6 *New Zealand Herald*, 14 May 2009.

7 ibid., and *Economist*, 23 May 2009, reported in De Schutter (2009).

8 Cotula et al. (2009: 73) claim that this land request is for sugarcane production in Bagamoyo district, whereas in fact it is for a second large-scale project in Rufiji district.

9 It was funded by FAO and IFAD. Various European donors, including the Norwegian Agency for Development Cooperation (Norad) and Sida, funded the field studies in Tanzania and Mozambique.

10 It is, however, true that sugarcane production also requires continuous water provision and is often related to irrigation systems. See, for instance, Sida's Helpdesk for Environmental Assessments (2009) 'Biofuels – potential challenges for developing countries', Uppsala. On 28 May 2009, Friends of the Earth International published a report that cast doubt on the notion that jatropha does not compete with food production for land and water (Burley and Griffiths 2009). This investigated the claims of UK biofuels company D1Oils about jatropha.

11 It is interesting to note that, on independence in the 1960s, many African states pursued and/or initiated plans for major multipurpose projects, combining food production (through irrigation) and hydropower development. For example, in Tanzania the FAO study (1961), *Report on the Preliminary Reconnaissance Survey of the Rufiji Basin*, addressed the trade-off between agriculture and hydropower production. When Japanese (Japan External Trade Organization in 1968) and Norwegian (Norconsult in 1972 and Hafslund in 1980) development assistance came on the scene, the focus of the project shifted entirely to hydropower production (Havnevik 1993: ch. 8). A similar development occurred with Tanzanian plans for multipurpose development, including agricultural irrigation, of the lower Wami river basin. When Swedish and other development assistance actors became involved, the project finally ended up as a single-purpose hydropower project at Kidatu, rather than a multipurpose project in the lower Wami basin (Öhman 2007).

12 The FAO has recently reformed its Committee for Food Security (CFS) which, alongside the World Bank and other institutions, promotes voluntary recommendations for land grabs, but without any analysis of power relations that can help the understanding of the limitations of such recommendations. In spite of such limited analyses, the FAO aims to make the reformed CFS 'a central actor for global governance of food and agricultural issues' (my translation from the Swedish). See FAO (2010a).

13 For a critical assessment of the World Bank's support to African agriculture over time and the *World Development Report 2008*, see Havnevik et al. (2007).

2 Biofuel governance

1 That is, the IEA, the FAO, the United Nations Framework Convention on Climate Change and the Intergovernmental Panel on Climate Change (IPCC).

2 Defined as development that meets the needs of the present without compromising the ability of future generations to meet their own needs.

3 Peak oil and climate change

1 Information from ASPO's home page, www.peakoil.net/. ASPO, the Association for the Study of Peak Oil and Gas, is an independent organization for the study of peak oil, initiated by Colin J. Campbell, who has worked for the oil industry for more than 40 years. It publishes the bulletin *Peak Oil Review*, which can be downloaded from its home page.

2 The EIA defines 'proved reserves' as 'estimated quantities that geological and engineering data indicate can be recovered in future years from known reservoirs, assuming existing technology and current economic and operating conditions' (EIA 2009: 31). Of course, the costs of exploiting 'proved reserves' may rise dramatically in the future.

3 The EIA reports three sources on the magnitude of 'proved reserves', viz. British Petroleum (2007): 1,239 billion barrels; *Oil and Gas Journal* (2009): 1,342 billion barrels; and *World Oil* (2007): 1,184 billion barrels. (See www.eia.doe. gov/international/reserves.html) However, it seems to settle on the highest figure. According to the EIA, 56 per cent of the world's proved oil reserves are in the Middle East, while North America has 15 per cent, most of it in Canadian tar sands (EIA 2009: 31).

4 In 2007, world production of oil amounted to about 4,093 million tonnes, while that of gas amounted to about 2,512 million tonnes of oil equivalent (IEA 2009: 74). In other words, to replace the present level of oil production, the production of natural gas would have to increase by a factor of 2.6 to 6,600 million tonnes of oil

equivalent per year, causing the RPR for gas to fall to 23 years.

5 My thanks to David Zilberman for providing me with these threshold prices during a discussion of the paper referred to here.

6 It may be noted that 76 per cent of the world's estimated exploitable reserves of coal are concentrated in only six countries: USA, Russia, China, India, Australia and New Zealand.

7 CO_2 emissions depend, of course, on the carbon content of the fuel in question. The atomic weight of carbon is 12, and that of oxygen is 16. Therefore, the atomic weight of carbon dioxide is 44. Based on the ratio $44/12 = 3.667$, and assuming complete combustion, 1 kg of carbon will produce 3.667 kg of CO_2, while 1 kg of oil will produce about 2.8 kg, and 1 kg of natural gas will produce about 2 kg of CO_2.

8 Emissions from fossil fuel burning, cement manufacture and gas flaring, calculated from data in http://cdiac.ornl. gov/trends/emis/meth-reg.html/

9 The world's light-vehicle road fleet numbers in the region of 900 million and is increasing by about 50 million units a year. Car production in China, and less so in India, contributes considerably to this annual increase. In the period 2002–06, car production in China rose by an annual 45.8 per cent. With a production of 7.3 million units in 2006, China overtook Japan as the world's second-largest car market, after the US – see *Peak Oil Review*, 3(2) (2008): 6; web edition of *China Daily*, 22 September 2007, available at: www.chinadaily.com.cn/china/; *Asia Times Online*, 17 August 2007, available at: www.atimes.com/atimes/

10 See also EIA: www.eia.doe.gov/ emeu/cabs/China/

11 In the US, cars, lorries and other vehicles are responsible for more than 25 per cent of greenhouse gas emissions (Earley and McKeown 2009: 9).

12 'In 2006, countries around the world spent an estimated $11 billion to support biofuel production through

subsidies and quotas' (Sexton and Zilberman 2010: 6).

13 In the overall picture, biofuels still play an entirely insignificant role and sequestrate a negligible amount of the world's cultivated land. In 2008, biofuel production reached 0.8 million barrels of oil equivalent per day, representing less than 1 per cent of total world oil production and about 1.7 per cent of total fuel consumption in road transport. In spite of this, estimates of the biofuel-induced increase in food prices in 2008 range from 10 per cent to nearly 50 per cent. The director of the FAO blamed biofuels for the food crisis, and politicians around the world demanded a re-examination of biofuel promotion policies (IEA 2009: 87–8; Sexton and Zilberman 2010: 7).

4 Attracting foreign direct investment

1 The authors acknowledge the research support provided by Sheila Chikulo, Gospel H. Matondi, Cuthbert Kambaje, Caroline Takawira and Sylvia Chahwanda.

2 In defining development, we are aware of Todaro's (1993) model of development for achieving economic growth. The debate on Africa's development has received much attention from Yash Tandon. We also take Walter Rodney's famous work *How Europe Underdeveloped Africa* (1964) as an important reference point in the politics of multinational corporations' operational mandate.

3 These are large conglomerates which have huge financial reserves. They normally invest in Africa and Asia and are interested in natural resource endowments. They take their profits back home.

4 The debate on globalization has economic, social and political ramifications which we consider in the biofuels boom. Joseph Stiglitz (2002) notes that it is mainly about the West benefiting excessively from the Third World.

5 Most studies on biofuels have overlooked the labour debate and hence we raise it from a rights-based and livelihood approach to show how it affects the less powerful – the labourers who do not have much bargaining power.

6 Many African countries, such as Zambia and Zimbabwe, have resisted the importation of genetically modified seeds or unprocessed products, on precautionary grounds, to protect the indigenous seed banks.

7 This is due to a lack of an appreciation of the resources they have and the extent to which policy-makers can bargain favourably for their people.

8 It is only recently that many countries have started the process of land registration. Namibia, Mozambique, Tanzania, Uganda, Rwanda and others are now in the process of implementing registration of land using land management information systems.

9 Markets in international trade are shaped by the politically and economically powerful, in this case the MNCs and host governments.

5 Smallholder-led biofuel production in Ethiopia

1 Other crops include *Pongamia pinnata* (a plant used in the production of biofuel and industrial chemicals) and palm trees.

6 Biofuel, land and environmental issues

1 The authors are grateful to the Swedish International Development Cooperation Agency (Sida)/Nordic Africa Institute programme on 'Inequalities and poverty in Africa' for funding this research. We are also grateful to Jumanne Abdallah, PhD, from Sokoine University of Agriculture, for participation and contributions during fieldwork in Tanzania in October 2009. Our institutions, the Nordic Africa Institute and the University of Agder's Centre for Development Studies, have supported the study throughout. We are also grateful to all the stakeholders who have given their time to assist us and to be interviewed,

or who provided relevant information to the project, both in Tanzania and Sweden. Longer interviews in Sweden were conducted with Melinda Fones-Sundell of the Stockholm Environment Institute (SEI); Linda Engström, Sida Helpdesk, Sveriges lantbruksuniversitet (SLU); and Per Giertz, ORGUT Consulting AB. Björn Edström, the former chief executive of SEKAB, Sweden, was interviewed by email. In Tanzania, interviews were conducted with, among others, Anders Bergfors, SEKAB Bioenergy Tanzania Ltd (SEKAB T), Dr Mato, Ardhi University, and Mr Ruriga, National Environmental Management Council (NEMC), as well as with villagers living on and adjacent to the Razaba farm in Bagamoyo district. Parts of the information presented in this chapter are also based on presentations and discussions at a number of seminars and workshops conducted between 2006 and 2010 (see the preface to this book).

2 For more insights see Chapter 1.

3 A SEKAB press release of 18 March 2009, entitled 'Sustainability award for SEKAB', reports that the company had been awarded a 'Sustainability Bioethanol Award'. This prize was given to SEKAB for its contribution in developing 'verifiable sustainable ethanol and second generation ethanol based on cellulose'. SEKAB is clearly, therefore, at the forefront in these areas and is an attractive partner for countries and businesses that aim to develop clean and alternative vehicle fuels.

4 Havnevik personal communication with Carstedt at SEKAB T's office, Dar es Salaam, October 2007.

5 Roberntz et al. (2009). SEKAB had originally planned to build three large ethanol factories in northern Sweden. However, due to lack of raw materials, the decision was made to start production in Africa (information provided by Eva Fridman, chief executive officer for biofuel region, to Swedish television's *Västerbottensnytt*, printed in the internet edition of *Dagens Nyheter*, Stockholm, 10 September 2007).

6 SEKAB's work in Sweden to develop alternative vehicle fuels has also been noted by the US embassy in Stockholm, which included the company on its list of 'Partners for cleaner energy – alternative energy opportunities in Sweden'. The document states that SEKAB's main mission is 'to create the conditions for actively promoting sustainable transport for the future with the help of long-term sustainable biofuels' (US Embassy 2009: 44). It goes on to say that SEKAB's ethanol produced in Sweden is biological and the raw materials for production consist, among other things, of sugar solution obtained from paper pulp production and oxygen from the air.

7 See Marie Widengård (2009b) – the notes are of a seminar at Stockholm University in May 2009, organized by the Nordic Africa Institute, in collaboration with WWF, Sweden; Department of Physical Geography and Quaternary Geology, Stockholm University; and the Swedish Interdisciplinary Research Network on Livelihoods and Natural Resource Governance.

8 SVT (Swedish Television), Stockholm, 11 June 2009. Based on information provided by SEKAB's chief executive, Björn Edström, to the *Mittnytt* programme.

9 The conflict over SEKAB's international investments was also played out at the local level, in the northern Swedish municipalities of Örnsköldsvik, Skellefteå and Umeå, which were the part owners of SEKAB (70 per cent). Municipal politicians from the three areas commissioned a report to investigate SEKAB's international investments. This was presented in Umeå on 4 November 2009. The report, compiled by the consultancy company Sweco, criticized the municipal energy companies for not having informed the municipal owners about SEKAB's international investments, but otherwise it was claimed that the municipalities had been given reasonable information on which to make decisions and there was no serious breach of the owners' directive for SEKAB. However, an opposition politician, Dan

Olsson, was reported to have stated that he found the report substandard and 'it looks as if it was done to protect those responsible' (our translation). Reported at www.SVT.se, 5 November 2009.

10 Among others, SEKAB T had recruited several competent aid practitioners from the successful Sida-supported Land Management Programme, which was conducted in Babati district between 1994 and 2008. See, for example, Havnevik (2006: ch. 7). In addition, young and competent Tanzanian development practitioners from this project were recruited to implement SEKAB T's activities in Rufiji district. To address rights perspectives in its activities, SEKAB T recruited, among others, a highly competent Sida official with long experience of this area. Based on several meetings in Dar es Salaam between Kjell Havnevik and some of the above-mentioned SEKAB T officials during November 2008, it appeared that a strong commitment and belief in SEKAB's biofuel expansion in Rufiji was emerging.

11 Communication between Jan Grafström, Sida, and Havnevik, June 2010. Grafström had been an official at Sida, Dar es Salaam, with responsibility for the energy sector, including biofuels, during the years 2005–08. To support the knowledge base for development of bioenergy in Tanzania, the Swedish embassy in Dar es Salaam also, among other things, initiated and funded a major study on the sector – Mwamila et al. (2009).

12 Personal communication between Havnevik and a member of the National Biofuel Task Force, Dar es Salaam, November 2008. See also *The East African*, 5 October 2009, which reported that more than 40 companies had biofuel investments in Tanzania. Kamanga (2008: 39) also provides figures on the number of companies registered with the Ministry of Energy and Minerals for biofuel investments. He reported (in 2008) that a total of 37 companies were registered, of which 13 were foreign, six were local and four were joint foreign–local interests, and

that most of these companies were planning to grow jatropha. For 14 companies, there was no information about origin and organizational structure. Only two of the 37 companies had indicated an intention of assisting smallholders in growing the crops. The land area requested by 16 of the companies registered totalled 641,170 hectares and 1,150 acres, while 21 companies had unspecified land needs.

13 This was, however, the only recommendation that the Tanzanian government acted on from the report.

14 This discussion is based on Haugen (2008).

15 www.worldbank.org/data/country-data/countrydata.html.

16 According to Fones-Sundell (n.d.), it was not until 2001 that ESIA guidelines were published by the African Development Bank as *Environmental and Social Assessment Procedures for AfDB Public Sector Operations*. As indicated in the title, these guidelines were limited to public-sector operations.

17 Ethical issues regarding the independence of this research need to be addressed as well. The research project of which this chapter is part originally also included a section that aimed specifically at investigating what the experience of biofuel developments can contribute to the establishment of better and more transparent ESIA procedures. Melinda Fones-Sundell, currently of the SEI and formerly with ORGUT, was to participate in this latter part of the project. However, since Fones-Sundell played an important role in the process around SEKAB T's ESIA for Bagamoyo (she was ORGUT's lead consultant for the feasibility studies leading up to the preliminary ESIA), she could not herself be a member of a research team that also investigated the ESIA process. We therefore decided to divide the project into two parts; Fones-Sundell will take part only in the second stage of the project, which has yet to be completed. Instead, she became an informant for the first part of the research project and was interviewed by

us, in the same way as other informants. With reference to ethical issues, it should also be mentioned that in 2005 one of the authors of this chapter, Kjell Havnevik, entered into a three-year consultancy contract with ORGUT. Within this contract, a four-week consultancy project was carried out, focusing on support to Suledo community forestry in Kiteto district. ORGUT has also supported Havnevik in technical ways during other fieldwork he undertook in Tanzania in 2007 and 2008. ORGUT's office in Dar es Salaam also helped establish contact between Havnevik and SEKAB T in November 2007. As mentioned earlier, this project has been funded through Sida support to the Nordic Africa Institute programme 'Inequalities and poverty in Africa', coordinated by Mats Hårsmar of the Nordic Africa Institute.

18 Large institutions such as banks, development agencies and donors normally have procedures to ensure that this is done, while private companies in many cases are seen to fast-track the process. See Fones-Sundell (2009).

19 Interview with Mr Ruriga, NEMC, 2 November 2009.

20 Interview with Mr Ruriga, NEMC, 2 November 2009.

21 Interview with Mr Ruriga, NEMC, 2 November 2009.

22 Interview with Mr Ruriga, NEMC, 2 November 2009.

23 These documents related to a contract between ORGUT Consulting AB and SEKAB Bioenergy Tanzania Ltd dated 3 August 2007, and included: 1. Terms of Reference for an Environmental Impact Assessment of the proposed SEKAB-BT Biofuel Development Project in Bagamoyo, Tanzania, 2. Preliminary Environmental and Social Impact Analysis (ESIA) of BioEthanol Production on the former Razaba Ranch, 3. Baseline Study 2.2.1 Inventory of Existing Terrestrial Wildlife, 4. Baseline Study 2.1.3 Industrial Processing Component, 5. Baseline Study 2.3.1 Policy Framework, 6. Inventory of Fauna and Flora in the Intertidal Area in Kitame, Bagamoyo, 7. An Analysis of the Socio-Economic Environment, 8. Land Use Report, 9. Vegetation Survey of Proposed Sugar Cane Plantation, 10. Specialist Studies: Water Resources, 11. Environmental Impact Statement (EIS), and 12. Stakeholders Consulted. These products were accepted and paid for by SEKAB T in full on 10 October 2008. ORGUT 'regard the above documents as delivered on May 8, 2008 to be accurate and of the required professional standard, given the information available' (ORGUT, untitled, undated).

24 This sub-consultancy contract was dated 12 November 2007 and was valid until 4 February 2008. The work was paid for by ORGUT on 12 February 2008. After February 2008, 'ORGUT has had no contractual relationship with ARU nor have any payments whatsoever been made to ARU or any of the individual consultants involved' (ORGUT, untitled, undated: 2).

25 Apparently ORGUT needed to recruit a local counterpart, as Tanzanian regulations require foreign firms to work in association with Tanzanian firms (interview with Dr Mato, ARU, 30 October 2009).

26 Interview with Dr Mato, ARU, 30 October 2009.

27 Interview with Dr Mato, ARU, 30 October 2009.

28 Interview with Per Giertz, head of ORGUT, 22 June 2010.

29 Interview with Dr Mato, ARU, 30 October 2009.

30 SEKAB statement on Bagamoyo BioEnergy project, 3 April 2009.

31 Interview with Dr Mato, ARU, 30 October 2009.

32 Interview with Dr Mato, ARU, 30 October 2009.

33 This is documented by various NGO studies in the rural areas affected by SEKAB T's projects in Bagamoyo and Rufiji districts, in particular: ActionAid (2009) and Roberntz et al. (2009). Such investigative reports, although based on short-term field studies, are important, since they can add important information

about critical environmental aspects and the situation of local people, and about contacts with and perceptions of the investing companies (in this case SEKAB T) that engage with them. But the speed of such investigations also makes them susceptible to misunderstandings and factual errors. For instance, the ActionAid (2009) report's discussion of food security (section 8) claims that: 'If the Rufiji delta was being utilized for food production instead of biofuel production, it could provide the whole of the capital, Dar es Salaam, and the surrounding areas, in excess of five million people, with food' (our translation). It might be pointed out that the Rufiji delta is, and has been for generations, intensively cultivated with food crops, in particular rice. The limiting factors for production are the mangrove swamps and the salinity of the tidal water that penetrates the delta. The planned biofuel plantations of SEKAB T in Rufiji do not target the delta, but rather the central or western part of Rufiji district, and the higher ground to the north and south of the flood plain. Cultivation in these areas is rain fed, and productivity would thus be enhanced by irrigation. The problem of some of SEKAB T's plantations in Rufiji district is thus not the areas of their planned location, but their size and the volume of water that needs to be drawn from the river. In addition, some of the planned sugarcane cultivation areas proposed by SEKAB T were located in wooded areas and had not taken into account the climate effect, while other cultivation areas were targeted for areas earmarked by village land use plans for village food production. In essence, SEKAB T was ill advised about the size and location of some of the planned sugarcane cultivations, but not about the activity itself – for more documentation about the complexity of the flood plain and higher ground agriculture, see Havnevik (1993: chs 3 and 4); Hoag (2003); Öhman (2007); Duvail and Hamerlynck (2007). Smaller-scale production of sugarcane on 'unused' or underutilized land employing some kind of irrigation techniques could make a contribution to village livelihoods.

34 Web site of National Land Use Planning Commission (www.nlupc.org/), April 2009.

35 SEKAB T's official response, dated 25 June 2009, to the draft report by WWF-Sweden (Roberntz et al. 2009). Here it is claimed that SEKAB T 'from the start stated that sustainability is a top priority and realises that difficult compromises to social and environmental challenges are necessary'. Further: 'SEKAB is interested in a serious dialogue on how to best achieve social and environmental sustainability.' SEKAB T does not feel, however, that 'the WWF assumptions, statements and guesses' can be a base for a constructive dialogue for 'true development' and 'sees no reason to discuss them in detail in this forum' (i.e. the response of 25 June). To this, our comment is that a constructive dialogue has little space to develop if one of the partners has the blueprint for 'true development'. Roberntz et al. (2009) provided a good opportunity for SEKAB T to provide information and to explain why its plans had taken the path they had and why there were discrepancies between visions and planning operations on the ground. The history of development assistance and investments is full of such discrepancies, which need to be discussed by all stakeholders if the objectives are to be attained.

36 See note 33 above about the need to take a critical approach to the information provided by NGOs and advocacy groups based on short-term field visits. This is taken into account when we provide our analysis and base it on Roberntz et al. (2009).

37 Such a strategy of creating atomized villages with limited scope for co-operation between them is nothing new in the Tanzanian context. The Tanzanian government itself employed such a strategy in its 'villagization' programme from 1969 onwards. Although the official motto was to instil development from below, the

creation of atomized villages was also an integral part of strengthening political control of the countryside. See Havnevik (1993: 195–214).

38 That trusted working relationships have been established between SEKAB T and local communities is strongly questioned by ActionAid (2009: section 5, focusing on how SEKAB negotiated directly at the village level) and by Roberntz et al. (2009). The criticism directed at SEKAB T by ActionAid is that it paid villagers to participate in the village assembly meeting that was organized to vote on whether to provide land to SEKAB T for biofuel production. For this, each person participating was paid Tsh 8,000 (SEK 45). Furthermore, SEKAB T paid Tsh 5,000 to each villager who participated in a meeting and discussion with representatives from SEKAB T. We argue that paying villagers to take part in critical democratic decisions at the village level is wrong, and hence we agree with Action-Aid's criticism on that point. But to pay villagers for taking part in a discussion with SEKAB T, which may distract them from their work or other activities, seems reasonable and should not be criticized. What appears from some of the reports, e.g. ActionAid (2009), is that villagers themselves seem to be confused as to what organ at village level has the authority to decide what. For instance, when interviewed, Mrs Zauda Saidi Mbalapi, an agriculturalist in Nyanda-Katundu in Rufiji district, said: 'It is not my responsibility to decide on whether SEKAB shall come to our village. This is decided by the Village Council. Therefore, I cannot influence on the decision' (ActionAid 2009: section 8 on food security). This is wrong, according to Tanzanian laws and regulations for village governance. Such a decision has to be taken by the village assembly, where every person over 18 years of age has the right to vote. The village council is merely the administrative and executive organ of the village and does not have the right to alienate land from the village without a decision

being taken in the village assembly which is subsequently supported by the District Land Officer and finally decided upon by the Commissioner for Land.

39 Nowadays called Sida External Expert Advice for Environmental Assessment.

40 See EU RED (2009). The problems for SEKAB T's plans in relation to the EU RED criteria are particularly in relation to paras 3b, 3b (ii) and 4b.

41 WWF Rufiji Study; ESIA Bagamoyo (May version); SEI Rufiji risk analysis; Tanzanian Forestry Working Group report; National Biofuel Task Force document; Feasibility study of large-scale biofuel investment in Tanzania by local researchers; Maps of SEKAB investment plans and current land use; Policy framework and regulatory scan by Econ Pöyry; SEKAB sustainability approach; SEKAB statement on ESIA; and SEKAB Environmental Impact Assessment Certificate.

42 Sida's Department for Partnership Development/AKTSAM (2010). As well as those Sida officials who did the reporting, presenting and approving, nine other officials, representing various departments and competences within Sida, Stockholm, had signed under the heading 'consultation with'.

43 Such as guidelines and recommendations for large-scale land acquisitions and leases for biofuel development and food production proposed by IFPRI; by the IIED in cooperation with the FAO and IFAD (Cotula et al. 2009); and by the UN/SRRF (see Chapter 1).

7 Agro-investments in Zimbabwe

1 The research assistance provided by Patience Mutopo is sincerely acknowledged.

2 This is a political statement, and its consistent use has created a 'virtual policy', since there is no policy document to back it up in the public domain. However, important decisions have been made in terms of investments and credit agreements that have helped Zimbabwe. What the Zimbabwean government has

offered in return is not known, as the deals are not public.

3 This was disputed by the Libyans, who claimed that their import of beef from Zimbabwe could have been misconstrued as investment in land and agriculture (*The Herald*, 5 April 2002). Libya and the government of Zimbabwe had signed a protocol for a 5,000-tonne beef quota, with the potential for it to increase to 12,000 tonnes, as part of normal trade relations.

4 The A1 and A2 model farms were designed by the government in 2000 as a basis for distinguishing various classes of farms to be established on the large-scale commercial farms that government was acquiring compulsorily. The A1 farm was based on typically small farms of less than 12 hectares in natural regions I to III, and increased in size depending on the ecological region. These were meant for those without adequate resources, such as the poor from communal and urban areas. The A2 farm was to be a larger farm, with a minimum of 30 hectares, and also increased in size according to the ecological region. These were meant to be allocated to beneficiaries with their own resources to undertake commercial production.

5 The Zimbabwe Investment Authority is a merger between the Zimbabwe Investment Centre and the Export Processing Zones Authority.

6 IFPRI quotes the following figures for the amount of water is takes to yield one kilogram of various products: a) oven dry wheat grain – 715–750 litres of water; b) maize – 540–630 litres; c) soya beans – 1,650–2,200 litres; d) paddy rice – 1,550 litres; e) beef – 50,000–100,000 litres; clean wool – 170,000 litres (Meinzen-Dick 2010).

7 See www.greenfuel.co.zw/templates/ greenfuel/newsroom/greenfuel_plant_ construction_nearing_completion.pdf

8 Competition between biofuel and food?

1 Interview with Arne Helvig, one of the founders of BioFuel Africa Ltd, 2010.

2 Interview with Steinar Kolnes, one of the founders of BioFuel Africa Ltd, 2010.

3 Interview with Kusawgu-Wura, 2009, the chief of Kusawgu in the Central Gonja district.

4 Interview with Assemblyman of Alipe, Central Gonja district, 2009.

Conclusion

1 'Squeeze' in the sense that the smallholder sector in Africa has not received greater recognition, in spite of the fact that a large percentage of Africans depend on it. This is compared to the large-scale commercial sector, which receives the bulk of state subsidies and which has access to international markets for finance, inputs and outputs. With the land grabs, the smallholder sector usually suffers because some of the land under it may be targeted for biofuel expansion.

References

Aal, W., L. Jarosz and C. Thompson (2009) 'Response to P. Collier, "Politics of Hunger"', *Foreign Affairs*, November/ December.

ABN (African Biodiversity Network) (2007) *Agrofuels in Africa: The impacts on land, food and forests*, available at www.biofuelwatch.org.uk/docs/ABN_Agro.pdf

Achten, W. M. J., W. H. Maes et al. (2010) 'Jatropha: From global hype to local opportunity', *Journal of Arid Environments*, 74(1): 164–5.

ActionAid (2009) *SEKAB – Etanol till varje pris? Hur SEKABs biobränsleprojekt i Tanzania drabbar lokalbefolkningen*, October, Stockholm.

ActionAid-Ghana (2009) 'Re: The biofuel debate: Action Aid-Ghana responds to Rural Consult's allegations', *Daily Graphic* (Ghana), 6 July.

ActionAid International (2008) *Food, Farmers and Fuels: Balancing global grain and energy policies with sustainable land use*, Johannesburg.

— (2010) *Meals per Gallon: The impact of industrial biofuels on people and global hunger*, January, available at: www.actionaid.org.uk/doc_lib/meals_per_gallon_final.pdf

Adger, N. W., T. A. Benjaminsen, K. Brown and H. Svarstad (2001) 'Advancing a political ecology of global environmental discourses', *Development and Change*, 32: 681–715.

Agrawal, A. (2005) *Environmentality: Technologies of government and the making of subjects*. Durham, NC and London: Duke University Press.

Aide, E. (2008) *The Right to Food and the Impact of Liquid Biofuels (Agrofuels)*, Right to Food Studies, Rome: FAO.

Alemayehu Lirenso (1992) 'Economic reform and agricultural de-cooperativisation in Ethiopia: Implications for agricultural production in the 1990s', in Mekonen Taddesse (ed.), *The Ethiopian Economy: Structure, problems and policy issues*, Proceedings of the First Annual Conference on the Ethiopian Economy, Addis Ababa, Ethiopia, pp. 81–104.

Alemneh Dejene (1987) *Peasants, Agrarian Socialism, and Rural Development in Ethiopia*, Oxford: Westview Press.

All Africa News (2010) 'Petroleum companies to build ethanol blending plants', 27 March, available at: http://en.ethiopianreporter.com/index.php?option=com_content&task=view&id=2423&Itemid=26

Amanor, K. S. (1999) *Global Restructuring and Land Rights in Ghana*, Uppsala: Nordiska Afrikaininstitutet.

Amigun, B., R. Siamoney and H. Blottniz (2008) 'Commercialisation of biofuel in Africa: a review', *Renewable Energy & Sustainable Energy News*, 12: 690–711.

Anderson, T. and M. Belay (eds) (2008) *Rapid Assessment of Biofuels Development Status in Ethiopia and the Proceedings of the National Workshop on Environmental Impact Assessment and Biofuels*, Publication No. 6, Addis Ababa: Melca Mahiber.

AREX (Department of Agricultural Research and Extension) (2006) *Jatropha Production*, Harare.

Ariza-Montobbio, P., S. Lele et al. (2010) 'The political ecology of jatropha plantations for biodiesel in Tamil Nadu, India', *Journal of Peasant Studies*, 37(4): 875–97.

Arndt, C., R. Benfica et al. (2008) 'Biofuels, poverty and growth: A computable general equilibrium analysis of Mozambique', IFPRI Discussion Paper 00803, October, Washington, DC: IFPRI.

Atakilte Beyene (2003) 'Soil conservation, land use and property rights in Northern Ethiopia: Understanding environmental change in smallholder farming systems', PhD thesis, Swedish University of Agricultural Sciences, Uppsala, Sweden.

Bäackstrand, K. and E. Lövbrand (2007) 'Climate governance beyond 2012: Competing discourses of green governmentality, ecological modernization and civic environmentalism' in M. E. Pettenger (ed.), *The Social Construction of Climate Change: Knowledge, norms, discourses*, Ashgate eBook.

Barrow, C. S. (1997) *Environmental and Social Impact Assessment*, London: Arnold.

Barry, J. (1999) *Environment and Social Theory*, London and New York: Routledge.

Benjaminsen, T. A. and I. Bryceson (2009) 'Klimakolonialismen', *Dagbladet* (Norway), January 28.

Benjaminsen, T. A., I. Bryceson and F. Makanga (2008) *Climate Change in Tanzania: Trends, policies and initiatives*, Aas, Norway: Norwegian University of Life Sciences.

Benjaminsen T. A., I. Bryceson, A. Dahlberg et al. (2009) 'Svenskt bistånd ska rädda miljöfarligt etanolprojekt', *Dagens Nyheter* (Sweden), 14 April.

Berry, R. A. and W. R. Cline (1979) *Agrarian Structure and Productivity in Developing Countries*, Baltimore, MD: Johns Hopkins University Press.

Berry, S. (1993) *No Condition is Permanent: The social dynamics of agrarian change in sub-Saharan Africa*, Madison: University of Wisconsin Press.

Binswanger, H. and J. McIntire (1987) 'Behavioral and material determinants of production relations in land-abundant tropical agriculture', *Journal of Economic Development and Cultural Change*, 36 (1): 73–99.

BioFuel Africa Ltd (2008) 'BioFuel Africa (Ltd.) gains EPA approval for the cultivation and planting of Jatropha', press release, available at: www.biofuel.no

Biofuels Digest (2009) 'A Biofuels Digest Special Report', 23 January.

Boamah, F. (2010) 'Competition between biofuel and food? The case of a jatropha biodiesel project and its effects on food security in the affected communities in Northern Ghana', Master's thesis, University of Bergen.

— (2011) 'Livelihood impacts of biofuels: Analyses of evidence from hot spots of biofuel investments', presentation made at Energy Center, College of Engineering, Kwame Nkrumah University of Science and Technology, January 2011.

Böhler, T. (2004) 'Vindkraft, landskap och mening', PhD thesis, Department of Environmental and Regional Studies of the Human Conditions, Human Ecology section, Gothenburg University.

Bolwig, S., P. Gibbon and S. Jones (2009) 'The economics of smallholder organic contract farming in tropical Africa', *World Development*, 37(6).

Borras, S. M., P. McMichael and I. Scoones (2010) 'The politics of biofuels, land and agrarian change: editors' introduction', *Journal of Peasant Studies*, 37(4): 575–92.

Bruce, J. and S. Migot-Adholla (eds) (1994) *Searching for Land Tenure Security in Africa*, Washington, DC, and Iowa: World Bank and Kendall/Hunt.

Buch-Hansen, M. and H. Marcussen (1982) 'Contract farming and the peasantry: Cases from Western Kenya', *Review of African Political Economy*, 9(23): 9–36.

Burley, H. and H. Griffiths (2009) *Jatropha: Wonder Crop? Experience from Swaziland*, Friends of the Earth, available at: www.foe.co.uk/resource/reports/jatropha_wonder_crop.pdf

Byerlee, D. and A. de Janvry (2009) 'Smallholders unite', *Foreign Affairs*, March/April.

CAADP (Comprehensive Africa Agriculture Development Programme) (2002) *New Partnership for Africa's Development (NEPAD)*, November 2002, available at: ftp://ftp.fao.org/docrep/fao/meeting/005/y8023e/y8023e00.pdf

Campbell, C. J. (2005) 'The end of the first half of the age of oil', presentation at the ASPO conference, Lisbon, May.

Campbell, C. J. and J. H. Laherrère (1998) 'The end of cheap oil', *Scientific American*, March.

Carney, A. (1994) 'Contracting a food staple in the Gambia', in P. Little and M. Watts (eds), *Living under Contract: Contract farming and agrarian transformation in sub-Saharan Africa*, Madison: University of Wisconsin Press.

Chakrabortty, A. (2008) 'Fields of gold', *Guardian*, 16 April.

Chikari, O. (2008) 'Mugabe to grow sugar cane in Lowveld', *Zimbabwe Times*, 31 October.

Cline, W. R. (2007) *Global Warming and Agriculture – Impact Estimates by Country*, Washington, DC: Center for Global Development/Peterson Institute for International Economics.

Cocks, F. H. (2009) *Energy Demand and Climate Change: Issues and resolutions*, Weinheim: Wiley-VCH Verlag.

Cohen, J. and D. Weintraub (1975) *Land and Peasants in Imperial Ethiopia: The social background to a revolution*, Assen, Netherlands: Van Gorcum.

Colchester, M. and M. F. Ferrari (2007) 'Making FPIC work: Challenges and prospects for indigenous peoples', Forest Peoples Programme, available at: www.forestpeoples.org/documents/asia_pacific/bases/philippines.shtml

Collier, P. (2008) 'The politics of hunger', *Foreign Affairs*, November/December.

Colombant, N. (2010) 'Activists, researchers raise alarm on Africa's "Land Grab"', *Pan Africa*, 28 January.

Comar, V. and J. M. Gusman Ferraz (2007) 'Brazil's sugar cane ethanol: villain or panacea?' Institute for Environment and Development and EMBRAPA/CNPMA, mimeo.

COMPETE (2009). 'Summary' of COMPETE International Conference on Bioenergy Policy Implementation in Africa, Fringilla Lodge, Zambia, May.

Cotula, L. and B. Neves (2007) 'The drivers of change', in L. Cotula (ed.), *Changes in 'Customary' Land Tenure Systems in Africa*, London: IIED.

Cotula, L., N. Dyer and S. Vermeulen (2008a) 'Bioenergy and land tenure: The implications of biofuel for land tenure and land policy', Land Tenure Working Paper 1, FAO.

— (2008b) *Fuelling Exclusion? The biofuels boom and poor people's access to land*, London: FAO and IIED.

Cotula, L., S. Vermeulen et al. (2009) *Land Grab or Development Opportunity? Agricultural investment and international land deals in Africa*, London/Rome: IIED/FAO/IFAD.

Council for Agricultural Science and Technology (2006) *Convergence of Agriculture and Energy: Implications for research and policy*, CAST Commentary QTA 2006-3, available at: www.cast-science.org/websiteUploads/publicationPDFs/QTA2006-3.pdf

Coyle, W. (2007) 'The future of biofuels: A global perspective', *AmberWaves*, November, available at: www.ers.usda.gov/AmberWaves/November07/Features/

CSDI, TASGA et al. (2008) *The Sugarcane Smallholder/Outgrower Scheme (SUSO) in Tanzania: A concept for inclusion of potential small and large scale farmers in a sugarcane production scheme in Tanzania*, Final Report, prepared for SEKAB Bio-Energy Tanzania Ltd, produced by Centre for Sustainable Development Initiatives, Tanzania Sugarcane Growers Association and Katani Ltd, Dar es Salaam.

D1 Oils (2009) 'Agreement with BP on D1-BP fuel crops', 17 July, available at: www.d1plc.com/news.php?article=197

Dakarai, M. (2009) 'BIPPA and policy position', presentation at Ministry of Lands and Rural resettlement (MLRR) conference Towards a Comprehensive Land Policy in Zimbabwe, Caribbea Bay Hotel, Kariba, 11–13 June.

DANIDA (2010) *Zimbabwe Transitional Programme*, Phase II: 2010–2012, *Agro-based Private Sector Recovery (APRISER)*, Harare: Ministry of Foreign Affairs.

Dauvergne, P. and K. J. Neville (2010)

'Forests, food, and fuel in the tropics: The uneven social and ecological consequences of the emerging political economy of biofuels', *Journal of Peasant Studies* 37(4): 631–60.

De Keiser, S. and H. Hongo (2005) 'Farming for energy for better livelihoods in Southern Africa – FELISA', presentation at the PfA-TaTEDO Policy Dialogue Conference on the Role of Renewable Energy for Poverty Alleviation and Sustainable Development in Africa, Dar-es-Salaam, 22 June.

De Schutter, O. (2009) 'Large-scale land acquisitions and leases: a set of core principles and measures to address the human rights challenges', 11 June, available at: www2.ohchr.org/english/issues/food/docs/BriefingNotelandgrab.pdf .

— (2010) 'Responsibly destroying the world's peasantry: Land grabbing's grim reality', in Right to Food Watch, *Land Grabbing and Nutrition: Challenges for global governance*, available at: www.rtfn-watch.org/fileadmin/media/rtfn-watch.org/ENGLISH/pdf/Watch_2010/watch_engl_innen_final_ a4.pdf

De Soto, H. (2000) *The Mystery of Capital: Why capitalism triumphs in the west and fails everywhere else*, London: Black Swan.

Dean, M. (1999) *Governmentality: Power and rule in modern society*, London: Sage.

Dehue, B. and W. Hettinga (2008) *The GHG Performance of Jatropha Biodiesel*, Utrecht, Netherlands: Ecofys.

Dessalegn Rahmato (1996) *Land and Agrarian Unrest in Wollo, Northeastern Ethiopia, Pre- and Post-Revolution*, IDR Research Report No. 46, Addis Ababa University.

DfID (Department for International Development) (forthcoming) *Zimbabwe Market Opportunities Study Report*, London.

Djurfeldt, G., H. Holmén, M. Jirstrom and R. Larsson (2005) *The African Food Crisis: Lessons from the Asian Green Revolution*, Wallingford: CABI Publishing.

Dove (2007) *Jatropha Curcas L. An International Botanical Answer to Biodiesel Production and Renewable Energy*, Dove Biotech, available to order from: www.dovebiotech.com

Downs, Erica (2006) *China*, Brookings Energy Security Series, New York: Brookings Institution.

Dryzek, J. S. (1997) *The Politics of the Earth: Environmental discourses*, Oxford: Oxford University Press.

Dufey, A., S. Vermeulen and B. Vorley (2007) *Biofuels: Strategic Choices for Commodity Dependent Developing Countries*, London: Common Fund for Commodities, Institute for Environment and Development.

Duvail, Stéphanie and Olivier Hamerlynck (2007) 'The Rufiji River flood: Plague or blessing?', *Journal of Biometeorology*, 52: 33–42.

Earley, J. and A. McKeown (2009) *Smart Choices for Biofuels*, Washington, DC: Worldwatch Institute/Sierra Club.

Eaton, C. and A. Shepherd (2001) *Contract Farming: Partnerships for growth*, FAO Agricultural Services Bulletin No. 145, Rome: FAO.

EIA (US Energy Information Administration) (2009) *International Energy Outlook 2009*, Washington, DC: US Department of Energy.

Eicher, C. K. (1995) 'Zimbabwe's maize-based Green Revolution: Preconditions for replication', *World Development*, 23: 805–18.

— (2001) 'Africa's unfinished business: Building sustainable agricultural research systems', Staff paper No. 2001-10, Department of Agricultural Economics, Michigan State University.

Eide, A. (2008) *The Right to Food and the Impact of Liquid Biofuels (Agrofuels)*, Rome: FAO.

Ellis, F. (1982) 'Agricultural pricing policy in Tanzania', *World Development*, 10(4): 263–83.

— (1993) *Peasant Economics: Farm households and agrarian development*, Cambridge: Cambridge University Press.

Elobeid, Amani and Chad Hart (2007)

'Ethanol expansion in the food versus fuel debate: How will developing countries fare?', *Journal of Agricultural & Food Industrial Organization*, Special Issue, 5(6).

ENA (Ethiopian News Agency) (2010) '84 investors to engage in bio-fuel development', 11 August, available at: www.ena.gov.et/EnglishNews/2010/Aug/11Aug10/119021.htm

Engström, L. (2009) 'Liquid biofuels opportunities and challenges in developing countries', Sida Helpdesk for Environmental Assessment, MKB-centrum, available at: www.sol.slu.se

EU Renewable Energy Directive (RED) (2009) 'Environmental sustainability criteria for biofuels and other bio-liquids', Article 17, April 23.

Europa Regional Surveys of the World (2009) *Africa South of the Sahara 2009*, London: Routledge.

Fairhead, J. and M. Leach (1995) 'False forest history, complicit social analysis: Rethinking some West African environmental narratives', *World Development*, 23(6).

Fanon, F. (1965) *The Wretched of the Earth*, Harmondsworth: Penguin.

FAO (2006) *Compendium on Food and Agricultural Indicators 2006*, Rome.

— (2007) FAO press conference on the Sustainable Energy Report, Rome, May.

— (2008) *The State of Food and Agriculture. BIOFUELS: prospects, risks and opportunities*, Rome.

— (2010a) 'CFS is requesting action against hunger and the price variability for foodstuffs', FAO Press, 20 October.

— (2010b) 'Rising food prices can lead to import costs of over one billion dollars', FAO Press, November 17.

FAO, IFAD, UNCTAD and the World Bank Group (2010) 'Principles for responsible agricultural investment that respects the rights, livelihoods and resources', discussion paper, available at: http://siteresources.worldbank.org/INTARD/214574-1111138388661/22453321/Principles_Extended.pdf

FAO, IIED and IFAD (2009) *Land Grab or Development Opportunity? Agricultural investment and international land deals in Africa*, available at: www.fao.org/docrep/011/ak241e/ak241e00.htm

FARA (Forum for Agricultural Research in Africa) (2007/08) 'Bi-monthly bulletin', December/January, p. 2

— (2008) 'Bioenergy value chain research and development. Stakes and Opportunities', discussion paper, Ouagadougou, Burkina Faso.

Fargione, J., J. Hill et al. (2008) 'Land clearing and the biofuel carbon debt', *Science*, 319: 1235–38.

Fischer, G., H. van Velthuizen and F. Nachtergaele (2002) *Global Agro-Ecological Assessment for Agriculture in the 21st Century*, Rome: FAO.

Fischer, G., E. Hizsnyik et al. (2009) *Biofuels and food security*, OPEC Fund for International Development (OFID) and International Institute for Applied Systems Analysis (IIASA).

Flammini, A. (2008) *Biofuels and the Underlying Causes of High Food Prices*, Global Bioenergy Partnership Secretariat.

Follath, E. and A. Jung (eds) (2006) *Der neue kalte Krieg – Kampf um die Rohstoffe*, Munich: Deutsche Verlags-Anstalt.

Fones-Sundell, M. (2009) 'ESIA as a tool for public participation in decision making. Some experiences from Bagamoyo, District', presentation at seminar on Biofuel and Smallholders in Africa, Nordic Africa Institute, Uppsala, 17 September.

— (n.d.) 'Lessons learned from ESIA implementation in Africa with special reference to the bioenergy sector (in Tanzania)', mimeo.

Foucault, M., M. Bertani et al. (2003) *'Society Must be Defended': Lectures at the Collège de France, 1975–76*. New York: Picador.

Franco, J., L. Levidow et al. (2010) 'Assumptions in the European Union biofuels policy: frictions with experiences in Germany, Brazil and Mozambique', *Journal of Peasant Studies*, 37(4): 661–98.

Franzel, S., L. Dadi, K. Colburn and G. Degu (1992) 'Grain-marketing policies and peasant production', in S. Franzel and H. Houten (eds), *Research with Farmers: Lessons from Ethiopia*, Addis Ababa: Institute of Agricultural Research.

Gallagher, E. (2008) *The Gallagher Review of the Indirect Effects of Biofuels Production*, Renewable Fuels Agency, available at: www.unido.org/fileadmin/ user_media/UNIDO_Header_Site/Sub sites/Green_Industry_Asia_Conference _Maanila_/GC13/Gallagher_Report. pdf

Garcez, C. A. G. and J. N. D. S. Vianna (2009) 'Brazilian biodiesel policy: Social and environmental considerations of sustainability', *Energy*, 34(5).

Gasela, R. (2009) 'Zimbabwe dilemma: growing food for people, or cars?', *New Zimbabwean*, 11 December, available at: www.newzimbabwe.com/pages/ farm72.18220.html

General Motors (2010) 'GM partners with US Department of Energy to develop jatropha-to-biodiesel project in India', PR Newswire, 30 March, available at: http://www. prnewswire.com/news-releases/ gm-partners-with-us-department- of-energy-to-develop-jatropha-to- biodiesel-project-in-india-89531022. html

Ghana Local Government (2006) 'Ghana districts: A public–private partnership programme between Ministry of Local Government and Rural Development and Maks Publications & Media Services', available at: www.ghana districts.com/districts/?news&r=6&_=91

Giampietro, M., S. Ulgiati and D. Pimentel (1997) 'Feasibility of large-scale biofuel production', *BioScience*, 47(9).

Gibbon, P. (1992) 'The World Bank and African poverty 1973–91', *Journal of Modern African Studies*, 30(2).

Gibbon, P. and S. Ponte (2005) *Trading Down. Africa, Value Chains, and the Global Economy*, Philadelphia, PA: Temple University Press.

Giles, J. (2007) 'Climate Change 2007: How to survive a warming world', *Nature*, 446: 716–17.

GRAIN (2007a) 'The new scramble for Africa', *Seedling*, July, available at: www.grain.org

— (2007b) 'Jatropha the agro-fuel of the poor', *Seedling*, July, available at: www. grain.org

— (2008) 'Seized: The 2008 land grab for food and financial security', GRAIN Briefing, available at: www.grain.org/ briefings/?id=212

— (2010) 'Stop land grabbing now', available at: www.grain.org/o/?id=102

Greenpeace (2006) 'Eating up the Amazon', available at: www.greenpeace.org/ international/press/reports/eating-up- the-amazon

— (2007) 'How the palm oil industry is cooking the climate', 8 November, available at: www.greenpeace.org/ international/en/publications/reports/ cooking-the-climate-full/

GTZ (German Technical Cooperation) (2005) *Liquid Biofuels for Transportation in Tanzania: Potentials and implications for sustainable agriculture and energy in the 21st century*, Dar es Salaam.

Hajer, M. (1996) 'Ecological modernisation as cultural politics', in S. Lash, B. Szerszynski and B. Wynne (eds), *Risk, Environment and Modernity: Towards a new ecology*, London: Sage.

— (2009) 'Ecological modernisation as cultural politics', in A. P. J. Mol, D. A. Sonnenfeld and G. Spaargaren, *The Ecological Modernisation Reader: Environmental Reform in Theory and Practice*, Oxford and New York: Routledge.

Hall, R. (2010) 'Background and introduction', presentation to the regional workshop on the Commercialisation of Land and 'Land Grabbing' in Southern Africa, Clara Anna Fontein Game Reserve and Country Lodge, Cape Town, South Africa, 24–25 March.

Hamza Abdurezak and Azanaw Tadesse (1995) 'Structural adjustment policy and Ethiopian agriculture: An assessment of short-term response and structural problems', in Dejene Aredo and Mulat Demeke (eds), *Ethiopian Agriculture: Problems of transformation. Proceedings of the Fourth Annual Conference on the Ethiopian economy*, Addis Ababa, Ethiopia.

Harvey, D. (2006) *Spaces of Global Capitalism*, London: Verso.

Haugen, Hans Morten (2008) 'Biofuel potential and FAO's estimate of available land: The case of Tanzania', mimeo.

Havnevik, K. (1987) *The IMF and the World Bank in Africa. Conditionalities, impact and alternatives*, Uppsala: Nordic Africa Institute.

— (1993) *Tanzania: The limits to development from above*, Uppsala, Sweden: Nordic Africa Institute.

— (2006) 'Successful community based forest management in northern Tanzania: Reflections and theoretical implications', in Kjell Havnevik, Tekeste Negash and Atakilte Beyene (eds), *Of Global Concern – Rural livelihood dynamics and natural resource governance*, Sidastudies No. 6, Stockholm.

— (2010) 'Guidelines for biofuel expansion – the legitimizing of new forms of colonialism?', introduction to panel at Nordic Africa Days, Åbo, Finland, 20 September–1 October.

Havnevik, K., D. Bryceson, L.-E. Birgegård, P. Matondi and Atakilte Beyene (2007) *African Agriculture and the World Bank. Development or impoverishment?* Policy Dialogue No. 1, Uppsala: Nordic Africa Institute.

Hazell, P. (2007) 'Bioenergy: Opportunities and challenges', presentation to the Sweet Sorghum Consultation, IFAD, Rome, November.

Hermann, S. M. and C. F. Hutchinson (2005) 'The changing contexts of the desertification debate', *Journal of Arid Environments*, 63.

Herring, R. J. (2008) 'Whose numbers count? Probing discrepant evidence on transgenic cotton in the Warangal district of India', *International Journal of Multiple Research Approaches*, 2.

Hien, O. (2008) 'Biofuels: Danger or new opportunity', *Mail and Guardian* (South Africa), 9 December, available at: http://mg.co.za/article/2007-12-09-biofuels-danger-or-new-opportunity

Hoag, H. (2003) 'Designing the delta: A history of water and development in the Lower Rufiji Basin, Tanzania, 1945–1985', PhD dissertation, Boston University, Graduate School of Arts and Sciences.

Hollander, G. (2010) 'Power is sweet: sugarcane in the global ethanol assemblage', *Journal of Peasant Studies*, 37(4): 699–721.

Hoogvelt, A. (2001) *Globalization and the Postcolonial World, the New Political Economy of Development*, Basingstoke: Palgrave.

Horta, L. (2008) *The Zambezi Valley: China's first agricultural colony?*, Washington, DC: Centre for Strategic International Studies, available at: http://forums.csis.org/africa/?p=120

Hubbert, M. K. (1974) 'Oil, the Dwindling Treasure', *National Geographic*, June.

Huber, J. (2008) 'Technological environmental innovations (TEIs) in a chain-analytical and life-cycle-analytical perspective', *Journal of Cleaner Production*, 16(18): 1980–86.

Hunsberger, C. (2010) 'The politics of Jatropha-based biofuels in Kenya: Convergence and divergence among NGOs, donors, government officials and farmers', *Journal of Peasant Studies*, 37(4): 939–62.

IEA (International Energy Agency) (2002) 'World oil outlook to 2030', available at: www.iea.org/speech/2001-2002/birol.pdf

— (2009) *World Energy Outlook 2009*, Paris: OECD/IEA.

IFAD (International Fund for Agricultural Development) (2009) 'Governing Council roundtables: Challenges and opportunities for smallholder farmers in the context of climate change and new demands on agriculture', available at: www.ifad.org/events/gc/32/round tables/index.htm

IFPRI (International Food Policy Research Institute) (2007a) *IFPRI's Africa Strategy: Toward food and nutrition security in Africa*, available at: www.ifpri.org/publication/ifpris-africa-strategy-toward-food-and-nutrition-security-africa

— (2007b) 'The World Food Situation: New driving forces and required actions', IFPRI's bi-annual overview of the world food situation presented to the CGIAR Annual General Meeting, Beijing, 3 December.

— (2008) *Biofuels and Food Security: Balancing needs for food, energy and feed*, Washington, DC.

IPCC (Intergovernmental Panel on Climate Change) (2000) *Land Use, Land-Use Change and Forestry*, edited by R. Watson et al., Cambridge, Cambridge University Press, available at: www.ipcc.ch/ipccreports/sres/land_use/index.php?idp=0

— (2005) *Special Report on Carbon Dioxide Capture and Storage*, edited by Bert Metz et al., New York: Cambridge University Press.

— (2007a) *Climate Change 2007: The physical science basis*, edited by Susan Solomon et al., New York: Cambridge University Press.

— (2007b) *Climate Change 2007: Synthesis report – summary for policymakers*, available at: www.ipcc.ch/

IRIN (2010) 'In brief: Cereal export ban lifted in Ethiopia', IRIN News, 13 July, available at: www.irinnews.org/Report.aspx?ReportId=89811

Irwin, S. H. and D. R. Sanders (2010) 'The impact of index and swap fund on commodity futures markets: Preliminary results', OECD Food, Agriculture and Fisheries Working Papers No. 27, available at: www.oecd-ilibrary.org/agriculture-and-food/the-impact-of-index-and-swap-funds-on-commodity-futures-markets_5kmd4owl1t5f-en

Jayne, S., D. Mather and E. Mghenyi (2006) 'Smallholder farming under increasingly difficult circumstances: Policy and public investment priorities for Africa', MSU International,

Development Working Paper No. 86, Michigan State University, USA.

Joireman, S. (2000) *Property Rights and Political Development in Ethiopia and Eritrea*, East African Studies, Oxford: James Currey.

Jones, P. D. and M. E. Mann (2004) 'Climate over Past Millennia', *Reviews of Geophysics*, 42(RG2002), May.

Kahiya, V. (2009) 'Party big wigs locked in Nuanetsi Ranch turf war', *Zimbabwe Independent*, 17 December.

Kamanga, K. C. (2008) *The Agrofuel Industry in Tanzania: A critical enquiry into challenges and opportunities*, Final version, Land Rights Research and Resources Institute and Joint Oxfam Livelihood Initiative for Tanzania, March.

Kanter, J. (2008) 'Europe may ban imports of some biofuel crops', *New York Times*, 15 January.

Kawadza, S. (2010) 'U.S.$600 million ethanol plant under construction', *The Herald*, 5 March.

Kennedy, A. (2007) 'Concept and measurement of human development', HDRO/RBA Regional Technical Workshop on Measuring Human Development, Nairobi, September.

Kidane, W., M. Maetz and P. Dardel (2006) *Food Security and Agricultural Development in sub-Saharan Africa: Building a case for more public support*, Rome: FAO.

Kirsten, J. and K. Sartorius (2002) 'Linking agribusiness and small-scale farmers in developing countries: Is there a new role for contract farming?' *Development Southern Africa*, 19(4): 503–29.

Ki-Zerbo, J. (1995) '"Which way Africa?" Reflections on Basil Davidson's The Black Man's Burden', Development Dialogue No. 2, Uppsala: Dag Hammarskjöld Foundation.

Kofi, T. and A. Desta (2008) *The Saga of African Underdevelopment: A viable approach for Africa's sustainable development in the 21st century*, Trenton, NJ: Africa World Press.

Kreft, H. (2007) 'Chinas Politik der

Energie- und Rohstoffsicherung als Herausforderung für den Westen', *Internationale Politik und Gesellschaft*, Heft 2.

Kuchler, M. (2010) 'Unravelling the argument for bioenergy production in developing countries: A world-economy perspective', *Ecological Economics*, 69(6): 1336–43.

Lakew, H. and Y. Shiferaw (2008) 'Rapid assessment of biofuels development status in Ethiopia', in T. Anderson and M. Belay (eds), *Rapid Assessment of Biofuels Development Status in Ethiopia and Proceedings of the National Workshop on Environmental Impact Assessment and Biofuels*, Addis Ababa: Melca Mahiber, available at: www.melca-ethiopia.org/Biofuel%20Dev't.html.pdf

Lane, J. (2010) 'Jatropha 2.0 arrives: Koch's FHR, LIFE Technologies invest in SG Biofuels', 14 September, available at: http://biofuelsdigest.com/bdigest/2010/09/14/jatropha-2-0-arrives-kochs-fhr-life-technologies-invest-in-sg-biofuels/

Langhelle, O. (2009) 'Why ecological modernization and sustainable development should not be conflated' in A. P. J. Mol, D. A. Sonnenfeld and G. Spaargaren (eds) *The Ecological Modernisation Reader: Environmental reform in theory and practice*, Oxford: Routledge.

Lawrence, R. Z. (2010) 'How good politics results in bad policy: The case of biofuel mandates', Discussion Paper 2010-10, Belfer Center for Science and International Affairs/CID Working Paper No. 200, Center for International Development, Cambridge, MA: Harvard University, available at: http://belfercenter.ksg.harvard.edu/files/Lawrence%20Biofuels%20Mandates%20DP%20final%20for%20web.pdf

Leahy, S. (2009) 'Foreigners lead global land rush', IPS News website, 5 May, available at: http://ipsnews.net/news.asp?idnews=46724

Leopold, A. (2009) 'Agrofuels: Discursive shifts and discursive rifts over time

and space', paper prepared for the 4th Interpretive Policy Analysis Conference 'Discourse and Power in Critical Policy Studies', 25–27 June, Kassel, Germany.

L'Essor (2008) 'Projet MCA-Mali d'Aménagement a l'Office du Niger: 5 ha, dont 2 gratuits', 13 August.

Little, P. and M. Watts (eds) (1994) *Living under Contract: Contract farming and agrarian transformation in sub-Saharan Africa*, Madison: University of Wisconsin Press.

Lockwood, M. and J. Davidson (2010) 'Environmental governance and the hybrid regime of Australian natural resource management', *Geoforum*, 41(3): 388–98.

Loewenson, R. (1992) *Modern Plantation Agriculture: Corporate wealth and labour squalor*, London: Zed.

Lund, C. (2001) 'Questioning some assumptions about land tenure', in T. A. Benjaminsen and C. Lund (eds), *Politics, Property and Production in the West African Sahel*, Uppsala: Nordic African Institute.

Mackenzie, J. M. (1997) 'Empire and the ecological apocalypse: The historiography of the imperial environment', in T. Griffiths and L. Robin (eds), *Ecology and Empire: Environmental history of settler societies*, Keele University Press and University of Natal Press.

Mandebvu, L. (2010) 'Chiefs embrace ethanol project', *The Herald*, 28 June.

Mapako, M. (1998) 'Energy applications of *jatropha curcas* oil', in N. Foidl and A. Kashyap (eds), *Exploring the Potential of Jatropha curcas in Rural Development and Environmental Protection*, Harare.

Mathews, J. A. (2007) 'Biofuels: What a biopact between north and south could achieve', *Energy Policy*, 35(7): 3550–70.

Matinga, M. (2008) 'A biofuels prenuptial: Questions for policy makers before the marriage', *Renewable Energy for Development*, 21(1).

Matondi, P. B. (2010) 'Agro-investment and land grabbing in Zimbabwe' presentation at the regional workshop on the Commercialisation of Land and 'Land Grabbing' in Southern Africa, Clara Anna Fontein Game Reserve and Country Lodge, Cape Town South Africa, 24–25 March.

Matondi, P. B., P. Masanganise, C. T. Khombe and C. Sukume (2011) 'Complexities of understanding agricultural production outcomes in Mazowe, Shamva and Mangwe Districts', in Prosper B. Matondi (ed.), *Inside the Political Economy of Redistributive Land and Agrarian Reforms in Mazowe, Shamva and Mangwe Districts, in Zimbabwe*, Harare, Zimbabwe (forthcoming).

Maxwell, S. and M. Smith (1992) 'Household food security: A conceptual review', in S. Maxwell and T. R. Frankenberger (eds), *Household Food Security: Concepts, indicators and measurements*, United Nation's Children's Fund and International Fund for Agricultural Development.

McCann, J. (1995) *People of the Plow: An agricultural history of Ethiopia, 1800–1990*, Madison: University of Wisconsin Press.

McMichael, P. (2010) 'Agrofuels in the food regime', *Journal of Peasant Studies*, 37(4): 609–29.

Mebratu, D. (1998) 'Sustainability and sustainable development: Historical and conceptual review', *Environmental Impact Assessment Review*, 18(6): 493–520.

Mebratu, D. and M. Tamire (2002) *Energy in Ethiopia: Status, Challenges and Prospects: Proceedings of the energy conference*, Addis Ababa, Ethiopia.

Meinzen-Dick, R. (2010) 'Overview of "land groups": Global trends, categories, outcomes' presentation to regional workshop on the Commercialisation of Land and 'Land Grabbing' in Southern Africa, Clara Anna Fontein Game Reserve and Country Lodge, Cape Town South Africa, 24–25 March.

Meskir Tesfaye (2007) 'Bio-fuels in Ethiopia', presentation to the Eastern and Southern Africa regional workshop on bio-fuels, 28–29 June, Nairobi, Kenya.

Mittal, Anuradha (2010) 'Land grabs: cheap deals for rich countries', *Farming Matters*, September, interview available at: www.landcoalition.org/cpl-blog/?p=8061

MLRR (Ministry of Lands and Rural Resettlement) (2009) 'Major themes proposed for the Kariba', planning retreat on Towards a Comprehensive Land Policy in Zimbabwe, Caribbea Bay Hotel, Kariba, 11–13 June.

MME (Ministry of Mines and Energy) (2008) *Ethiopian Biofuels Development and Utilization Strategy*, Addis Ababa, Ethiopia.

Moe, Terry M. (2005) 'Power and political institutions', *Perspectives on Politics*, 3: 215–33.

Mol, A. P. J. (2007) 'Boundless biofuels? Between environmental sustainability and vulnerability', *Sociologia Ruralis*, 47(4).

— (2010) 'Environmental authorities and biofuel controversies', *Environmental Politics*, 19(1): 61–79.

Msangi, S. (2007) 'Biofuel revolution threatens food security for the poor', SciDev.Net website, 6 December, available at: www.scidev.net/en/climate-change-and-energy/biofuels/opinions/biofuel-revolution-threatens-food-security-for-the.html

Mwamila, Burton et al. (2008) 'Feasibility of large-scale bio-fuel production in Tanzania', August, mimeo.

— (2009) 'Feasibility of large-scale biofuel production in Tanzania. Study Report', April.

Neumann, R. P. (2004) 'Nature-state-territory: Toward a critical theorization of conservation enclosures', in R. Peet and M. Watts (eds), *Liberation Ecologies: Environment, development, social movement*, Oxford: Routledge.

Nhantumbo, I. and A. Salomao (2009) 'Biofuels, land access and new business models for rural livelihoods in Africa – the Mozambican case', Maputo: Centro Terra Viva and IIED (unpublished).

Nkomo, J. C., A. O. Nyong and K. Kulindwa (2006) 'The impacts of climate change in Africa', commissioned research for the Stern Report, www.hmtreasury.gov.uk/media/3/A/Chapter_5_The_Impacts_of_Climate_Change_in_Africa-5.pdf

North, D. (1990) *Institutions, Institutional Change, and Economic Performance*, Cambridge: Cambridge University Press.

Nyari, B. (2008) 'Biofuel land grabbing in Northern Ghana', Report by Regional Advisory and Information Network Systems (RAINS), available at: www.gaiafoundation.com

Obama, B. (2010) 'Obama energy policy address', 1 April, available at: http://biofuelsdigest.com/bdigest/2010/04/01/complete-text-of-obama-energy-policy-address/

Odén, Bertil (2006) *Biståndets Idéhistoria. Från Marshallhjälpen till milleniemål*, Studentlitteratur.

OECD (Organisation for Economic Co-operation and Development) (2008) 'Rising food prices: Causes and consequences', paper prepared for the DAC High-Level Meeting, 20–21 May.

OFID (OPEC Fund for International Development) (2009) 'Biofuels and food security implications of an accelerated biofuels production: Summary of the OFID study prepared by IIASA', Vienna, available at: www.ofid.org/publications/PDF/pamphlet/ofid_pam38_Biofuels.pdf.

Öhman, May-Britt (2007) 'Taming exotic beauties. Swedish hydropower construction in Tanzania in the era of development assistance, 1960s–1990s', doctoral thesis in History of Science, KTH, Stockholm.

Olukoshi, A. (1998) 'The elusive Prince of Denmark: structural adjustment and the crisis of governance in Africa', Research Report No. 104, Nordic Africa Institute, Uppsala.

Oscarsson, P. (2009) 'The land process in Tanzania', mimeo.

Oxfam (2008) 'Another inconvenient truth: How biofuel policies are deepening poverty and accelerating climate change', Oxfam Briefing Paper 114, June, available at: www.oxfam.org.uk/resources/policy/climate_change/bp114_inconvenient_truth.html

Oxfam Australia and Ruzivo Trust (2011) *Mainstreaming Livelihoods into Gender, HIV and AIDS Programming*, Harare, Zimbabwe (forthcoming).

Palmer, R. (2010) 'Would Cecil Rhodes have signed a Code of Conduct? Reflections on global land grabbing and land rights in Africa, past and present', paper delivered at the African Studies Association of the UK, biennial conference, Oxford, 16–19 September, available at: www.oxfam.org.uk/resources/learning/landrights/downloads/would_cecil_rhodes_have_signed_a_code_of_conduct.pdf

Partners for Africa (2005) 'Developing African renewable energy sectors for poverty alleviation, emphasis on bioenergy', 14th European Biomass Conference, 17–21 October, Paris.

Peskett L., R. Slater, C. Stevens and A. Dufey (2007) 'Biofuels, agriculture and poverty reduction: Natural resources', *Perspectives*, 107.

Petroleum Economist (2006) 'Addicted to oil', December.

Pimentel, D. et al. (2009) 'Food versus biofuels: Environmental and economic costs', *Human Ecology*, 37(1), available as: DOI: 10.1007/s10745-009-9215-8.

Platteau, J.-Ph. (1996) 'The evolutionary theory of land rights as applied to sub-Saharan Africa: A critical assessment', in *Development and Change*, 27(1): 29–86.

Porter, G. and K. Phillips-Howard (1997) 'Comparing contracts: An evaluation of contract farming schemes in Africa', *World Development*, 37(11).

Practical Action Consulting (2009) 'Small-scale bioenergy initiatives: Brief description and preliminary lessons on livelihood impacts from case studies in Asia, Latin America and Africa', PISCES and FAO, available at: www.pisces.or.ke/pubs/pdfs/FAO-PISCES%

20Case%20Studies%20Executive%20
Summary%2005020o9.pdf

Prowse, M. and T. Braunholtz-Speight (2007) 'The first Millennium Development Goal, agriculture and climate change', *ODI Opinion*, 85.

Pye, O. (2010) 'The biofuel connection: Transnational activism and the palm oil boom', *Journal of Peasant Studies*, 37(4): 851–74.

Rajagopal, D. et al. (2007) 'Challenge of biofuel: Filling the tank without emptying the stomach?', *Environmental Research Letters*, 2, available at: http://ecnr.berkeley.edu/vfs/PPs/Sexton-SteE/web/challenge.pdf

Reardon, T. and C. Barrett (2000) 'Agro-industrialisation, globalization and international development: An overview of issues, patterns and determinants', *Agricultural Economics*, 23.

Republic of Mozambique (2009) *Biofuels Policy and Strategy*, Resolution No. 22/2009, Ministry of Energy, Maputo: Ministry of Energy with support of DfID.

Republic of Zambia (2009) *Revised Draft Policy Biofuels Strategy for Zambia*.

Roberntz, P., T. Edman and A. Carlson (2009) 'The Rufiji landscape. The sweet and bitter taste of sugarcane grown for biofuel', draft report prepared for World Wildlife Fund, Sweden.

Rodney W. (1964) *How Europe Underdeveloped Africa*, London: Macmillan Press.

Roe, E. (1991) 'Development narratives, or making the best of blueprint development', *World Development*, 19(4).

— (1999) *Except Africa: Remaking development, rethinking power*, Edison, NJ: Transaction Books.

Rukuni, M., P. Tawonezvi, C. Eicher, M. Munyuki-Hungwe and P. Matondi (eds) (2006) *Zimbabwe's Agricultural Revolution*, 2nd edn, Harare: University of Zimbabwe Publications.

Runge, C. F. and B. Senauer (2007) 'How biofuels could starve the poor', *Foreign Affairs*, May/June.

Rural Consult (2009a) 'The biofuel debate', *Daily Graphic* (Ghana), 10 June.

— (2009b) 'Action Aid and biofuels. Rural Consult responds yet again', *Daily Graphic* (Ghana), 23 July.

Sawe, E. N., TaTEDO and WWF Tanzania (2008) 'Scoping exercise on the biofuels industry within and outside Tanzania', Dar es Salaam, Energy for Sustainable Development, available at: www.wwf.se/source.php/1203701/WWF_Tanzania_Scoping_Report_Biofuels.pdf

Scott, J. (1985) *Weapons of the Weak: Everyday forms of peasant resistance*, New Haven, CT: Yale University Press.

Searchinger, T. et al. (2008) 'Use of US croplands for biofuels increases greenhouse gases through emissions from land-use change', *Science*, 319(29): 1238–40.

SEI (Stockholm Environment Institute) (forthcoming) *Biofuel: A Guide for the Confused*, Norwegian Peoples Aid, SEI and Renetech AB.

SEI/IRA (Institute of Resource Assessment, University of Dar es Salaam) (2009) 'Initial assessment of socio-economic and environmental risks and opportunities of large-scale biofuels production in the Rufiji District', a report prepared for SEKAB T, Stockholm and Dar es Salaam.

SEKAB (2009a) 'Hållbarhetspris till SEKAB', press release, 18 March.

— (2009b) 'Sustainability award for SEKAB', press release, 18 March.

— (2009c) 'SEKAB sells subsidiaries in Tanzania and Mozambique to EcoDevelopment in Europe AB', press release, October 23.

SEKAB Bioenergy Tanzania (2009) 'SEKAB BioEnergy Tanzania Ltd – Application for Credit Enhancement Guarantee', Dar es Salaam, July 28.

Sen, A. (1981) *Poverty and Famine: An essay on entitlement and deprivation*, Oxford: Oxford University Press.

Sengers, F., R. P. J. M. Raven and A. van Venrooij (2010) 'From riches to rags: Biofuels, media discourses and resistance to sustainable energy technologies', paper delivered to the SPRU

Energy Conference Programme, Sussex University, 25–26 January.

Sexton, S. and D. Zilberman (2010) 'The economics of agricultural biotechnology adoption: Implications for biofuel sustainability', paper delivered to the National Bureau of Economic Research Conference, available at: www.nber.org/confer/2010/AGs10/Sexton.pdf

Shut, M., M. Slingerland et al. (2010) 'Biofuel developments in Mozambique. Update and analysis of policy, potential and reality', Energy Policy, 38: 5151–65.

Sibanda, T. (2010) 'Villagers face eviction to make way for biofuel cultivation', SW Radio Africa News, 30 March.

Sida Helpdesk for Environmental Assessment (2009) 'General environmental assessment comments', September 30.

Sida's Department for Partnership Development/AKTSAM (2010) 'Decision on assessment and preparation', October 29.

SIRDC (Scientific and Industrial Research Development Council) (1998) 'The potential of jatropha curcas in improving rural livelihoods and environmental protection – An exploration', concept paper – Final Draft, Harare, Zimbabwe.

Smith, G. (1993) Impact Assessment and Sustainable Resource Management, London: Longman.

Stiglitz J. (2002) Globalization and Its Discontents, Cambridge, MA: Harvard University Press.

Sulle, E. and F. Nelson (2009a) 'Developing biofuels through securing local livelihoods and land rights', information brief, Tanzania Forestry Working Group, Tanzania Natural Resources Forum.

— (2009b) Biofuels, Land Access and Rural Livelihoods in Tanzania, London: IIED.

Sunday Mail (Zimbabwe) (2010) 'Villagers, investor clash over land', 30 May.

Svarstad, H. (2002) 'Analyzing conservation-development discourses: The story of a biopiracy narrative', Forum for Development studies, 1.

Swift, J. and K. Hamilton (2001) 'House-hold food and livelihood security', in S. Devereux and S. Maxwell (eds), Food Security in Sub-Saharan Africa, London: ITDG Publishing.

Teketel Abebe (1998) '"Tenants of the state": The limitations of revolutionary agrarian transformation in Ethiopia, 1974–1991', dissertation, Lund, Sweden.

Tigere, T. A. et al. (2006) 'Potential of jatropha curcas in improving smallholder farmers' livelihoods in Zimbabwe: An exploratory study of Makosa Ward, Mutoko District', Journal of Sustainable Development, 8.

Todaro, M. (1993) Economic Development, Oxford: Oxford University Press.

Tompsett, C. (2010) 'Fuelling development? A critical look at government-centered jatropha cultivation for biodiesel as promoted by the biofuel policy in Rajastan, India', unpublished Master's thesis, University of Bergen.

Toulmin, C. (2008) 'Securing land and property rights in sub-Saharan Africa: The role of local institutions', Land Use Policy, 26.

Toulmin, C. and J. Quan (eds) (2000) Evolving Land Rights Policy and Tenure in Africa, London: IIED.

Ulmanen, J. H., G. P. J. Verbong et al. (2009) 'Biofuel developments in Sweden and the Netherlands: Protection and socio-technical change in a long-term perspective', Renewable and Sustainable Energy Reviews, 13(6–7): 1406–17.

UN (2007) Sustainable Bioenergy: A framework for decision makers, available at: http://esa.un.org/un-energy/pdf/susdev.Biofuels.FAO.pdf

UNAC&JA (2009) 'Jatropha! A socio-economic pitfall for Mozambique', Maputo: UNAC (União Nacional de Camponeses) and JA (Justiça Ambiental).

UNCTAD (2006) FDI in Least Developed Countries at a Glance, available at: www.unctad.org/en/docs/iteiia20057_en.pdf

— (2007) 'Globalization for development: Opportunities and challenges, Report of the Secretary-General of UNCTAD

to UNCTAD XII', available at: www.
unctad.org/en/docs/td413_en.pdf

— (2008) *World Investment Report 2008
– Transnational Corporations and the
Infrastructure Challenge*, available at:
www.unctad.org/en/docs/wir2008_
en.pdf

— (2009) *World Investment Report:
Transnational Corporations, Agricultural
Production and Development*, available at: www.unctad.org/en/docs/
wir2009_en.pdf

UNDP (2007) *Human Development Report
2007/2008: Fighting climate change*, Basingstoke: Palgrave Macmillan, available at: http://hdr.undp.org/en/media/
HDR_20072008_EN_Complete.pdf

United Nations, Department of Economic
and Social Affairs (2007) 'Small-scale
production and use of liquid biofuels
in sub-Saharan Africa: Perspectives for
sustainable development', Background
Paper No. 2, DESA/DSD/2007/2, New
York.

URT (United Republic of Tanzania)
(2010) 'Giudelines for available liquid
biofuels development in Tanzania',
Dar es Salaam: Ministry of Energy and
Minerals.

US Embassy (2009) 'Partners for cleaner
energy – alternative energy opportunities in Sweden', June 30.

Utete Report (2003) *Report of the Presiden-
tial Land Review Committee under the
Chairmanship of Dr Charles M. B. Utete*,
Vol. I: *Main Report*, Harare.

Via Campesina (2003) 'What is food sovereignty?' 1 January, available at: www.
viacampesina.org/IMG/_article_PDF/
article_216.pdf

— (2007) 'Small scale sustainable farmers
are cooling down the earth, a Via
Campesina background document on
global warming', available at: www.
viacampesina.org

Vidal, J. (2010) 'How food and water are
driving a 21st-century African land
grab', *Guardian*, 7 March.

von Braun, J. (2007) *The World Food Situation: New driving forces and required
actions*, Washington, DC: IFPRI,

available at: www.ifpri.org/publication/
world-food-situation-2

— (2008) *Food and Financial Crises:
Implications for agricultures and the
poor*, Food Policy Report No. 20,
Washington, DC: IFPRI.

von Braun, Joachim and Ruth Meinzen-
Dick (2009) ' "Land grabbing" by for-
eign investors in developing countries:
Risks and opportunities', IFPRI Policy
Brief, 13 April.

von Braun, Joachim and R. K. Pachauri
(2006) 'The promises and challenges
of biofuels for the poor in developing countries', IFPRI, available at:
www. ifpri.org/sites/default/files/
publications/ar05e.pdf

Wall Street Journal (2009) 'BP gives
up on jatropha for biofuel', available at: http://blogs.wsj.com/environ
mentalcapital/2009/07/17/bp-gives-up-
on-jatropha-for-biofuel/

Wamukoya, N. (2007) 'Biofuels sustainability: Towards solutions', paper
presented at the High-level Biofuels
Seminar in Africa, organized by the
African Union, the Brazilian Government and UNIDO, Addis Ababa,
30 July.

Warwick, C. (2008) 'Environmental effects
of biofuels crops must be weighed,
researchers say', News Bureau Illinois
website, available at: http://news.il-
linois.edu/NEWS/06/0922biofuels.html

Watts, M. (2004) 'Violent environments,
petroleum conflict and the political
ecology of rule in the Niger Delta,
Nigeria', in R. Peet and M. Watts,
*Liberation Ecologies: Environment,
development, social movements*, Oxford:
Routledge.

WCED (World Commission on Environment and Development) (1987) *Our
Common Future*, New York.

Weidemann Associates, Inc. (2010) *Zimbabwe Agricultural Sector Market Study*,
Harare: USAID.

White, B. (1997) 'Agroindustry and
contract farmers in upland West Java',
Journal of Peasant Studies, 24(3): 100–36.

White, B. and A. Dasgupta (2010) 'Agrofuels capitalism: A view from political economy', *Journal of Peasant Studies*, 37(4): 593–607.

Widengård, M. (2009a) Personal notes from COMPETE International Conference on Bioenergy Policy Implementation in Africa, Fringilla Lodge, Zambia.

— (2009b) Seminar notes from May 25 on Aspects of SEKAB's plans for large scale biofuel production in Tanzania. Based on presentations and discussions in a seminar organized by the Nordic Africa Institute, Uppsala.

— (2010a) Personal notes from seminar on Bioenergy Sustainability and Tradeoffs: Does Global Sustainability Threaten Local Sustainability?, Sida, Stockholm.

— (2010b) Personal notes from WWF regional workshop on Renewable Energy – Biofuels in Southern Africa (Miombo), Victoria Falls, Zimbabwe.

Windfuhr, M. and J. Jonsén (2005) 'Food sovereignty: Towards democracy in localized food systems', FIAN Working Paper, ITDG Publishing.

Wolde-Georgis T. and M. H. Glantz (2008) 'People-focused biofuels development in Africa', *Fragile Ecologies*, 20 November, available at: www.fragilecologies.com/nov20_08.html

Wood, C. (2003) 'Environmental impact assessment in developing countries: An overview', Conference on New Directions in Impact Assessment for Development: Methods and Practice, mimeo.

World Bank (1989) *Sub-Saharan Africa: From crisis to sustainable growth*, Washington, DC.

— (2007) *World Development Report: Agriculture for development 2008*, Washington, DC.

— (2010) *Rising Global Interest in Farmland: Can it yield sustainable and equitable benefits?*, available at: http://siteresources.worldbank.org/INTARD/Resources/ESW_Sept7_final_final.pdf

World Resources Institute (2003) 'Biodiversity and protected areas – Tanzania', mimeo.

WWF (World Wildlife Fund) (2003) 'Soy expansion – losing forests to fields', available at: http://assets.panda.org/downloads/wwfsoyexpansion.pdf

Wyeth, P. (2002) *Jatropha or Physic Nut: An industry and market study on six plant products in Southern Africa*, Pullman: Washington State University, USA.

York, R. and E. A. Rosa (2003) 'Key challenges to ecological modernization theory', *Organization and Environment*, 16(3): 273–88.

Young, J. (1997) *Peasant Revolution in Ethiopia. The Tigray People's Liberation Front, 1975–1991*, Cambridge: Cambridge University Press.

Young, O. R., F. Berkhout et al. (2006) 'The globalization of socio-ecological systems: An agenda for scientific research', *Global Environmental Change*, 16(3): 304–16.

Ziegler, Jean (2007) 'The right to food, Report of the Special Rapporteur on the right to food', UN General Assembly A/62/289, 22 August 22, available at: http://www.righttofood.org/new/PDF/A62289.pdf

Zimbabwe Standard (2008) 'Little oil trickles out of bio-diesel plant', 22 November, available at: www.thestandard.co.zw/business/19256-little-oil-trickles-out-of-bio-diesel-plant.htm

Other contributors

Festus Boamah (MSc) is a Ghanaian with a BA degree in Geography and Resource Development from the University of Ghana. He worked with the Centre for Migration Studies, University of Ghana, and in 2010 obtained his MPhil in Resources and Human Adaptations from the University of Bergen, Norway. Boamah's interest is to promote rethinking of both contemporary and historical 'received wisdom' as it relates to environment, energy use and development, by situating analysis within specific local contexts, in order to contribute to a more nuanced debate on globalization and climate change.

Marie Widengård (MSc) is a PhD student at the School of Global Studies, Gothenburg University, Sweden. Her research is centred on bioenergy as a potential sustainable driver for rural development. She has done work in Angola, Cameroon, Kenya, Malawi, Mozambique, Namibia, Nicaragua, South Africa, Sweden, Zambia and Zimbabwe. Her areas of interest include participatory research and development, civil society, environmental engineering, bio law, seed systems, demand-driven extension and adult education methodologies.

Patience Mutopo (MSc) is a programmes research fellow with the Ruzivo Trust in Harare, Zimbabwe. She is currently a PhD candidate at the African Studies Centre, University of Cologne, Germany. Her research interests are gender studies, land, environmental governance and the theory and practice of human rights in Africa. She is a member of the Legal Empowerment of the Poor network, which is run by the Centre for Environment and Development, in conjunction with the Norwegian Centre for Human Rights.

Hanne Haaland (PhD) is an associate professor at the Centre for Development Studies, University of Agder, Kristiansand, Norway. She worked earlier as a researcher at the Norwegian Institute for Nature Research, Oslo, focusing on conflicts related to the use and protection of nature, both in Norway and in developing countries. She earned her PhD from the University of Life Sciences, Norway, exploring the links between land rights, identity and forms of knowledge in a community in southern Mozambique. Her current research interests focus on land politics and smallholder rights in Southern Africa, as well as on local mobilization and social movements in the democratization processes in Bolivia.

Rune Skarstein (PhD) is an associate professor in the Department of Economics at the Norwegian University of Technology and Natural Sciences, Trondheim. His specializations are macroeconomics, development economics and political economy. Over many years, he has conducted research on rural and agrarian change and broader development issues in Tanzania and other African countries, Argentina, India and Norway. Skarstein has published numerous books and articles in Norway and abroad. He is an experienced lecturer and has supervised and mentored many students in Norway and Africa researching the economics of development.

Index

National Oil Company of Zimbabwe (NOCZIM), 140, 143–4
natural gas, production of, 61
neo-colonialism, 2
neoliberalism, 3, 180; challenges to, 181–3
New Partnership for Africa's Development (NEPAD), 24
new land colonization, use of term, 1
Niyari, Bakari, 85
non-governmental organizations (NGOs), 133, 173, 190
Norad, 133
North–South relations, 88, 178
Norway, 161

oil: discoveries of new reserves, 61; prices of, rising, 22 *see also* peak oil
Organisation for Economic Co-operation and Development (OECD), 30, 113
ORGUT consultancy company, 109, 110, 116–21, 122, 132
outgrower schemes, 125, 127, 188
Oval Biofuel company, 58

palm oil feedstock for biodiesel, 91
Palmer, Robin, 13
panicum virgatum (switchgrass), 74
Paraguay, 73
Paris Declaration (2005), 177
participation and participatory approach, 18, 88, 172
pastoralism, 8, 15, 183
patronage and kinship relations, 101
peak oil, 1, 2, 11, 60–7, 186
pesticides, use of, 74, 152
petroleum, substituted with biofuels, 94
Plant Oil Producers' Association (POPA), 143
plantation agriculture, 15; pitfalls of, 183–4
Poland, 107
poor: estranged from market, 80; sovereign rights of, 184–5
population: density of, 172; global, growth of, 182; of Africa, growth of, 25, 185
populist discourse on biofuels, 164–6
poverty, 81, 179, 184; reduction of, 17, 69, 80, 181, 187, 192
Praj Industries, 140
privatization: of land, 31; of natural resources, 53
profit repatriation, 70

promises of biofuel investment, 71–2, 78, 94–6, 157; in employment, 72–3
property rights, individual, 41
prosperous islands of biofuel development, danger of, 68
protected areas of land, 112

Qatar, 70; acquisition of land in Kenya, 35

rain-fed farming, 15, 160
Rajasthan, India, jatropha project in, 172
Rating Investments company, 153
recolonization of Africa, 89
Regional Advisory and Information Network Systems (RAINS), 161, 165, 168, 174, 190
rehabilitation of land, 50
relocation of farmers, 169, 172
renewable energy *see* alternative energy sources
Renman, Per, 117–20
reproduction of labour crisis, 9
Reserve Bank of Zimbabwe (RBZ), 145
right to strike, suspension of, 70
rights, reclaiming of, 74
Ruahi River forest reserve (Tanzania), 126
Rufiji district, Tanzania, biofuel project in, 32, 109, 122–8
rural change, theorization of, 193
Rural Consult Ltd, 163–4, 167–8
rural entrepreneurship, 192
rural poor, migration of, 73
Russia, 62

salinity of soils, 33
satellite imagery, use of, 49–50
Saudi Arabia, 26, 70
Scramble for Africa, 178
second-generation biofuel technologies, 23, 38, 40, 67, 107
secrecy of operations *see* transparency, lack of
SEKAB Bioenergy Tanzania Ltd (SEKAB T), 107, 110, 116, 123–31; application for Credit Enhancement Guarantee, 128–31
SEKAB International AB (Sekab), 6, 17, 27, 40, 53, 54, 106; biofuel plans, implications of, 131–3; operations in Tanzania, 32, 34, 106–33; resistance to, 13
Sen, Amartya, 34
settler society, new form of, 5

greenhouse gas emissions of, 63;
support for biofuels, 66
unused and underutilized land, 8, 16, 25,
31, 49, 74, 75, 93, 94, 99, 112, 136, 138,
142, 149, 164, 169, 172, 179, 183; allocated
to landless people, 100
US Energy Independence and Security Act
2007 (revised), 66

Varun International, acquisition of land
in Madagascar, 26
Via Campesina network, 51
victims *see* heroes, victims and villains
village land, 31; loss of, 150; use plans for,
126–7
Village Land Act (1999) (Tanzania), 42, 112
village land certificates, 123
vinasse, 119

water plunder, use of term, 1
water resources: access to, 8, 93, 115, 147,
154, 178; availability of, 33, 65, 119,
121; changing usage patterns of, 12;
damage to, 185; diverted from food
crops, 82, 152; depletion of, 22; impacts
on, 38; over-use of, 74; pollution of, 79;
shortages of, 12
weather events, irregular, 12
wetlands, draining of, 79
white land owners in Zimbabwe, 149
win-win solutions, 86, 87, 164, 172, 176, 190;
conditionalities of, 53–5; construction
of, 51–3

women, 145; as farmers, 10, 18, 152, 188;
as household breadwinners, 160; as
petty traders, 171; economic activity
of, 166; excluded from job market, 151;
fuelwood activities of, 104, 147, 160; in
food industry, 154; weaker claims of,
100
wood biomass, health implications of, 104
workers, recruitment of, 161–2 *see also*
skilled workers
World Bank, 29, 31, 43, 77, 113, 190;
report on land ownership, 3; World
Development Indicators, 112; *World
Development Report*, 14, 57, 181, 183
World Commission on Dams, 38
World Food Programme (WFP), 144
World Wildlife Fund, 190
World Wildlife Fund (WWF)-Sweden,
123–7

Zambia, 52, 74; jatropha production in,
57–8; smallholder agriculture in, 52–3
Zanzibar, 108
Zimbabwe, 16, 70–1, 74, 75, 185, 194; agro-
investments in, 134–58; biofuels in,
17–18; foreign land ownership in, 137–9;
fuel crisis in, 142; land policy in, 14
Zimbabwe African National Union –
Patriotic Front (ZANU-PF), 142
Zimbabwe African People's Union –
Patriotic Front (ZAPU-PF), 136, 142
Zimbabwe Bio-Energy Ltd (ZBE), 135, 136,
140–1, 142, 147, 148, 152

About Zed Books

Zed Books is a critical and dynamic publisher, committed to increasing awareness of important international issues and to promoting diversity, alternative voices and progressive social change. We publish on politics, development, gender, the environment and economics for a global audience of students, academics, activists and general readers. Run as a co-operative, Zed Books aims to operate in an ethical and environmentally sustainable way.

Find out more at:

www.zedbooks.co.uk

For up-to-date news, articles, reviews and events information visit:

http://zed-books.blogspot.com

To subscribe to the monthly Zed Books e-newsletter, send an email headed 'subscribe' to:

marketing@zedbooks.net

We can also be found on **Facebook**, **ZNet**, **Twitter** and **Library Thing**.